MODERN HOUSING FOR AMERICA

HISTORICAL STUDIES OF URBAN AMERICA
A series edited by James R. Grossman and Kathleen N. Conzen

Smoldering City: Chicagoans and the Great Fire, 1871–1874
Karen Sawislak

Parish Boundaries: The Catholic Encounter with Race in the Twentieth-Century Urban North
John T. McGreevy

MODERN HOUSING FOR AMERICA

Policy Struggles in the New Deal Era

Gail Radford

The University of Chicago Press ▪ Chicago and London

GAIL RADFORD is assistant professor of history at the State University of New York–Buffalo.

The University of Chicago Press, Chicago 60637
The University of Chicago Press, Ltd., London
© 1996 by The University of Chicago
All rights reserved. Published 1996
Printed in the United States of America

05 04 03 02 01 00 99 98 97 96   1 2 3 4 5

ISBN 0-226-70222-7 (cloth)
0-226-70223-5 (paper)

Library of Congress Cataloging-in-Publication Data

Radford, Gail.
    Modern housing for America: Policy struggles in the New Deal era
/ Gail Radford.
        p.   cm. — (Historical studies of urban America)
    Includes bibliographical references and index.
    ISBN 0–226–70222–7 (alk. paper). — ISBN 0–226–70223–5 (pbk. :
alk. paper)
    1. Housing policy—United States—History—20th century.   2. New
Deal, 1933–1939.   I. Title.   II. Series.
    HD7293.R28   1996
    363.5'8'0973—dc20   96-21155
                                                              CIP

For Stephen Hart

CONTENTS

ACKNOWLEDGMENTS

Writing this book has been a rewarding experience, not least because of the chance to meet many talented and public-spirited people. A number of them appear in the following pages, as they played a part in developing the modern housing policy initiative. While most were not living when I began this work, I nevertheless relish the hours spent in their company as I sat in libraries and archives researching their work. There were two principals in this story who were alive when I began, and I deeply regret that William Jeanes, Sr., who helped plan and later managed the Carl Mackley Houses, and John Lewis Wilson, the last surviving member of the architectural team that designed the Harlem River Houses, will not be able to see this project in its completed form. It was a privilege to meet and talk with both of them. I would also like to acknowledge the invaluable help of the many residents and supporters of the two developments who spoke with me at length, sometimes on several occasions, particularly Irene and Bernard Cohan, Vincent Hammond, William Jeanes, Jr., Helen Jeanes, Priscilla Reed, Isadore Reivich, and Larry Rogin.

Kenneth T. Jackson, my dissertation advisor at Columbia, has been a loyal mentor and friend over many years. He introduced me to key issues in urban and policy history, helped me maneuver the shoals of graduate school and the job market, and has immensely improved this book by advice when the project was being formulated and close readings of the manuscript since. I also owe a debt to Richard Abrams and Paula Fass for inspiring me to pursue my graduate education and supporting my effort to do so. I want to acknowledge Elizabeth Blackmar and Joshua Freeman for their efforts before, during, and after their service on my dissertation committee. Gwendolyn Wright and Richard Plunz provided important input during early stages of work.

A great many colleagues and friends have helped in various ways over the years. Many thanks to: Henry Binford, Eugenie Birch, Charles Byler, Mary Ann Clawson, Roger Daniels, Gary Dymski, Michael Ebner, Robert Fishman, Deborah Gardner, Tim Gilfoyle, Howard Gillette, Scott Henderson, Susan Henderson, Charles Hoch, Clifton Hood, Janet Hutchison, Ann Keating, Judy Kramer, Gene Lewis, Carolyn Loeb, Stanley Mallach, Margaret Marsh, Jon Peterson, Wendy Plotkin, Susan Rugh, Eric Sandeen, Ron Schatz, Joel Schwartz, Paula Schwartz, Paula Silver, Frank Stricker, Kristin Szylvian, Marc

Weiss, Cindy Wells, Kim Wilson, and Komozi Woodard. Participants in two writing groups deserve special mention: in Chicago, Susan Stall and Martha Thompson, and in Milwaukee, Margo Anderson and Genevieve McBride.

The project was supported by a Taft Postdoctoral Fellowship at the University of Cincinnati and the Julian Park Publication Fund of the State University of New York at Buffalo. During my year in Cincinnati, I participated in the lively and stimulating Frontiers in Urban History Seminar led by Zane Miller. I benefitted from careful reading of my work by Zane and other members of the seminar, especially Fritz Casey-Leininger, Roger Hansen, and Judy Spraul-Schmidt. The Department of History at SUNY-Buffalo, and especially its chair, Jonathan Dewald, have provided an extremely supportive environment for completing this work.

James A. Ulrich and Joanne Parrish at the outstanding Art and Photographic Services Department at SUNY/Buffalo provided invaluable help with the illustrations. At the University of Chicago Press, my series editors Kathleen Conzen and James Grossman were sympathetic but rigorous readers. The book fell mainly in Kathy's bailiwick, and I am grateful for her insight and her many excellent suggestions for improvement. Douglas Mitchell, my editor at the Press, has been a wonderful person with whom to work. I would also like to thank Matthew Howard and Kathryn Kraynik for the effort and intelligence they have put into improving this manuscript.

As a token of my appreciation for many happy years of companionship and the sustained support he has given to this project, I dedicate this book to Stephen Hart.

INTRODUCTION

"A housing movement based purely on hand-outs from the top down, with all the driving power coming from talk about 'crime and disease', will never be basically popular in this country, and will necessarily be limited in scope."[1] So warned housing activist Catherine Bauer as the struggles of the New Deal years over federal housing policy drew to a close. Just as Bauer predicted, the American public was always lukewarm about housing programs that were aimed specifically at poor people, and in recent years support has cooled almost to the freezing point. Yet, while many Americans think of federal housing policy primarily in terms of such programs, there is in fact another, less visible, but far more important group of federal programs that deal with housing. These are the programs that support the commercial market and middle- and upper-class consumers of housing. They, too, originated in the 1930s, but unlike programs for the poor they have grown steadily in size and popularity since their creation. During the period when this bifurcated pattern was being developed, Bauer worked with an organization called the Labor Housing Conference to put forward a very different vision for how the government would deal with the housing question, a plan termed "modern housing." The modern housing program called for making a publicly supported, broadly targeted, noncommercial housing sector the centerpiece of federal housing policy. In contemporary terms it was a proposal for a "universalistic" policy.

This book tells the story of this policy initiative, its successes, and its eventual defeat. It is a story about housing, but it is also about the development of American government. The program for modern housing posed a clear alternative to the direction in which expanded government activity was generally moving in the interwar period, namely toward the now-common two-tier pattern of well-legitimized, relatively generous state support for the middle and upper segments of the population and poorly regarded, poorly funded programs for the least affluent. As with tiered frameworks in other policy arenas, this pattern with regard to housing has systematically disadvantaged the poor, with the result that government activity itself has been an important factor in recreating and even expanding inequalities in American society.

The plan for modern housing was a conscious effort to move in another direction. As Bauer freely acknowledged, "It is not a 'reform' within the old

1

pattern."[2] The proposal failed politically, but its history is nonetheless important. Ideas associated with the program were taken seriously during the 1930s. Its design features and emphasis on local community life influenced the initial phase of direct federal housing activity in the New Deal under the Public Works Administration (PWA). And despite the strength of home ownership ideals associated with freestanding single-family homes, PWA housing proved attractive to many people. The story of this effort helps to illuminate the policy structure that "won," so to speak, a framework typically taken so much for granted that it is often hard even to perceive. In addition, this story suggests possibilities for, as well as barriers to, achieving public policies that operate more fairly, coherently, and democratically than those routinely devised within the American political system.

Through exploring issues such as these, this study seeks to contribute to new trends in American history. In recent years scholars seeking to understand twentieth-century politics in the United States have increasingly turned from a focus on presidents and electoral activity to questions concerning the development of the state, such as why and how it has expanded into new spheres of formerly private activity. Analyses of the origins, implementation, and outcomes of public policies have been central to this new orientation.[3] In addition, some scholars have been investigating the connections between social movements and state activity.[4] While the recent turn toward questions involving the state has produced much valuable work, urban policies generally and government involvement in residential real estate specifically have received little attention. This is despite the fact that housing is a central sector of the economy and that, starting in the New Deal era, it has been significantly shaped by federal programs.

Much of the new scholarship on the history of state has probed the origins and outcomes of the tiered pattern of policy development referred to above, particularly in relation to income-support programs where social security has become highly differentiated from so-called welfare programs.[5] State activity with regard to housing manifests a similar structure, with an upper tier composed of mortgage guarantee programs, quasi-public secondary mortgage markets, highway building, and tax subsidies that support private homeowners, businesses in the real estate sector (developers, contractors, brokers, etc.), and financial institutions. Far fewer resources go into programs aimed at the poor, such as public housing. The extreme disparity between the two tiers is illustrated by the fact that during the 1980s directly subsidized housing programs were cut approximately 80 percent to a level of around $12 billion per year. Meanwhile, in this same budget-sensitive period, subsidies through the tax code for owned housing in the form of mortgage-interest and property-tax deductions soared to approximately $50 billion per year with hardly a word of

2

criticism.[6] As this example illustrates, bottom-tier programs, despite the lower levels of public resources they receive, are extremely vulnerable during periods of fiscal austerity. Obviously this can be explained largely by their small and relatively powerless constituency, but they are also vulnerable because they generally consist of direct federal expenditures and operations. By contrast, upper-tier programs tend to be indirect, with their fiscal impact relatively invisible. Partly because of this invisibility, government activity that supports the commercial housing market is not only well-legitimated, but has come to seem almost natural.

Tiered patterns of federal activity are so usual in the United States as to seem almost inevitable. Yet, in reality, they are the outcome of political choices. As in many other sectors, the basic decisions that established the general pattern of state intervention related to housing were made during the 1930s. These decisions have had a variety of implications. The programs that resulted modernized and revitalized the commercial housing industry, which in turn helped drive the prosperity of the postwar years. Also, they played an important role in buttressing social stability. Many Americans enjoyed higher living standards as a result of mass suburbanization made possible by policies first put into effect during the 1930s. But over time the particular character of the New Deal housing settlement has played a major role in undermining a majority coalition in favor of activist government. Given that the mechanisms to reorganize the financial system used by New Deal housing programs were largely invisible to the average person, many core Democratic constituencies came to believe that they were not receiving any public help. Meanwhile, these groups perceived themselves to be paying for programs to benefit groups they regarded as less hardworking and deserving than themselves. As it worked out, then, most Americans came to credit the market and their own efforts for the increase in living standards that occurred after the New Deal.

How did this tiered pattern of federal activity in housing become established? Previous histories of the origins of federal housing policy have usually assumed rather than tried to explain this outcome, focusing either on the development of programs aimed at the poor or on those that supported the market. The account told here probes the causes for and consequences of the split by looking at the fate of the modern housing initiative to establish a single focus for federal activity in the housing arena.

As noted, advocates of modern housing wanted to make direct government support for noncommercial residential building the principal thrust of federal policy, and they envisioned this housing being built to a standard of majority acceptability. Their conception involved using innovative architectural and site design ideas, moving a sizeable proportion of housing out of the market, and invigorating local community life. To minimize costs and keep land open for nearby park areas and playgrounds, supporters of this program assumed that individual living units would be grouped together—similar to garden apartment or rowhouse construction, or what is today termed "clustered" development. They hoped to supply the new neighborhoods with a variety of conveniently accessible shared amenities, such as day care for young children and recreational opportunities for older children and adults. While individual apartments might be more compact than was the norm for upscale suburban homes, they would not have to be minimal, either, given the savings possible compared with that of typical residential development patterns. These residences could be of a size and quality that would appeal to the majority of the population. Thus, the nation would be able to afford to make good housing of a similar character available to everyone rather than supporting one style for the majority and a quite inferior and visually stigmatizing one for poor people.

Bauer and others associated with the Labor Housing Conference thought that the new way of building they espoused would have a number of other desirable outcomes, as well. They believed that the denser patterns of urban development would move the country toward more aesthetically satisfying and ecologically sensitive land-use patterns than low-density construction. Also, they thought that residential districts built along the lines they suggested, with high-quality shared facilities, would encourage interaction beyond the family, thereby creating an atmosphere of sociability that would prove personally satisfying and constructive for the society as a whole. Lively and child-friendly, these neighborhoods would provide advantages that housing within the market could not match. Such living arrangements would thus appeal to many middle-income families and not just those with too little money to purchase decent commercially produced shelter. As a result, there would be the basis for cross-class coalitions in support of this policy direction. Finally, advocates of modern housing thought that large-scale programs of direct government activity—building housing itself and providing assistance to private noncommercial groups on terms and at times determined by national policy—would provide a major macroeconomic lever by which to influence the level of domestic investment and help maintain high levels of employment.

The narrative begins in chapter 1 with an overview of the active and responsive, even if anarchic and technologically static, housing production system of the late nineteenth century. This system was disrupted by economic and political changes in the early twentieth century. Chapter 2 recounts how, as a result of these disruptions, business interests as well as advocates for the poor and liberal policy analysts put forward proposals in the 1920s for ways in which government activity should expand into the housing arena. Each group had a distinctive view of what constituted the American housing problem and how to solve it, but they were united in wanting a more activist state. This chapter explores the paradox of growing skepticism, even at a time when the private market was generating a large volume of construction, about the capability of the market to upgrade residential standards for the many families of low-wage industrial workers. In fact, it was during the twenties that a number of observers came to believe that profit-driven activity would never solve the housing problems of a large proportion of the population. Chapter 3 tells the story of Catherine Bauer, the aspiring art critic turned policy intellectual and political activist, who accepted this radical critique and best articulated a constructive response in a program she termed "modern housing." Bauer did not invent the various elements of the modern housing approach. These ideas for architectural and economic innovation in the field of residential development had been circulating internationally for some time. Her special contribution was to present them in a coherent and appealing fashion to an American audience.

Chapter 4 moves into the period of the early New Deal. It shows how the new political context allowed some of the ideas associated with the modern housing program, when supported by social movements, to have an impact on the temporary, experimental housing program of the Public Works Administration. Case studies in chapters 5 and 6 provide an in-depth look at two of the most acclaimed housing developments built through the PWA: the Carl Mackley Houses of Philadelphia and the Harlem River Houses of New York City. Both complexes show the influence of social and architectural ideas associated with the modern housing program. The experiences and reactions of people who lived in these two projects are explored using oral interviews.

The story next moves to the national level, charting the political struggle over the character of permanent policy. Chapter 7 describes the unsuccessful efforts of the Labor Housing Conference to have the modern housing approach institutionalized through permanent legislation and the reasons for this failure. The conclusion discusses outcomes of the policy direction chosen at the end of the 1930s, stresses that the American housing system currently faces, and recent initiatives to expand affordable housing. It also considers the legacy of the modern housing policy initiative.

Put briefly, the most important legacy of this initiative is that it suggested ways of breaking through barriers to more egalitarian public policies in the United States. Policy intellectuals, labor unionists, and some of the residents of the experimental PWA projects were involved in shaping a new vision for American housing that did not take for granted so many central characteristics of the existing system. The program they advocated did not assume a zero-sum competition for the type of housing already being created by commercial activity. Instead, it put forward plans for a radically new urban living environment, where design innovations and social activity would create satisfactions not available through the market. In addition, Bauer was sensitive to the importance of allowing for significant self-determination and influence for residents and nongovernmental organizations such as unions and cooperatives. Ideas for this kind of democratic quality in housing provision suggested possibilities for a version of the welfare state that could command wider public support in America, given a political culture that prizes individual initiative and local control.

Was this a hopelessly utopian vision? Would ordinary Americans have liked living in neighborhoods built along the lines suggested by modern housing ideals? Conventional wisdom suggests that Americans never would have abandoned their cherished dream of owning their own home, preferably a free-standing, single-family house in the suburbs. Yet some scholars have argued that this seemingly transhistorical commitment to homeownership in the United States was considerably strengthened if not actually created in its present form during the interwar period.[7] Also, evidence from the case studies of the PWA housing developments in this book suggests that many Americans might well have enjoyed living at least some part of their lives in good quality, economical garden apartment buildings or rowhouses surrounded by attractive landscaping and generously provided with recreational opportunities and social services within easy walking distance.

In fact, Americans were never given such a choice, so it is impossible to tell how they would have reacted. Only some of the PWA developments that were built successfully embodied much of the spirit of the modern housing idea, and few Americans ever saw one of these. Encouraged by the housing industry, conservative forces in Congress made sure that there would be no federal support for this policy direction in the permanent legislation that ultimately emerged from the turmoil of the 1930s. As we will see, this vision for American housing had limitations and ambiguities. Yet, the problems it sought to solve have not disappeared, and many of the ideas it put forward could help us today as we try to craft solutions to our contemporary dilemmas.

ONE

American Housing before the Depression

W alter Stabler, who headed the Metropolitan Life Insurance Company's urban mortgage department, told a special Senate committee in 1920 that "the housing question" constituted the most serious problem "that this country has ever seen" and warned that it was "growing worse steadily."[1] He argued for federal action in the form of lifting taxes on income from residential real estate investment. Stabler was only one of many prominent figures in this era who believed that the government needed to intervene in some way to improve the functioning of the housing market. Long before the Great Depression, leaders of major institutions in the housing industry as well as reform-oriented intellectuals and charity workers voiced serious misgivings about the American system of housing provision. Not surprisingly, given their different viewpoints, critics often did not agree as to what constituted key problems, much less underlying causes. But a significant proportion of reform proposals, including those from business groups, involved some form of state intervention.

To understand the sources of these new attitudes about how the federal government should relate to the housing sector, we need to know how the housing system worked and was changing. This chapter describes housing production in the late nineteenth century, explains the pressures that were destabilizing that system, and concludes by looking at the housing situation in Chicago as a way of gaining a better understanding of what the market was delivering for modest-income families at a point when it was operating at high volume and high profitability.

American Housing in the Late Nineteenth Century

In the decades after the Civil War, North American cities experienced "extraordinary waves of shelter construction."[2] All but three of the country's twenty-eight largest cities increased their supply of dwellings by at least 50 percent from 1880 to 1900. In some cases, growth was spectacular; Denver's housing stock, for instance, expanded by 413 percent in this period.[3] Such extreme growth was possible only in smaller and newer cities, but even the more typical rates were high. Of course, the country's population was increasing rapidly at the same time, but residential building expanded even faster. During the 1890s, the first period for which we have national housing data, the 21 percent population growth was outpaced by a 26 percent expansion of residential units. This was despite a major depression during the decade.[4]

Affordability was the key to this construction boom. Before the turn of the century, a variety of factors made the ratio of housing costs to income more favorable than in other industrial countries. Transportation innovations continually opened new tracts of inexpensive land on the fringes of U.S. cities, and prices for building materials fell. The result was that construction costs for North America as a whole actually dropped by a quarter from 1870 to 1895. Meanwhile, American workers made higher wages. This combination of circumstances has led some analysts to dub the late nineteenth century "the golden age of housing for the common people" of North America.[5]

Within this context, affluent families improved their living conditions dramatically. Many moved to suburban towns like Swarthmore, Pennsylvania; Lake Forest, Illinois; and Scarsdale, New York where they could commute to central cities by rail. Elite suburbs provided attractive living environments, with handsome homes set well back from quiet tree-lined streets on large landscaped lots. The houses themselves were very commodious. Typically two stories tall, upscale Victorian-era suburban homes had numerous rooms, many quite specialized, such as pantries, sleeping porches, and libraries. Full basements and attics provided even more space. These residences routinely came equipped with central heating, flush toilets, and hot and cold running water piped to several rooms.[6]

With regard to working people in this period, the well-publicized tenement-house situation of New York City has led many to assume that a high proportion of low-income families throughout the country resided in small, dark, rather airless rooms in multistory buildings. But, in fact, the extreme densities characteristic of cheap accommodations in New York were unique, a function of the atypically high land costs in Manhattan. In other urban centers, small freestanding wooden houses were the most usual type of inexpensive shelter (see figure 1.1). There were some regional traditions of denser building types—for example, row housing in mid-Atlantic cities like Baltimore and Philadelphia, three-deckers in New England, and the two-flats of Chicago—but these kinds of structures were not common in the country as a whole.[7]

Set close together on narrow lots and stretching mile after mile, the great masses of inexpensive tiny houses that mushroomed so quickly on the outskirts of late nineteenth-century American cities did not cumulate into charming neighborhoods. Nor did they offer their inhabitants a high level of physical comfort. Typically these structures were little more than flimsy, drafty "shells" with no running water or indoor toilets. Heat came only from the kitchen stove. Nor did these small dwellings necessarily provide all that much

FIG. 1.1 This Chicago neighborhood of small wooden homes was actually more typical of inexpensive urban housing in the late-nineteenth-century American cities than the famous tenement houses of New York City. Initially, such structures were often little more than drafty shells, with only stoves for heat and no running water or indoor toilets. While they appear to be single-family dwellings, they were routinely divided between two or more families. Their deficiencies as individual units could be significantly rectified over time, however, as owners invested money and their own labor in upgrades of various kinds. A more problematic outcome of the housing delivery system of this era was the monotony and density of the larger neighborhood environment, with few landscaped open spaces available for visual relief or recreation. Photograph reproduced courtesy of the Chicago Historical Society.

family privacy. To increase income, owners routinely took in boarders or subdivided their small homes into multiple units. In Chicago and Milwaukee, builders commonly cut costs by not fully excavating basements. The practice meant that residents had to climb a flight of stairs to reach their front doors, but it also meant that basements were easily converted into rental units with private entrances. Crude and cramped as these homes were, however, they did offer their residents more light, ventilation, and fire safety than working-class families could obtain in the densely packed cores of industrial cities.[8]

With respect to the housing delivery system in this period we have only fragmentary evidence, but it seems to be the case that most residential financing and building happened on a piecemeal basis. Individuals would acquire a parcel of land and hire a builder to put up a specific structure that the owner planned to inhabit or use as rental property. Purchasers normally financed the operation using some combination of savings and personal loans.[9] The builders they hired generally did not operate self-contained businesses. Having typically started as carpenters, most builders functioned as general contractors who coordinated a variety of specialized trades. During this period, there was a plethora of small residential construction companies. The field was an easy one to enter, since a lot of people knew the fundamentals of simple wood-framing and expensive machinery was not required. These factors explain why there were so many small enterprises and also why many families became their own builders for all or part of the job.[10]

Some entrepreneurs did produce finished houses to sell to unknown buyers, but they were a distinctly minor force in this era. Most often, residential real estate speculation took the form of selling lots in districts that were more or less "improved," meaning they contained such features as paved roads, sidewalks, water and sewer mains, and plantings. Those entrepreneurs who did build for the market usually worked on a very small scale, most likely as a sideline enterprise. Historian Sam Bass Warner found that approximately three-quarters of the builders working in the streetcar suburbs of Boston in the late nineteenth century put up no more than one dwelling per year and less than twenty total over a thirty-year period.[11]

There were a few large operators. The most successful in terms of sheer numbers was probably the flamboyant land speculator and sometime playwright Samuel E. Gross, who built almost ten thousand houses in and around Chicago in the 1880s. But the scale of Gross's operations seems to have been truly remarkable nationally as well as in the Chicago area. More commonly, a "large" builder was one who put up a block of houses at a time.[12]

In sum, then, the American urban housing delivery system of the late nineteenth century was extremely responsive. The many small builders were more than able to keep pace with the shelter needs of rapidly expanding cities. They produced housing that, for all of its disadvantages, was better than that which the working class was able to obtain in other advanced industrial countries. This building pattern, however, did oftentimes create bleak cityscapes, particularly when builders were working at the low end of the market.

Changing Conditions in American Housing

Around the turn of the century, the framework of housing provision just described began to experience significant disequilibrating pressures. Construction costs increased dramatically, financing patterns shifted, and new public activities were initiated in the years of Progressive-Era state building. These changes made things much more difficult for investors and builders as well as consumers and created the context for debates about the role of the federal government in the housing sector.

Despite the new pressures, American builders continued to be highly active in the early twentieth century. Evaluated on the basis of number of housing units and viewed by decades, the residential construction industry seems to have been not only robust, but constantly improving. The first ten years of the new century saw an average of 361,000 housing starts each year, compared with 294,000 during the 1890s. In the next few years, there was so much construction that despite an almost complete cessation of activity during the war the yearly average for the decade of the 1910s rose to 359,000 starts. The 1920s broke all previous records with an average of 703,000 starts per year.[13] In each of these three decades residential units multiplied faster than population.[14] These totals are impressive, but they mask profound shifts in the housing delivery system that created difficulties for both providers and consumers.

Increasing Costs of Construction

Probably the single most important destabilizing force was the dramatic upsurge of construction costs. From 1895 to 1914, the cost of residential building increased by 50 percent, compared with an overall rise in consumer prices of 20 percent.[15] Both labor and materials became more expensive. Wood, the largest single component of an American house, was the major problem. From the turn of the century, when the great timber stands of the Midwest were exhausted, until 1920, when the introduction of truck transport began to lower costs of Southern and Pacific Northwestern lumber, the cost of wood increased by almost fivefold. Rising wages in the construction trades without corresponding productivity gains also tended to drive up overall costs. Hourly rates went up only slightly more than in manufacturing industries, but the impact was greater because labor comprises a larger proportion of the cost of construction than it does in most other industries.[16]

Housing providers would have had problems enough if they had confronted only the challenge of higher costs while trying to supply the same product. But they also faced dramatically rising expectations. Tighter local building codes and new consumer demands transformed concepts of what constituted an acceptable minimum standard for new housing. Thus, the most basic dwelling unit became much more expensive to produce. Supplying plumbing and central heating systems, for instance, accounted for approximately one-quarter of the total cost of a housing unit.[17]

Builders responded in a variety of ways. For one thing, they saved money by cutting back size, an economy that impacted buyers' comfort less than it might have given that family size was also shrinking.[18] In addition, they built more housing units in the form of apartments, resulting in considerable savings compared with freestanding houses. From 1922 through 1929, forty-one percent of all new housing units were in multiple unit structures, compared with thirty-three percent in the years 1900 through 1907.[19] Finally, the increasing use of automobiles meant that builders could use land parcels that were less expensive as a consequence of not being contiguous to public transportation. The growth of suburbs indicates the popularity of this strategy. During the decade of the 1920s, the population of fringe districts within the largest metropolitan areas increased at twice the rate of the cities at their cores.[20]

Such maneuvers did cut costs, but they did not represent actual increases in efficiency. Why did housing not conform to the general "New Era" model of increased productivity and falling prices? In 1908 when Ford made his first Model T's, he sold the cheapest models for $825. In 1927, when the last of the "Tin Lizzies" rolled off the production line, they went for as little as $290, despite auto workers' wages having gone up.

As we have seen, during these same years trends in residential construction were moving in exactly the opposite direction. One reason that residential builders could not hope to compete with the mass production achievements of the country's lead industry was the utterly different scale of their firms. In the mid–1920s, the Ford Motor Company alone was producing approximately two million cars a year. Ford spent around $30 million merely to replace the electrical equipment at the giant River Rouge plant as part of the 1927 changeover to the Model A. The factory's machine tools alone were worth an estimated $45 million.[21]

By contrast, homebuilding truly was, in the words of its critics, a collection of "picayune businesses." A survey by the Commerce Department for 1929 revealed that approximately 80 percent of residential builders did an annual volume of business of less than $9,000. Given the cost of typical dwellings, this was equivalent to constructing approximately one–and–one-half houses a year. Even the comparatively large builders (who represented 20 percent of the total) only erected an average of fifty houses per year.[22] Individual firms simply had too little capital to mechanize their operations, let alone mount research projects to develop productivity-enhancing innovations. Balloon framing had been the last "true paradigm shift" in housing production, and it had been introduced in the mid-nineteenth century.[23]

Financial Changes

New trends in financing were a second major force transforming American housing. In the nineteenth century, purchasers paid for most residential building either directly out of their own savings or else with loans from relatives, friends, or small local lenders. After the turn of the century, purchasers relied increasingly on commercial loans to finance their housing, and institutional lenders supplied an increasing proportion of housing capital. During the 1890s, debt financing went up by approximately 27 percent. Over the following thirty years, mortgage debt increased by a factor of almost 10, reaching 28 billion dollars by 1930. Institutional lenders, such as savings and loan (originally called "building and loan") associations, commercial savings banks, mutual savings banks, and life insurance companies, held 49 percent of the nation's outstanding mortgage debt in 1900. By 1930, institutional lenders had increased their share to 62 percent.[24]

Changes within the housing sector interacted with developments in the larger economy to fuel these new financing patterns. For example, higher housing prices meant that purchasers needed to take on more debt to bridge the gap between savings and the cost of a home. At the same time, financial institutions were increasingly on the lookout for more outlets for their funds, as the amount of money in savings accounts and life insurance policies ballooned in the decades after the Civil War. In 1867 the total amount deposited in mutual savings banks, savings and loans, commercial banks, and life insurance policies stood at approximately $425 million. By 1900 the total had risen to somewhat over $5 billion. Then, in the next three decades, these kinds of deposits expanded to $52 billion, growing three times as fast as the overall economy.[25]

During this same period, behavior patterns of individual investors were also shifting in ways that impacted housing. Traditionally, the urban middle class had used modest urban residential properties as outlets for savings. But the late nineteenth century's new middle class of managerial, technical, and professional workers tended to favor interest-bearing accounts with financial institutions over the rigors of life as a small landlord. By the early twentieth century, individual investors began entering national capital markets. For many people, the enormously successful Liberty and Victory bond campaigns of the World War I era served as an introduction to these new kinds of opportunities. During the 1920s, national corporations did their best to encourage individuals to buy securities. Anxious to build support for utopian visions of a business-led society of abundance and equality, big companies courted small investors with low-denomination stock issues.[26]

One type of security that proved particularly appealing to small investors in these years was the mortgage bond, a new financial instrument invented around the turn of the century. Mortgage bonds were backed by a single whole mortgage or a package of several mortgages bundled together. They came in denominations as small as $100, yielded relatively high returns, and had a reputation for safety (unfounded as it turned out). Investment in mortgage bonds is estimated to have soared from $150 million before World War I to approximately $10 billion by the early 1930s.[27]

These transformations in the operation of financial markets and changes in real estate financing practices had profound effects on American housing. Trends toward using institutions for savings and participating in national capital markets meant that a smaller proportion of individual investments financed small rental properties. Meanwhile, the increasing role of institutional actors in real estate together with new financial instruments like mortgage bonds made it easier for entrepreneurs to secure financing for expensive large-scale projects, such as big apartment complexes and fully developed residential subdivisions.[28] More participation by sophisticated institutional lenders also meant an increasing focus on the high-end, high-profit segment of the market. Cost trends illustrate this emphasis. Although wholesale prices of building materials held steady during the building boom of the 1920s, housing units were, on average, 21 percent more expensive in 1929 than they had been in 1922.[29] Meanwhile, production of modest types of urban rental properties declined significantly as a proportion of the overall mix of new housing.[30]

The Changing Role of the State

The third major change for residential building was the expansion of the national state in the Progressive Era. The federal government did not move into the housing sector directly until the emergency conditions of the First World War. However, sweeping innovations aimed at other key sectors of the economy introduced during Woodrow Wilson's first administration had important repercussions for housing.

The creation of the Federal Reserve in 1913 is a good example of the way that Progressive Era economic reforms were not aimed specifically at housing but impacted it nevertheless. In order to encourage banks to join the Federal Reserve System, Congress liberalized prohibitions against real estate lending by nationally chartered banks. Commercial banks welcomed these legal changes, as their traditional corporate customers were relying increasingly on internal profits or else issuing securities when they needed capital. After the new regulations went into effect, commercial banks moved aggressively into urban real estate. Between 1922 and 1929 they increased the size of their mortgage portfolios by a factor of ten.[31]

The introduction of the income tax marked another major federal intervention into the economy with important implications for real estate. Following the general outlines of the original Civil-War era federal income tax legislation, the 1913 act made interest payments and taxes deductible from income. These features of the internal revenue code would come to affect a large proportion of the population and account for what, in effect, would be subsidies for homeowners after the income tax became a mass tax during World War II. Initially, however, these provisions were rather unimportant, since only high-income individuals were subject to income taxes and rates were low. The significant issue at the time for housing had to do with the regulations in the tax code that exempted income from state and local bonds.

Since income from real estate investment was not accorded any such exemption, developers found it harder to raise capital for residential construction.[32]

The Federal Farm Loan Act of 1916 represented another Progressive-Era economic innovation not directly related to housing, but with important implications for this sector, nevertheless. A public program to lower the cost of long-term credit to farmers had been the dream of a generation of Populists. Passage of this legislation meant that the federal government accepted responsibility for channeling low-cost capital to economic activities deemed essential to the public interest. This would prove to be an influential precedent for businesses involved with residential financing.[33]

While the federal activities just described were not aimed explicitly at housing, the expanding Progressive state did enter the housing market directly during the First World War. This "departure from the custom of the country," as one senator termed it, was politically possible because many federal officials became convinced that housing problems were compromising the success of industrial mobilization. While it is not clear to what extent housing shortages were to blame, it was indeed the case that parts of the economy were functioning quite poorly by 1917.[34]

War orders from the Allies had led to rapid and chaotic expansion of the economy even before the United States joined the fighting. As new high-paying jobs opened up in industry, the number of manufacturing workers rose from 8.2 million in 1915 to 10.2 million in 1918.[35] Existing housing stock around shipyards and war production plants quickly filled to overcapacity. Yet commercial builders were unable to respond. Most private capital was pouring into industrial expansion or war bonds, making it almost impossible to secure financing for homebuilding. In addition, beginning in early 1918, the government began officially restricting nonessential construction.[36] Only about half as many new housing units were built in 1917 as in the year before, and by 1918 the total again shrank by half.[37]

The economic expansion disrupted industrial labor relations as well as the housing market. For workers, the war prosperity meant a welcome reprieve from the pressures of corporate efficiency programs and union busting that had marked the previous several years. Labor historian David Montgomery points out that once labor shortages began in 1916, workers changed "jobs freely in search of better earnings, while putting in many more days of work and many more hours of overtime than in normal years." Meanwhile, the number of strikes shot up to historic highs.[38] This new freedom for workers translated into difficult conditions for management. For example, after the United States entered the war, Bethlehem Steel in Pennsylvania experienced a monthly turnover rate of almost 40 percent. The company was so shorthanded it had to operate some shifts as much as a thousand workers short.[39] Between 1915 and 1918, labor productivity rates declined; this was the first time this had happened in American history except during deep depressions.[40]

During the harsh winter of 1917–18, the situation became acute. Railroad transport became snarled, Eastern cities suffered fuel shortages, and steel production declined. National leaders worried about the success of the war effort, especially after congressional hearings exposed the level of administrative confusion in the War Department and the amount of crowding and labor turnover in defense production centers. Anxiety ran so high that congressional Republicans even tried to wrest leadership from President Wilson and install a bipartisan War Cabinet. Wilson managed to retain control, but only by bold initiatives that brought the economy more firmly under executive authority.[41]

The crisis atmosphere in Washington prompted action on the housing question. Legislation authorizing the United States Shipping Board to initiate housing programs at shipbuilding centers passed in March 1918. In May, Congress passed a more general bill directing the Labor Department to provide dwellings for "such industrial workers as are engaged in . . . industries connected with and essential to the national defense, and their families."[42] Despite the general conviction that housing shortages were undermining the mobilization effort, the legislation was controversial. The basic source of worry was, as one congressman explained, that the temporary wartime programs would "be a stepping stone to a permanent plan for this government to provide housing for labor people generally after the war."[43]

To carry out the housing programs, the United States Shipping Board established the Emergency Fleet Corporation (EFC) and the Labor Department created the United States Housing Corporation. Before embarking on any construction, each agency tried to promote more efficient use of existing housing stock in affected areas by upgrading transportation services. The Housing Corporation also set up vacancy registration bureaus and organized local "fair rent" committees to discourage rent increases.[44]

When it came to actual building, both agencies initially attempted to work through local operators rather than becoming developers and landlords themselves. The EFC practiced this strategy successfully by supplying loans to realty subsidiaries of shipbuilding companies. It did, however, as one of its reports noted, retain powers "broader than that of a mere mortgagee or banker," including design control and management oversight of the rental properties it financed.[45] At the outset, the Labor Department's Housing Corporation also hoped to operate through privately controlled local development companies, but it found it difficult to locate "public spirited interests" capable of taking on the necessary tasks. The problem was that in munitions manufacturing locales there were generally a number of different companies operating, each with its own idea of how and where new residential facilities should be constructed. Thus, it turned out to be simpler, although more time-consuming, for the Housing Corporation itself to plan the operation, directly supervise contractors, and then retain title to the finished housing.[46] Partly for this reason and also because it had received funds four months later than the EFC, the Labor Department's more ambitious program was further from realization when the armistice was signed in November. (See figures 1.2 and 1.3.)

Ultimately, the Housing Corporation finished only 5,998 of the nearly 25,000 family dwellings it had projected as a goal. The EFC completed 9,185. The two programs together also provided temporary quarters for approximately 15,000 single men. The family homes were permanent construction, most in attractively planned residential developments. After the war, these were sold off to private buyers.[47]

Besides curtailing nonessential private construction and mounting building programs, the federal government also intervened in the housing market during the war with rent control laws. While more sweeping national proposals failed, Congress did approve the Soldiers' and Sailors' Civil Relief Act of 1918 which forbade eviction of military dependents from nonluxury rental housing. Also, in response to the massive influx of white-collar personnel into the Capitol, Congress passed rent control laws for the District of Columbia beginning in 1918. This legislation developed a large and enthusiastic constituency, and Congress continued it after the war was over. Rent control in the district continued in effect until late 1924, when landlords were successful in getting the Appellate Court to declare that there was no longer constitutional authority for such measures.

Six states also passed laws aimed at controlling rents during the war, but most local efforts occurred without benefit of formal government action. In many centers of congestion, leading citizens formed committees to hear complaints and determine fair rents. Landlords who failed to cooperate would find themselves written up in the local newspapers, apparently quite an effective sanction given that rents in large cities held quite steady until the end of hostilities.[48]

Housing in the 1920s: The Case of Chicago

In the early twentieth century, higher costs, shifts in financing patterns, and a more activist state altered the environment for housing production. What was the impact of this new environment on industry actors and on consumers, especially moderate- and low-income families?

For the most part, scholars have answered this question by looking at national data on overall levels of housing production. These levels were strikingly high. But the aggregate rate of building does not tell us about those aspects of the housing situation that concerned contemporaries and affected

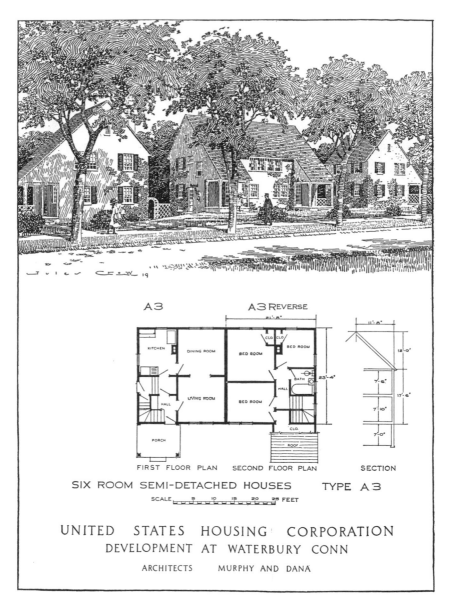

Fig. 1.2 (see p. 19 for legend)

their thinking about the appropriate role for government, such as trends toward increasingly expensive production and the difficulties that many wage-earners faced in trying to afford decent shelter. By looking at the market in a particular city—in this case, Chicago—we can observe its functioning in greater detail.

Figs. 1.2 and 1.3 The United States Housing Corporation development at Waterbury, Connecticut, built during World War I. Figure 1.2 is an architect's drawing of exteriors and interior plans. Figure 1.3 is a photograph of the same housing under construction. The development was built within walking distance of two different companies involved in military production. It was slated to include housing for 205 families, although only fifty-five dwellings were built by the time the program was discontinued. While only semidetached (double) and freestanding houses were constructed at Waterbury, other federal developments included short rows of four and six attached homes, as well as some apartment buildings. To insure that all interior spaces received some sunlight, units were never more than two rooms deep. The interior layouts of the homes were highly standardized, but the simplified English cottage motif was easy to manipulate so as to avoid visual monotony from the street.

Chicago is a good place to look in order to understand what was happening with American urban housing and how modest-income families were living in the years immediately before the Great Depression. The economic dynamism of the city means that conditions were probably as good there as anywhere in the country. Moreover, researchers connected with the University of Chicago studied their city intensively, leaving us with probably more data on housing than for any other city in the country except New York City. Yet, unlike the much-studied but unique New York, Chicago possessed all the variables identified by historians as differentiating North American housing from that of other parts of the industrialized world, namely: "higher wages, coupled with the availability of land, wood, and simple techniques of construction."[49]

Post-War Difficulties in the Housing Market

Contemporaries assumed that residential building throughout the country would make a rapid recovery when the war ended. All restrictions on con-

Fig. 1.4 Streetscape of Chicago bungalows constructed in the 1920s. Built of brick and provided with indoor plumbing, electricity, and central heating, these homes were significantly more comfortable than the crude wooden residences of previous decades. Nevertheless, methods of subdividing continued to result in long narrow lots. Thus, bungalows were quite long and usually set close to the property lines on their sides, an arrangement that compromised possibilities for interior sunlight as well as pleasant views from windows. Furthermore, although these houses were some of the least expensive built in the 1920s, they still cost much more than the entry-level homes of previous decades and were not easily affordable for people of modest incomes. Photograph: Bungalows on 9100 block of South Colfax Avenue, Chicago, Illinois, 1962; photographed by Ralph E. Tower. Reproduced courtesy of the Chicago Historical Society.

clearly they were enormously more comfortable than their simple, flimsy predecessors. They were also significantly more expensive. While the overall cost of living had not quite doubled in the forty years between 1885 and 1925, the price of an entry-level new house had grown five and one-half times.[59] This increase is partly explained by the higher costs of materials and labor without offsetting gains in productivity and partly by escalating standards such as water and sewer hookups. But a good part of the higher price tag was a simple function of producing an inherently more luxurious commodity. The bungalow was targeted at a more prosperous segment of the market than the worker cottage had been.

The trend toward more expensive production characterized all kinds of residential building in Chicago. The dramatic increase in luxury apartment houses in the 1920s provides a particularly striking example of this tendency. In this period, it was the biggest buildings that were aimed at the highest-paying clientele, since local building codes required more expensive steel and concrete fireproof construction once a residential structure went over three stories. Most of the high-rise construction was concentrated along the "Gold Coast" of Lake Michigan to the north of the city's central business district. Gold Coast apartment buildings were the ultimate in luxury. The lobby at 900 North Michigan was modeled after a Versailles palace dining room, for example. At 1400 Lake Shore Drive, tenants had all the amenities of a grand hotel, with a barber shop, florist, newsstand, beauty shop, commissary, cigar store, drugstore, giftshop, restaurant, and even a small golf course staffed by a full-time instructor in the building.[60] Not surprisingly, rents in such buildings were steep, averaging between $500 and $1,200 a month at a time when the median housing cost in the city was $55 a month.[61] In the twenty years preceding the war, developers had only put up eighty-five buildings with forty or more units in the city. In the twenties they built 890.[62]

Meanwhile, at the other end of the new construction mix, the pattern reversed itself. The "two-flat," a residential building with two vertically stacked units, had typically served the lower part of the rental market and was a mainstay of Chicago's housing market in the early twentieth century. Before the war, two-flat apartments made up approximately 25 percent of new housing units in the Windy City each year, but in the 1920s they accounted for only 12 percent.[63]

These production trends, combined with the higher expectations for basic amenities, meant that housing was relatively more expensive in the 1920s. The increasing availability of mortgages did make it possible for many families to purchase new or used housing equipped to the standards of the day. Yet even installment buying could not make up the discrepancy between the small incomes of most industrial workers and the true cost of well-maintained urban shelter equipped with contemporary plumbing and heating systems.

Chicago philanthropists inadvertently dramatized the extent of the gap between modest incomes and the price of even moderate standards by their efforts to construct affordable housing in this period. Julius Rosenwald built Michigan Boulevard Garden Apartments as a model of good housing for African Americans and the trustees of the fortune of another leading Chicago merchant constructed Marshall Field Gardens as a demonstration aimed at modest-income white families. Neither complex was luxurious. Both contained more landscaped space than most commercial developments, but they were each five stories with no elevators, and their ceilings were only eight feet high, instead of the eight-and-one-half-foot ceilings required by the city building code. Yet, even when these design concessions were combined with painstaking planning, minimal profit expectations, and low-interest capital, both developments needed to charge tenants an average of over $62 a month at a time when median housing costs in the city were $55.[64] These experiments clearly illustrate why private developers, who expected profits of "at least 10, 15, and preferably 25 percent" to offset their business risks and high borrowing costs, preferred to avoid even the middle of the market.[65]

That entrepreneurs did not build expressly for lower-income families, however, did not in itself preclude improvement in conditions over time. According to the theoretical model of housing market processes often termed "filtering," even though most new housing is built for the more affluent, everyone benefits. As the more wealthy move into newly built homes, it is assumed that their used housing filters down to people less well off. As a result of an increase in total supply, everyone moves up a notch.[66]

However, for those who were paying low rents in Chicago in the twenties, the market did not operate according to this model. In 1926, canvassers for the Department of Welfare found that the tight market from the war years was indeed easing for those who could afford over $30 a month. For those paying between $25 and $30 a month, however, rents essentially had held steady during the year. In the below $25 rental bracket, the general pattern reversed itself. Overall, these rents advanced 3 percent. For housing that had cost between $15 and $19 in 1925, the increase was 4 percent. What these data suggest is that new building was indeed making housing less expensive for many consumers.[67] But the rent increases for the less expensive rentals implies that the supply of these dwellings may actually have been contracting. In any case, the same quality of housing was becoming more expensive in the part of the market available to those in the bottom income quartile.

Conditions for Low-Income Families

Within the general framework described, what kind of accommodations could people with low incomes obtain in the years before the Great Depression? To envision conditions for modest-income urban families, it is necessary to estimate what they were paying to rent or purchase housing. (Most, in fact, were renting. In Chicago, over two-thirds of families rented in the twenties.[68]) Experts of this era assumed that people of modest means could afford to pay a maximum of 20 percent of their yearly income for housing.[69] A low percentage of small incomes was advised, because, as Chicago housing reformer Benjamin Rosenthal explained, "when families must spend between a third and a half of their income to obtain shelter," the result was a "deprival of necessities of life."[70] On this basis, families at the 25th percentile would have paid $19 a month. Despite the admonitions of middle-class advisors, however, the city's poorest families spent a much higher portion of their income on housing. Census takers in 1930 found that housing costs at the 25th percentile were $35, or 36 percent of income.[71]

Even by devoting so much of their income to shelter, low-wage families obtained rather basic accommodations. At the top of the bottom quartile of rentals, dwellings were generally "cold water flats."[72] A typical Chicago flat was a long unit that ran the length of a two or three-story wooden building set on a 25 by 125 foot lot.[73] These structures tended to fill up most of the width of the property on which they sat, so only rooms in the front and back got much light. Most often the interior layout consisted of a kitchen, living room, and two bedrooms.[74] One could expect to find cold running water in the kitchen, although not in any other room.[75] Toilets, although not an original feature of old inexpensive buildings, had been added to most cheap rentals by the twenties. They were usually installed in small cubicles off the kitchen, where plumbing already existed. Built-in bathtubs were less common. At the 25th percentile of rent levels, families had about a 60 percent chance of obtaining some kind of facilities for bathing, although such arrangements would not usually be considered bathrooms by contemporary standards.[76]

Many Chicago houses and flats were centrally heated by the 1920s, but this amenity was only consistently available at rents above what half the families in the city paid.[77] In the cheaper housing stock, everyone used stoves for warmth and purchased their own fuel.[78] Renters had to pay for their own coal, plus any electricity, gas, and ice they used. These incidentals drove up shelter costs by approximately one-third, according to the Illinois Housing Commission.[79] One researcher observed that "in these thinly built frame houses the kitchen may be the only heated room in the house," which was not surprising given the labor and costs involved.[80]

At this rent level, residents could not expect much neighborhood charm. A large proportion of low-rent districts were close to industrial enterprises. In "the Bush," a South Chicago neighborhood that bordered steel mills, the air was "always laden, day or night, with the smoke from steel mills, whose furnaces never rest"[81] (figure 1.5). A study by the Illinois Housing Commission described a district north of Douglas Park, where rents between $25 and $37 predominated, in the following terms: "Old brick buildings, crowded together on narrow, dirty streets were the rule. Many of the alleys were indescribably

Fig. 1.5 A 1920s photograph of "the Bush," a south Chicago neighborhood adjacent to steel mills. Like other cheaply built residential areas, it had little in the way of "neighborhood charm." Also in common with other poor sections of the city, the Bush only seemed to decline in the prosperous twenties. Photo reproduced, with permission, from Edith Abbott, *The Tenements of Chicago, 1880–1935* (Chicago: University of Chicago Press, 1936).

filthy. Car lines and elevated tracks pervaded the district." The report also noted the presence of several factories and a railroad yard in the neighborhood.[82]

Of course, not everyone could afford even this level. As a group, African Americans fared most poorly, disadvantaged by the combination of a segregated housing market and low incomes resulting from a segregated job market. In 1925, researchers for the Department of Public Welfare described the situation of a six-person black family supported by a father who worked in a foundry. These people were living in two rooms for which they paid $10 a month. "The toilet was under the sidewalk; light at night was from oil lamps; both rooms served as bedrooms." Toilets installed under the sidewalk was a peculiar Chicago custom related to the raising of street grades. Such facilities, which often served more than one family, frequently became unusable during harsh Midwestern winters when outdoor plumbing would freeze.[83]

While African Americans inhabited the worst dwellings, in the mid–1920s "no group was free from the disadvantages of poor housing," according to Elizabeth Hughes, director of the city's Bureau of Social Research. As evidence for her contention, she cited the case of the "native white family of foreign parentage" consisting of ten persons, supported by the earnings of three adults. For $12 a month they rented four rooms, and though their flat did have an inside toilet, it was broken and would not flush. In fact, the plumbing throughout the building was defective and "the second floor toilet leaked through into the kitchen this family used."[84]

As this overview of housing conditions for the bottom quarter of Chicago families before the Depression makes clear, a large proportion of fully employed people were not significantly integrated into the emerging consumer economy. Nowhere was this more obvious than in housing, one of the most important commodities in determining people's standard of living. This was not only because the interiors of their homes lacked amenities, but also because low rental housing was located in ill-favored neighborhoods. Then as now, neighborhood context determined access to services both public and commercial, as well as to transportation networks that affected access to employment opportunities and much else.[85] Especially in an era when automobile ownership was not widespread among people of modest incomes, the character of the immediate neighborhood was crucial to the quality of life.

Conclusion

Viewed from a national perspective with a focus on profitability and sheer output, the housing market of the 1920s seemed healthy and effective. Although costs had gone up, those who could afford the price were able to purchase a high level of comfort and convenience.

Despite these achievements, many were critical of the way the market was operating. Contemporary observers worried about such issues as the lack of investment capital for residential building after the war and the inability of the industry to do a better job at supplying what they defined as an acceptable standard of urban housing to a large proportion of full-time working families. The next chapter describes the complaints of different groups, the analyses they developed to explain the problems they identified, and the proposals they put forward to solve these problems.

TWO

The Politics of Housing in the 1920s

Pressures on the housing industry and the harsh options many wage-earning families confronted in their search for good housing prompted a variety of proposals for remedial action in the early twentieth century. By the 1920s, groups from across the political spectrum were arguing that the national government needed to enter the housing arena, although there was no consensus as to why or how this should be done. The debate over the nature of the country's housing problem, its sources, and the proper role for government that took place in this era has been largely forgotten, with the result that the housing reforms of the New Deal seem practically inevitable. The Great Depression appears sufficient to explain their timing, while their goals and strategies—primarily to bolster the private market through indirect mechanisms—appear so unproblematic as to require little explanation.[1]

At the time, however, the direction of public policy with regard to housing did not seem so obvious, and a variety of ideas were considered. A number of prominent participants in these debates argued that profit-driven production would never generate the kind of housing that the country needed, both in terms of affordability and location. On the basis of their critique, they advocated public support for noncommercial development. In other words, they believed that federal policy should focus on creating what is sometimes termed "social housing." A few liberal intellectuals embraced this view even before the First World War, and it gained credence during the difficult economic period immediately after hostilities ended. Yet, ironically, it was during the heyday of the 1920s' building boom that skepticism about market-based solutions to housing problems grew strongest. What follows explores the range of ideas that were circulating before the depression regarding the federal government's proper role in housing. Chapter 3 will take a detailed look at the most completely developed alternative put forward to the direction that American policy eventually took.

Early Housing Reform Efforts

Anxiety about housing problems and debate over their sources certainly did not begin in the 1920s. From the beginning of large-scale urbanization in the United States, observers deplored squalid conditions in rapidly expanding cities. New York City, which grew faster within a more confined space than other American cities, was on the cutting edge of public concern as well as of the problems themselves. In one early effort to focus public awareness, the chief health officer drew attention to the city's high death rate in his 1834 report, attributing it to "the crowded and filthy state" in which so many city residents lived. As time went on, many of the city's elite did become worried about the slums, seeing these districts as breeding grounds for disease as well as defective character traits. Yet, efforts by groups like the New York Association for Improving the Condition of the Poor to solve problems entirely through voluntary action proved largely futile. An 1850 pamphlet distributed by the association urged immigrants to escape "the terrible ills of beggary" by moving to the country, advice that was doubtless no more effective than the organization's continuing admonitions to landlords to upgrade their property at their own expense.[2]

Low-wage workers in New York City and elsewhere experienced the slums firsthand, so they were not in need of official reports to apprise them of the existence of dismal conditions. Most often they expressed their grievances "with their feet." For individual families facing a rent bill they could not afford or a living environment that had become unbearable, the most practical protest was usually simply to vacate without paying. Political mobilization was difficult, in part because of the great legitimacy of private property rights in the United States, although some protest groups did form. For example, Irish radicals and land reformers organized the Tenant League of New York City in 1848. Proclaiming landlordism "one of the most blighting curses that ever was inflicted on the human race," the league called for laws restricting rent increases to 7 percent of a property's assessed value.[3] Such a response was atypical, however. In general during the nineteenth century it was reform-oriented wealthy and middle-class individuals who tried (however unsuccessfully) to improve living conditions for the urban poor.

By the turn of the century, efforts to upgrade urban housing relied chiefly on "model" tenements and restrictive legislation. The model tenement strategy assumed that a large supply of good, inexpensive housing could be produced by low-profit companies supported by wealthy investors. Enthusiasts promoted the program with slogans like "philanthropy and five percent." While architects associated with the movement did develop some creative new design concepts, model tenement companies never attracted enough capital for more than a few projects. Potential investors presumably found the low ceiling on earnings unappealing and were no doubt further discouraged when actual profit margins often turned out to be even more modest and sometimes nonexistent. In 1910, one critic of the movement calculated that in the preceding forty years model tenements built in New York City had housed fewer than 20,000 people, during which time speculative builders had put up enough tenements for over a million. Proponents tried to drum up enthusiasm among the wealthy by extolling the extra-financial rewards of providing affordable, good quality apartments to low-wage families but, as one housing historian has quipped, "capitalist society did not work by insight but by profit."[4]

Restrictive legislation, by contrast, aimed at using the state's police power to force builders and landlords to adhere to certain minimum specifications of design, construction, and maintenance. The first such law, passed by New York State in 1867, established standards such as one toilet for every twenty people and no cellar apartments without ceilings at least one foot above ground level. The Progressive-Era reformer Lawrence Veiller became the nationally recognized champion of restrictive legislation after his successful campaign to get the New York legislature to raise standards and add enforcement mechanisms to the state's Tenement House Law in 1901. Veiller spent years refining his recommendations for an ideal housing code and tirelessly advocating its adoption around the country, but he was a staunch opponent of more direct kinds of public involvement. Once minimum levels of comfort and safety were mandated by law, Veiller was sure the market would supply an adequate supply of housing unless interfered with by government competition.[5]

The new wave of criticism that began in the early twentieth century took restrictive legislation as a necessary first step, although not the final answer. As Edith Elmer Wood was fond of saying, restrictive legislation "may forbid the bad house, but it does not provide the good one."[6] Urban reformers in this era were disturbed by the failure of either philanthropic or commercial developers to provide what they saw as adequate living conditions at the lower end of the market. With regard to the definition of an acceptable standard, it should be noted that housing reform advocates in this era generally had more ambitious notions than their predecessors. Whereas physicians and charity workers had dominated earlier phases of the housing movement, this generation of reformers included a large proportion of architects and urban planners. Influenced in part by the English Garden City movement, they conceived of the domestic environment as consisting of the larger neighborhood as well as the individual home and assumed that such features as convenient social services and aesthetic charm were essential.

The Garden City idea, in its original formulation, had far-reaching goals like ending urban sprawl by establishing economically self-sufficient new towns and solving housing affordability problems through nonspeculative forms of real estate ownership. But it was as a new approach to the physical design of residential neighborhoods that the concept had its biggest impact in the United States. The design vocabulary associated with the Garden City

FIGS. 2.1 and 2.2 Rowhouses at Forest Hills Gardens being built (2.1) and completed (2.2). For some of the buildings, project architect Grosvenor Atterbury employed a system he had developed using large precast concrete blocks that were lifted into place with a crane. Atterbury advocated standardized plans, factory-made components, and mechanization to bring down the cost of housing. Through such techniques, he hoped to "do for the laboring man's house what Ford has done for the automobile" (Grosvenor Atterbury, "How to Get Low Cost Houses," *Housing Problems in America* 5 [New York: National Housing Association, 1916], 97). "Rowhouses at Forest Hills Gardens" is reprinted with the permission of Scribner, a Division of Simon & Schuster, from *Architecture Magazine* 73, no. 4 (April 1936). Copyright (c) 1936 by Charles Scribner's Sons, Renewed 1964.

featured short, often curving streets, a clear division between major thoroughfares and secondary streets, an emphasis on open space, and large blocks closed to vehicular traffic.[7]

Forest Hills Gardens in Queens, New York, was one of the first expressions of this new phase of housing reform thought. The Russell Sage Foundation began the venture in 1909 as a demonstration of the latest planning theories, but the effort also represented an attempt to realize a longstanding ideal of American residential planning: a rustic, but fully serviced environment where families could enjoy elements of both country and city life. Previous projects of this type, like Frederick Law Olmsted's Riverside, Illinois, were extremely expensive and therefore frankly aimed at "the more fortunate classes."[8] By contrast, the Sage Foundation directors hoped to provide for what they described as "people of moderate income and good taste." Foundation spokesmen stressed that the venture was not being subsidized, hoping that its success as a commercial venture would "encourage imitation" by real estate entrepreneurs throughout the country. The Sage directors felt sure that the model sub-

urb would clearly show how high levels of capitalization, large-scale planning, and new building technology could produce a superior environment at about the same cost as ordinary speculative operations.[9]

Project architect Grosvenor Atterbury, who characterized the residential construction methods of his day as essentially the same as those "perfected by the mound builders," welcomed the opportunity to experiment with more mechanized, capital intensive techniques at Forest Hills. He built several of the suburb's houses of large, factory-made, concrete panels into which electrical wiring had been embedded. Cranes at the site lifted these modules into place like giant building blocks.[10] Ironically, Atterbury used these innovations to build conventional Tudor-style houses (see figures 2.1 and 2.2).

In a certain sense, the entire effort at Forest Hills Gardens can be interpreted as a critique of speculative development practices of the time. In terms of physical design, the critique was widely hailed as a success. Frederick Law Olmsted, Jr.'s curvilinear streets, cul-de-sacs, and interior parks both respected the natural topography and created a distinct sense of place. The unified and attractive architectural treatment that Atterbury gave to the various buildings was a good complement to the plan (figure 2.3). Financially, Forest Hills Gardens was less convincing. The Sage directors had hoped to prove that high quality mid-range homebuilding could be profitable, but as things worked out, the foundation ended up losing money (approximately $360,000 out of a total investment of $4 million). It is unclear whether the project could have turned a profit even in a favorable economic climate, but as it happened, inflationary pressures from World War I undercut any possibility for demonstrating the directors' initial contention that "more tasteful surroundings and open spaces pay."[11]

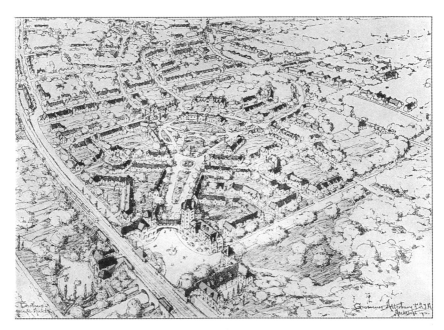

FIG. 2.3 Site plan for Forest Hills Gardens, drawn by architect Grosvenor Atterbury based on plans by Frederick Law Olmstead, Jr. The open area in the lower portion is the Station Square. The square, with an entrance to a commuter rail line linking the subdivision to Manhattan, an inn, and an arcaded shopping center, functions as an entrance to the development. The two major streets that lead from the square enclose common areas that form the core of the development. At the far end of the central commons is the public school. The design serves to integrate the whole project into a distinct enclave. This effect became more pronounced after the surrounding land was developed using rectangular urban blocks. Most buildings along the perimeter do maintain a conventional relationship with the surrounding streets, although the large grouped building just beyond the station square on the left-hand side of the plan does not. While some critics of publicly subsidized housing in the United States have blamed program problems on site designs that separated developments from the larger urban fabric, visual distinctiveness has clearly not been a problem for the wealthy New Yorkers who have made Forest Hills Gardens one of the city's most exclusive residential districts.

Beyond Regulatory and Private Solutions

In the search for ways to provide better and cheaper urban housing that was going on in this period, a few intellectuals began to look beyond experimenting completely within the framework of the private market, as at Forest Hills, and to consider some kind of active role for government. Programs in European countries frequently served as models.

In 1909, Benjamin Clarke Marsh, Executive Secretary of the Committee on Congestion of Population in New York, published *An Introduction to City Planning*, which favorably described the way in which many European municipalities purchased land within and beyond their city limits in order to contain costs of eventual development. The book also endorsed the special tax on increased land values levied by the city of Frankfurt am Main, whereby the public reaped part of the gain that Marsh described as having been created "chiefly through the presence and productive enterprises of all citizens."[12]

The well-known municipal reformer Frederick C. Howe was another exponent of European land-banking practices. Speaking to the third national conference on city planning in 1911, Howe drew special attention to German cities that, in addition to purchasing land on their peripheries, were involved in actually developing low-rent housing. He told the conference approvingly that "Germany has decided that the housing question is too important a problem to be left to the free play of capitalistic exploitation, and is beginning to substitute the municipal dwelling in competition with that of the private owner."[13]

Carol Aronovici, the Romanian-born city planner who directed the Philadelphia Metropolitan Planning Association, was another early advocate of public intervention. In 1913 he urged readers of the *National Municipal Review* to adopt what he termed "constructive housing reform" to cope with what he defined as the true American housing problem. The main difficulty with American housing, he insisted, was not the "pathological" situation in the largest cities, because big city slum conditions affected only 10 to 12 percent of the population by his calculations. Rather than slums, the real issue was the overall quality of houses and neighborhoods, which he regarded as low in relation to the country's wealth. He maintained that the housing movement, rather than focusing all its energies on legislating and enforcing minimum tenement standards, should develop strategies aimed at providing the majority of people with good quality, inexpensive homes in attractive, convenient neighborhoods.

Aronovici thought that private groups were capable of expanding the supply of good housing, but he believed that government activity held out greater possibilities. Public policy, he pointed out, could affect many underlying cost factors and also could create institutions capable of the kind of long-range, large-scale planning necessary for defining the character of urbanized regions. In terms of specific recommendations, he suggested that cities invest in better transportation systems and revamp their tax policies to reward suppliers of good housing. Also, like Marsh and Howe, he applauded the approach of European cities, which were taking control of undeveloped land on their outskirts so that the municipality could control development and cut out speculative land transaction costs that drove up the price of shelter.[14]

Another early convert to the idea of a more active public role in housing

tial development on a much broader scale. As we saw earlier, housing shortages for civilian workers in defense industries became a public issue during the
war years. Policymakers came to believe that the scarcity of housing around
defense plants was jeopardizing manufacturing productivity necessary to victory and, therefore, that the federal government needed to take action.

In retrospect, it seems clear that the sources of production problems went
far deeper than poor residential conditions.[21] Whether they knew this or not,
reformers who were already convinced of the necessity of public aid for
working-class housing seized the opportunity. Charles Harris Whitaker, editor
of the *Journal of the American Institute of Architects*, made emotional appeals for
federal action on the grounds that good housing was necessary for industrial
efficiency. "Peace has enunciated this economic principle with a voice which
has been drowned to a whisper. War shrieks the message to the nation and
makes it heard above all other cries," he insisted in the September 1917 issue
of the journal.[22]

The World War I federal programs, although they lasted less than a year
and were drastically curtailed after hostilities ended, still represented a great
opportunity for proponents of new methods of creating urban neighborhoods.
A large number of architects and planners were able to try their hand at building along lines suggested by the most advanced contemporary theories. As at
Lowell and Forest Hills Gardens, they hoped to demonstrate that comprehensively planned, large-scale operations could cut costs while at the same time
providing more attractive and better equipped neighborhoods. In addition,
designers were anxious to encourage what architect Walter H. Kilham described as a "spirit of common responsibility for the community welfare and
of neighborhood goodfellowship."[23]

The war housing planners shared with other reformist professionals of this
era the belief that active local communities were important, not only or even
primarily because they would be more interesting and pleasant places for their
inhabitants to live, but because they would help bring about a more cohesive
and democratic society.[24] For this reason, they emphasized giving an overall
aesthetic coherence to the residential districts they designed, so that residents
would have the sense of living in an identifiable place. Also, they included
parks, central squares, and recreation fields where people could meet and
socialize. In addition, planners frequently called for community buildings of
some sort. Of the forty-seven projects eventually built by the Emergency Fleet
Corporation and United States Housing Corporation, about a quarter included some kind of facility to serve as a neighborhood center (see table 2.1).
Approximately forty percent would have contained such a structure had it not
been for the cutbacks ordered at the end of the war.[25]

The ambitious plans for the community building proposed for the Shipping

TABLE 2.1 COMMUNITY CENTERS IN WORLD WAR I FEDERAL HOUSING

United States Housing Corporation

New England

CT	Bridgeport	No community center
	New London/Groton	No community center
	Waterbury	No community center
ME	Bath	No community center
MA	Quincy	Provided-new building
RI	Newport	No community center

Middle Atlantic

NJ	New Brunswick	Planned only
NY	Niagara Falls	No community center
	Watertown	No community center
PA	Erie	Planned only
	Philadelphia	No community center
	Tullytown	No community center

South Atlantic

MD	Aberdeen	No community center
	Indian Head	Provided by alterations
VA	Cradock	Provided-new building
	Truxton	Provided-new building
WV	Charleston	Planned only

East North Central

IL	Rock Island District	No community center
IN	Hammond	No community center
OH	Alliance	No community center
	Niles	No community center

West North Central and Pacific

CA	Vallejo	Provided-new building
IA	Davenport	No community center
WA	Bremerton	Provided by alterations

Emergency Fleet Corporation

New England

CT	Groton	Planned only
ME	Bath	No community center
NH	Portsmouth ("Atlantic Heights")	Provided by alterations

Middle Atlantic

NJ	Camden ("Yorkship Village")	Provided-new building
	Gloucester ("Noreg Village")	Provided by alterations
NY	Newburgh	No community center
	Port Jefferson	Planned only
PA	Bristol ("Harriman Village")	Provided-new building
	Chester ("Buckman Village")	Provided by alterations
	Chester ("Sun Village")	Planned only

TABLE 2.1 CONTINUED

	Emergency Fleet Corporation	
	Essington	No community center
	Philadelphia ("Elmwood")	No community center
	Philadelphia ("Island Road")	No community center
	South Atlantic	
DE	Wilmington ("Union Park Gardens")	Planned only
FL	Jacksonville	No community center
MD	Dundalk	No community center
VA	Newport News ("Hilton Village")	Provided-new building
	Quantico	No community center
	East North Central	
MI	Wyandotte	No community center
OH	Lorain	No community center
WI	Manitowoc	No community center
	Pacific	
CA	Clyde	No community center
WA	Vancouver	No community center

NOTE: This list of projects is based on information compiled by Miles L. Colean, in *Housing for Defense* (New York: Twentieth Century Fund, 1940), 155–56. Regions are as defined in this report. See note 25 for sources of information on community centers.

Board's Union Park Gardens in Wilmington, Delaware, gives a sense of the enthusiasm that many of the planners had for the idea of an active neighborhood life. This facility was to have included a 600-seat auditorium, a swimming pool with locker rooms, a full-service kitchen, medical offices, and game rooms for pool and card playing. In addition, the designers called for a club room for reading and lounging, which they thought could function as "a sort of round table" and "safety valve" where "workmen could congregate to express their personal opinions on matters of daily interest. . . ."[26] Congress cut off funding before this elaborate building could be constructed, but the scope of these plans demonstrates the commitment of the war housing planners to the goal of social interaction at the local level (figures 2.4 and 2.5).

In recent years, some scholars have raised questions about the social and political meaning of the World War I public housing experiment. From the nineteenth century on, according to historian Christian Topalov, the middle-class-led housing movement in the industrially developed countries represented an effort to reorganize the proletariat's environment of everyday life in such a way as to render working people more amenable to the goals of capital. With regard to the World War I housing program, he interprets the planners' explicit aspiration to create an "organized community" when they designed

FIG. 2.4 Architect's drawing of the central square of Union Park Gardens, Wilmington, Delaware, a World War I development of the Emergency Fleet Corporation. To the left is the projected community building (with clock tower). Facing it is a large apartment house. To the rear can be seen some of the short row units that account for most of the housing in the development. The community building was to have included a large auditorium, swimming pool, and a variety of rooms for leisure and social activities. The apartment buildings and houses were built, but funds were cut off before the community building could be erected. "Perspective View across Village Green, Union Park Gardens," from the Ballinger Collection at Athenaeum of Philadelphia, photo no. 2889.

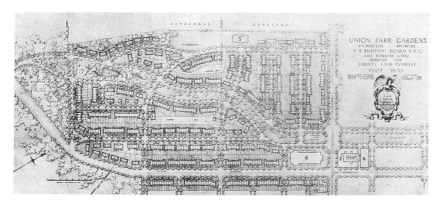

FIG. 2.5 Site plan for Union Park Gardens designed by John Nolan. Number 4 indicates the location of the community building. The size of the proposed structure suggests the importance of shared neighborhood facilities in the minds of the project's designers. Numbers 1, 2, and 3 mark apartment buildings. Number 5 labels the local school; Number 6, a parking garage. The plan shares a number of elements with Forest Hills Gardens, including winding, irregular streets and communal spaces designed to impart a sense of place. To cut down on road-building costs and increase green space, there are no alleys to the rear of houses. Also, no large thoroughfares cut the tract so as to reduce noise, pollution, and danger to children from traffic.

41

Fig. 2.6 The neighborhood center in Moorestown, New Jersey, built in the 1920s. Much like the facility envisaged for Union Park Gardens, it included a swimming pool, a gymnasium with stage, a children's health clinic, and meeting rooms to be used by local organizations. This commodious and well-appointed building provides evidence that affluent families were interested in having much the same kind of neighborhood amenities that housing reformers of the era desired to provide to those of more modest resources. In the 1990s, this building is still in use and in excellent condition.

a development as little more than an attempt to control the behavior of residents.[27]

Topalov is correct in pointing out that the planners subscribed to the common American faith in "the molding power of architecture." Like the nineteenth-century utopians before them, the builders of the war housing developments assumed that the design of their communities would influence the people who lived in them.[28] Also, as we have seen, it is true that planners thought community facilities and good neighborhoods would provide (among other things) more "cordial" class relations. However, it is important to recognize the ways in which the planners were not trying to repress working people in the interests of capital. At least since de Tocqueville, political analysts have stressed that a rich structure of civil society is a favorable condition for democratic political participation. Also, the planners' zeal for promoting local community life was not class-specific.[29]

This lack of focus on the working class in particular is evident given that Charles Harris Whitaker, who had spearheaded the campaign for federal war housing, was equally if not more eager to reform the living habits of the affluent. To middle-class readers of the *Ladies Home Journal* in 1919 he commended kitchenless homes and community food centers. His object was to cut back on household labor, since he believed that "freeing men and women for social contact is vitally more important than cloistering them in a home."[30]

While ignoring Whitaker's suggestions for kitchenless homes, wealthy communities often did support neighborhood programs and facilities for themselves. For instance, in the 1920s, the residents of Moorestown, New Jersey, built a neighborhood center at a cost of about $200,000 (figure 2.6). With its library, apartment for visiting nurses, clinic, suite of offices for the Church Federation, club rooms, men's smoking lounge, swimming pool, and gymnasium with stage and dressing rooms, the Moorestown Community House bore a striking resemblance to the facility envisioned for the Wilmington ship workers.[31]

The Postwar National Debate

The federal housing programs of the war years were legitimated as a means of securing military success, and congressional support evaporated with the signing of the armistice. Proposals for making the wartime programs permanent, even on a drastically scaled-down basis, met with antipathy in Congress. Superficially, American housing seemed back on its prewar footing, but in fact significant change had occurred. This can be seen in part by the widespread assumption during the postwar housing shortage and building slump that government should act. Even many businessmen took the position that the federal government needed to intervene to improve the situation. Throughout the twenties, Herbert Hoover attempted to improve performance in the housing industry through programs directed by the Commerce Department, and his efforts met with no complaints from the real estate industry. Thus, by the 1920s, a subtle but definite shift had occurred in which a variety of groups took for granted that there was a role for the government in the housing arena. The question was: what exactly was this role?

At first, discussion of housing issues at the national level centered on the fate of the federal housing programs put in place during the hostilities. Supporters argued that the government needed to continue to work in the field of low-cost housing, although only the American Federation of Labor (AFL) advocated direct government construction in peacetime. In its 1919 Reconstruction Program, the AFL asserted that municipalities and states, as well as the federal government, should "build model housing" to free home ownership "from the grasp of exploitative and speculative interests." Also, the AFL maintained its prewar position of support for a program of government-supplied low-interest loans to noncommercial builders.[32]

For Frederick L. Ackerman, former Chief of Design for the Emergency Fleet Corporation, the issue of whether government agencies should initiate construction was a "detail," in other words, a tactical question. The key point, he maintained, was that the war programs had demonstrated a recognition of public responsibility for "the problem of providing all men with adequate homes." To secure this goal, he argued for policies by which states and municipalities, and perhaps the federal government, would channel low-cost capital into particular kinds of nonprofit development. "At the root of this whole problem is the Land Question," he insisted, referring to nineteenth-century producerist and single-tax ideas associated with Henry George.[33]

Like Ackerman, Charles Whitaker was influenced by George's approach to urban economics. According to this perspective, property values were socially created and rightfully belonged to the whole community.[34] Whitaker believed that "the increase in land-values caused by the growth of the cities is one of the primary causes of high rent." Therefore all strategies to expand on a permanent basis the supply of low-cost shelter by means of "government loans, cheap forms of construction, or wholesale building operations" were destined to fail unless the new housing remained outside of the market.[35]

Accepting this analysis, a number of prominent housing reformers advocated plans by which the government would sell its war housing to nonprofit associations of residents or other noncommercial entities. Their hope was that the federally built developments would form the nucleus of a noncommercial housing sector, one that would expand as time went on. Advocates of this policy direction included a former president of the National Municipal League, an architect who had served on the Massachusetts Homestead Commission, and the director of the Philadelphia Housing Association. The group was able to win the approval of the Department of Labor's Advisory Committee on Living Conditions, but not that of Congress.[36]

By contrast, some reform-minded professionals suggested that public support for the housing sector be structured in such a way that initiative would be in private hands. For example, Frederick Law Olmsted, Jr., who headed the Town Planning Division of the U.S. Housing Corporation, felt that during normal times government housing operations "could hardly be expected to attain the exceptionally high standard of personnel" that had characterized the war agencies. In any event, he desired to avoid such a "dangerously revolutionary change of method." Olmsted's alternative was to create federal programs that would upgrade the functioning of private enterprise. He recommended, for instance, that the government make low-interest loans to residential developers and fund research into new building materials and techniques.[37]

With these suggestions, Olmsted was articulating once again the widely held assumption that the for-profit sector would be able to adequately respond to housing needs if only it was organized more like the mass production industries. As we have seen, faith in the potential of centralized planning, technical knowledge, and large, well-capitalized, carefully organized operations had animated the prewar housing experiments at Forest Hills Gardens and Lowell, as well as to some extent the federal programs of the war years. None had success in achieving the cost savings envisioned for them. In part, this was because all of them ran up against skyrocketing war inflation and also because they were actually quite small compared with the huge national firms in other industries that operated on a mass production basis. Probably the biggest barrier to success for all of these efforts was the expectation that costs could be brought down while producing a significantly higher-quality product. Despite the disappointing results from these experiments, many reformist professionals clung to their hopes for improving housing conditions through better organization of production, just as professionals in other fields during the early twentieth century subscribed to a belief in the ability of science and administration to solve other social problems. This was, in historian Samuel Hays' phrase, the "gospel of efficiency."[38]

As it turned out, Congress was hostile to every suggestion for continuing the war programs in any form and even seemed to regret having authorized them on a temporary basis. The plan to sell whole neighborhoods to residents to manage cooperatively on a nonprofit basis made absolutely no headway in Congress. Similarly, a bill to establish an agency within the Labor Department to promote better living conditions for working-class families got nowhere. Rather than support any such initiatives, Congress embarked on what one observer described as an "orgy of 'investigation'" into the operations of the war programs. Not surprisingly, it was the Labor Department's U.S. Housing Corporation which came in for the bulk of criticism, since this agency represented the most abrupt break with conventional practices by retaining ownership and direct control of its housing.[39]

Local Response to the Postwar Crisis

At the state and local level, there was little interest in the fate of the federal programs after the war ended, but severe shortages of rental housing did create pressure for government action to blunt the free play of market forces in this sector of the economy. In New York City, thousands of families were being evicted every month in 1919. Tenants swamped the courts with appeals for legal assistance, organized rent strikes, and staged demonstrations.[40] On the other coast, the California Commission of Immigration and Housing's 1921 report announced that from all over the state "comes the cry for more houses."[41] Grassroots agitation across the country encouraged individuals and groups to put forward a variety of proposals to ease the crisis, a few of which were enacted into law.

45

Most of these plans had little impact, even when they secured political support, with the exception of rent control laws, tax abatements in New York City, and an ambitious California program to help veterans buy homes. For example, North Dakota established a state agency in 1919 to produce houses to be sold for less than $5,000, but the operation never generated any construction.[42] In 1920, New York Governor Al Smith attempted to secure a constitutional amendment allowing the state to make low-interest loans to low-profit housing developers. Resistance from private financial institutions doomed the proposal, but state lawmakers did approve rent control and a property tax exemption that prompted new residential construction in New York City.[43] In California, the American Legion threw its weight behind the California Veterans' Farm and Home Purchase Act, which passed in 1921. Over the following decade, the legislation provided low-interest amortized home loans to over 7,000 families.[44]

In contrast to the limited number of programs that attempted (mostly unsuccessfully) to generate new housing, the defensive strategy of rent control was a pervasive response to the housing shortage. After the war, several states passed some form of rent control legislation, including New York, New Jersey, Massachusetts, Maine, Delaware, Illinois, Colorado, and Wisconsin. Cities such as Fresno, Los Angeles, New London, Jersey City, Atlanta, Chicago, Wichita, Baltimore, Newark, Buffalo, Cleveland, Dayton, Akron, Hamilton, Philadelphia, Seattle, and Washington, DC, all used rent laws extensively in the postwar period. Despite their wide popularity, rent control measures could be seen, in Edith Elmer Wood's ironic formulation, as "the most radical interference with the rights of private property of any housing measure adopted outside of Soviet Russia."[45] (Wood's problem with such laws, of course, was not that they interfered with the market, but that they would do nothing to solve underlying housing problems.)

To get around constitutional objections, state and local rent laws were justified as temporary responses to an emergency situation. Nevertheless, organized pressure kept some of this legislation on the books for several years. In New York State, where laws persisted the longest, tenant testimony as late as 1929 convinced the State Board of Housing that the situation of poor New York City renters was still critical. Despite the serious plight of the poor, however, in that year the board finally ruled against continuing with any form of rent control, reasoning that "the condition which confronts [the poor] is not temporary, . . . it does not arise out of the economic adjustments following the war, . . . [and thus it] is not an emergency in the meaning of the law." While this description of the situation was demonstrably true, political pressures on the board also affected its decision making. By 1929, only the cheapest apartments were being controlled, which meant a small and weak constituency for continuing the legislation.[46]

The grassroots movement for rent control in New York City was probably the strongest in the country, but significant support existed elsewhere. Regulations continued in Massachusetts until 1927. In Washington, DC, support was so broad-based that a bill to extend the District of Columbia Rent Act beyond 1925 even carried the endorsement of President Calvin Coolidge.[47]

Business Responds to Housing Problems

Business groups in real estate, while protesting that rent control laws "interfere with the laws of supply and demand," came forward with their own proposals for government intervention into the market.[48] The general thrust of these plans was to create privileged arrangements for mortgage finance, principally through tax exemptions. This was not the first time that elements of the real estate industry had looked to government to solve problems. For example, beginning in 1907 the California State Realty Board fought to tighten regulations on subdividers by strengthening state laws, while in 1908 the Los Angeles Realty Board spearheaded passage of the nation's first citywide zoning ordinance. The impetus for these efforts came from large investors who wanted to constrain small operators from erecting cheap buildings that might bring down property values generally.[49] By the 1920s, partly as a result of earlier growth of the national government in the Progressive Era, most business leaders looked not to the local or state level for help, but to the federal government.

In the midst of the postwar housing shortage and building slump, industry spokesmen argued that the federal government needed to come to the aid of the housing sector. Clarence H. Kelsey, president of a major New York mortgage firm, argued to Congress in 1920 that the government had a responsibility to help, since its actions were largely to blame for the failure of the market to respond to the obvious demand for housing. Exemptions on federal war bonds and municipal bonds meant, he maintained, that "money was running out of the mortgage market instead of into it." In Kelsey's view, federal tax policy had upset the "free-field" in capital markets.[50]

Industry leaders suggested methods by which Congress should act to create, in Kelsey's words, "an equal opportunity" for the mortgage borrower and even tilt capital flows toward residential construction.[51] In 1919, the United States League of Building and Loans (later called savings and loans), together with the Department of Labor and the National Federation of Construction Industries, drafted legislation to create a secondary market for mortgages. The aim was to create a federally organized system of regional banks to purchase mort-

47

gages, which traditionally had been illiquid assets. To bring new low-cost capital into the system, so that lenders could make more loans, the legislation called for regional banks to sell tax-free mortgage-backed bonds. The concept was consciously modeled on the Farm Loan Bank System established in 1916 to lower the cost of long-term credit for farmers.[52]

Meanwhile, the National Association of Real Estate Boards and large mortgage finance companies advocated legislation to exempt income on mortgage investments from federal taxes. Speaking on behalf of this proposal, J. Willison Smith, Vice-President of the Land Title and Trust Company of Philadelphia, told the House Committee on Ways and Means in 1920 that the mortgage market was "almost stagnant." Before the war, his company typically had financed fifty building operations during a year, but at this point it had loans out to only twelve. Like many in the real estate industry, Smith believed that the source of the problem was tax policy. Exemptions for some kinds of securities meant that large investors shied away from putting money into mortgages, he told the committee, "because the greater their income the smaller their net return when investing in mortgages."[53]

Congressman William A. Oldfield of Arkansas pressed Smith for an estimate of the tax losses that his proposal entailed. Like many rural representatives, Oldfield was unenthusiastic about expanding exemptions, given that the resulting loss of revenue might mean higher taxes for his hard-pressed constituents. "We have all sorts of trouble here [in the House Ways and Means Committee] trying to get enough money to run the Government. . . ," he told Smith. "Of course your business is hurt, . . . but it seems that everybody's business is hurt." Smith could not give an estimate as to what mortgage investment exemptions would cost the treasury, but he asserted in response to Oldfield's questioning that mortgage financing was not on the same footing as other commercial enterprises. A strong residential construction industry was as much a "public issue" as the well-being of cities, he maintained, and therefore mortgage investment deserved special treatment through the tax code just as much as investment in municipal bonds. If Congress failed to aid private developers through the tax system, he predicted that the housing industry might collapse, thereby forcing the government to take over housing production. "We may face the same condition that England has faced," he warned, "where she has put hundreds of millions of dollars into her housing program."[54]

Less politically powerful than the farm bloc, the real estate industry was not able to convince Congress to use tax exemption as a policy tool to help channel private capital into home building in the 1920s. Nor was it successful in its efforts to get the government to oversee institutional arrangements that needed public confidence to function, as with the proposed regional building loan bank system. Nevertheless, these efforts were significant. The policies business leaders proposed foreshadowed major policy directions adopted later, and, particularly with regard to the plan for a federal home loan bank system, demonstrated the role played by business groups in formulating specific mechanisms by which public authority could expand into new fields.

Despite all of the efforts just described, not everyone abandoned hope for purely private sector solutions in the tumultuous postwar period. In the early 1920s, businessmen around the country, often coordinated by their local Chambers of Commerce, tried to establish limited-profit companies to supply homes at prices working-class families could afford. Committees formed in over 150 cities to explore possibilities for such building, although only a few operations of any size actually got organized. Local businessmen subscribed to stock worth $1 million in companies in St. Louis; Indianapolis; Cleveland; Bridgeport, Connecticut; and Kenosha, Wisconsin. The Dallas business community, reportedly "actuated by the Texan spirit," put together $150,000 and erected 120 simple precut wood houses in 1920.[55] In Michigan, the giant automakers enrolled in the effort. General Motors' Modern Housing Corporation, initially capitalized at $3.5 million, built homes in Flint, Pontiac, and Detroit—3,200 in Flint alone between 1919 and 1933. In Dearborn, associates of Henry Ford, hoping to achieve cost breakthroughs using mass-production techniques pioneered by the car magnate, began the Ford Homes subdivision in 1919.[56]

The results of this movement proved disappointing and it soon petered out, prompting some in the business community to question their earlier assumptions about the viability of purely private-sector solutions. For instance, of the fourteen companies in Pennsylvania that got as far as building any houses, ten had collapsed by 1925. Only three built as many as 100 houses and just one was able to achieve even a modest profit ($50 per house). The rest went bankrupt.[57] At Ford Homes, as with Atterbury's earlier attempts at Forest Hills, the goal of significantly decreasing costs through modernized production techniques proved elusive. The houses sold in 1919 for a minimum of $6,750, and the price for the cheapest model rose the following year to $8,750. Such homes were too expensive for most working-class families in the area, given that at the height of prosperity in 1925 annual pay for autoworkers averaged only $1,625.[58] Efforts in Cleveland seem to have been particularly disillusioning. In 1923, the local Chamber of Commerce responded to a national survey of business opinion on housing issues by asserting that "private building enterprises under existing financial circumstances" could not provide shelter that wage-earning families could afford. The business association insisted that the problem was so dire that "either the community or the government must come to the rescue."[59]

In one city, the business community and local government did work together, although it was an uneasy alliance. This was in Milwaukee, where So-cialist mayor Daniel W. Hoan appointed a housing commission that rec-ommended that the municipality promote a housing program along English garden city lines. In addition to those aspects of garden city theory that had already been tried by Americans, such as comprehensive planning, large-scale building, and improved neighborhood design, the commission emphasized the importance of nonprofit cooperative ownership. "God be praised!" exclaimed Charles Harris Whitaker when he heard about the Milwaukee commission's intention to keep its housing permanently out of the for-profit sector. He called the plan the only one "that squarely and fairly attacked the problem at its roots."[60]

Local business leaders, while supporting the idea of more homes for wage earners, were wary of the very features of the proposal that most excited Whit-aker. They pressed for the more conventional approach of building inexpen-sive houses and selling them to individuals. But the mayor's Housing Commis-sion was not receptive to this alternative, having already gone on record against the "long harbored" American creed "that ownership of his home makes a man a better citizen." Indeed, the commissioners were convinced that long-term affordability was only possible if the homes were kept outside of the speculative market. The head of the commission, architect William H. Schuchardt, argued that "the selling of small homes at cost . . . does not offer a permanent solution of the housing problem as such but merely lets a few lucky individuals in on a philanthropic scheme." If such homes turned out to be attractive, Schuchardt predicted that the new owners would sell them at a profit, which meant that any plan for "procuring homes for wage earners at rock bottom prices and keeping them on a low price level is defeated." Although never enthusiastic about the noncommercial financial setup, local businessmen did abandon outright opposition and eventually even subscribed to over $77,000 worth of shares in the $550,000 venture.[61]

In 1919, the city created the Garden Homes Company of Milwaukee after the Wisconsin legislature approved a city-sponsored bill to allow formation of cooperative housing companies and municipal participation in such enter-prises. By 1923, the company had put up over 100 homes on a 29-acre tract. The development, with its park and curvilinear streets, turned out to be a physically appealing place to live. Emil Seidel, who had served as Milwaukee's first Socialist mayor from 1910 to 1912, was an early and enthusiastic resident. In a memoir written in the late 1930s, he described how visitors always re-marked on the charm of the neighborhood. "My, but you're living here like in Hollywood," one widely traveled guest told him when she arrived at his house.[62]

In contrast to its aesthetic success, the economic and legal dimensions of the plan did not work out well. Almost immediately after moving in, occupants began agitating for fee simple ownership. As one resident told a reporter, "I want my house and lot to be in my own name, not in the name of a corporation, in which I am a mere stockholder." Mayor Hoan, a leader in the national cooperative movement, believed that the pressure for individual deeds stemmed from inadequate education about the advantages of shared, nonprofit ownership. Later analysts have speculated that residents' desires to take advantage of the rising housing prices of this period may have been the undoing of the cooperative dimension of the development. Edith Elmer Wood, a strong believer in the potential of cooperative housing, hypothesized that the Milwaukee experiment may have suffered from lack of resident involvement at the outset. In a successful venture, she wrote, "there is almost necessarily some bond of friendship, of race, occupation, trade union or religion in the first place, a bond that has been greatly strengthened by the time they have gone through the processes of site purchase, plan making, financing and building."[63] Whatever the reasons, the pressure to privatize was intense. The company acquiesced in 1925, and two years later all of the property at Garden Homes had passed into private ownership.[64]

Housing Activities of the Commerce Department

Congress in the 1920s resisted moves to continue any version of the war housing programs aimed at working-class families and also ignored efforts by business groups in real estate who desired indirect subsidy programs. Nonetheless, the federal government did not return to its earlier stance of passivity in relation to the housing sector. Secretary of Commerce Herbert Hoover's 1921 request for congressional approval to establish a Division of Building and Housing within his department was easily granted. Hoover wanted to give special attention to residential building, as he perceived it to be critically important for the health of the entire economic system. A follower of the business cycle theories of economist Wesley C. Mitchell, Hoover thought the construction industry could serve as a balance wheel to stabilize the economy. But homebuilding was more than just a macroeconomic lever for the "Great Engineer." Hoover also wanted to promote homeownership because of what he saw as its "spiritual" impact on society.[65]

In his private correspondence, Hoover acknowledged that "on present wage levels and present building costs" there was "utterly no hope" of working-class families buying their own homes.[66] Therefore, in line with his efforts to improve efficiency throughout American industry, he tried to push residential builders in the direction of more streamlined production techniques so they could deliver cheaper houses. By this strategy he hoped to help the housing industry by expanding the market, while at the same time helping more people become homeowners. To achieve these goals, he had the Housing Division promote the standardization of construction materials as well as the adoption nationally of simplified and consistent building codes. The division also tried to encourage consumers to invest more in housing by publicizing the virtues of homeownership and encouraging municipalities to implement zoning laws in order to make buying a home a more secure investment. Hoover and his colleagues in the Housing Division had great hopes for their efforts. Launching the campaign in 1921 for the standardized building code developed by the division, a spokesman for the agency told the press that a savings of approximately $600 could be achieved on the average small house if local governments throughout the country would adopt a single code for fire-wall construction.[67]

Hoover tried to modify the operation of the housing market mainly through noncoercive techniques such as publicity campaigns and conferences. He was anxious to promote methods by which a large-scale, industrially advanced society could be managed effectively while still preserving the maximum of individual freedom. The Better Homes for America campaigns provide a good example of the kind of model he supported. Local volunteers in hundreds of Better Homes committees across the country distributed Commerce Department materials in their communities. They mounted yearly contests to develop enthusiasm for buying and maintaining houses. Hoover served as president of Better Homes, which was ostensibly a private organization although actually it was, in his words, "practically directed out of the [Commerce] Department."[68]

Hoover always emphasized his commitment to working cooperatively with business, but he did go beyond exhortation in his larger standardization campaign. After 1923, he began moving all federal agencies toward unified specifications in their contracts. This policy had the effect of forcing private companies that wanted federal business to adopt standards promoted by the Commerce Department, a development with far-reaching effects on American manufacturing.[69]

As with Hoover's larger standardization drive, the work of the Division of Building and Housing did result in efficiencies, but, for the most part, savings seem to have been absorbed into profits, rather than being passed along to consumers.[70] Noting this trend, Edith Elmer Wood commented with sarcasm after the division's efficiency campaign had been in effect for a decade that "we are still waiting to see it 'do for the poor man's home what Ford did for his car.'"[71]

The failure of Hoover's initiatives to achieve his goals for the housing sector should not lead us to underestimate their importance, however. As Commerce Secretary and later as President, Hoover was committed to using the

federal government to modify various features of the housing market. Report-
ers at the President's Conference on Home Building and Home Ownership
that Hoover called in 1931 noted that fourteen divisions of federal agencies were engaged in housing-related research. At this conference, Hoover
announced plans to introduce legislation for a system of federally supervised
home loan banks modeled on the plan proposed over a decade earlier by the
building and loan associations. Passed in the summer of 1932 as the Federal
Home Loan Bank Act, the bill became the first permanent federal housing legislation.[72]

That Hoover was able to pursue his goal of trying to influence the operation of the housing industry through government efforts demonstrates that
the issue in the postwar years was not whether, but how, the government
would get involved with housing. As it worked out, Hoover's programs were
important precursors to the policy direction that ultimately emerged from the
New Deal, with their focus on the importance of housing to the health of the
larger economy, their strategy of working cooperatively with business interests, and their method of affecting economic processes indirectly rather than
through overt intervention.

The Market Rebounds but Criticism Deepens

The recovery of building that began in mid–1921 turned into a boom, and the
next few years witnessed record levels of housing construction. At the close
of the decade, President Hoover made the no doubt accurate observation that
the United States possessed "a larger proportion of adequate housing than any
country in the world."[73] Yet, despite the achievements of the commercial market during this period, some observers were struck by the extent to which poor
conditions persisted in many urban neighborhoods. A few even thought the
housing situation was becoming more difficult for those with the lowest incomes. In 1926, Chicago businessman and housing reformer Benjamin Rosenthal told the press that for many low-wage working families in the city "the
situation in Chicago is worse than ever."[74] The failure of an active and prosperous real estate industry in the 1920s to make more of an impact on the
living conditions of many urban working families disillusioned many people
as to the capacity of the private market to achieve the kinds of changes they
believed were necessary.

As a group, social welfare professionals, with their firsthand experience of
the lives of the urban poor, were probably the least impressed with the results
of the general economic expansion of the 1920s. The uneven distribution of
the prosperity, which statistics recorded abstractly, was a concrete and compelling reality to social workers. "We talk about big profits and high wages as if
everybody was experiencing either the one or the other," wrote Philadelphia

social worker Karl de Schweinitz in 1928. Contrary to such impressions, he insisted that poverty "abounds in every great city." Of course, social workers had a professional interest in defining the living standards of the poor as inadequate but, as chapter 1 indicated, many families were indeed living at a meager level given the overall wealth of the country.[75]

Chicago, with its long tradition of social research, in particular its housing surveys, was a center for analysis of the urban housing question. Ever since 1900, when Robert Hunter began his report for the City Homes Association, waves of canvassers had regularly tramped door to door through the worst sections of the city, recording and tabulating conditions and then comparing their findings with those of the previous survey.[76] The bulk of these studies were supervised by Edith Abbott, dean of the Graduate School of Social Service Administration at the University of Chicago and a leader of the city's social welfare community.[77] Abbott's initial surveys were conducted in 1908–9 at the request of the new city sanitary inspector. In the 1920s, she supervised a recanvass of all of the neighborhoods previously surveyed.[78]

The new studies showed that although some families had moved out of the most deteriorated sections of the city (from 10 to 40 percent had left the worst districts, according to one estimate), many hung on.[79] Despite regular employment, some residents were seemingly trapped in squalid, deteriorating environments where no new investment happened. In 1926, after surveying a previously studied South Side neighborhood nicknamed "the Bush," Abbott's researcher wrote:

> It seems hard to realize that these houses, described as dilapidated and neglected in 1901, and said to be more so because of the lapse of years in 1905, should still be standing to be decried in 1911. That 1925 should find many of them occupied by families is almost unbelievable.[80]

Abbott was clearly discouraged by such results in this new round of surveys. Reporting the data, she lamented that "statistical tables portray very inadequately the discomforts and inconveniences of living in old frame tenements with old-fashioned coal stoves, with kerosene lamps, no bath, and an outside toilet."[81]

Abbott's colleague Elizabeth Hughes, director of the Bureau of Social Research for Chicago, was more blunt. In a study of living conditions of low-income families, particularly those of African-American and Mexican backgrounds, she talked about the "derelict" character of the housing stock at the lower rent levels. It was old. It had been cheaply built in the first place and poorly maintained since. Furthermore, the plumbing was "wretchedly inadequate." Living in the cheap rentals was so terrible, the outspoken Hughes contended, that "the tenants instead of the landlords should be paid because of the constant risk to health and limb which the houses force on their occupants daily."[82]

But to Chicago's social work community, the quality of housing at the lower rent levels—however "derelict" it might be—was not the most disturbing aspect of the city's housing situation. The worst problem was the failure of new building to significantly improve conditions for those at the bottom of the economic ladder. The surge of construction during the 1920s had "done nothing for the small-wage earner and his family," Hughes wrote in a report to the city in 1925. While newly built residential units were obviously too expensive for this group, she explained how supply and demand theory predicted that the expansion of more expensive housing stock should make an impact on prices throughout the market. Yet this had not happened. Hughes's rent survey (described in chapter 1) revealed that by mid-decade, rents were falling only above a certain level. At the lower levels, rents were actually continuing to rise. Granting that the new construction may have relieved "some little pressure from the economic group just above," she concluded that the benefits for low-income families were "possibly counterbalanc[ed]" by the loss of available cheap rentals due to deterioration.[83]

The lesson for the Chicago social researchers was that the actual cost not only of new housing, but also of older urban housing in decent condition, was simply too high for the slender resources of many working families. Landlords would not drop their prices below the cost of owning, or if they did, they would let buildings deteriorate in order to still make a profit. Speaking for many of her colleagues, Hughes concluded: "Private enterprise and restrictive legislation alone have proved themselves incapable of meeting the needs of small-wage earners for adequate housing."[84]

A few American analysts, most notably Edith Elmer Wood, had been making this argument for some years.[85] Ironically, it was prosperity, high building rates, and profitability for the real estate industry in the 1920s that helped expand the constituency for such a thoroughgoing critique of commercial housing provision. By the end of the decade, even the traditionally conservative "professional housers," who staffed big-city housing improvement associations, were losing faith in pure private-sector solutions. Bleecker Marquette, director of the Cincinnati Better Housing League, complained publicly in 1929 that despite twenty-five years of reform efforts "little progress . . . has been made in getting rid of what is commonly called slum conditions." Lawrence Veiller, long a vocal opponent of any government intervention beyond restrictive legislation, also modified his stance. In 1929, he urged the city of Cincinnati to buy up portions of its West End slum district, clear away derelict structures, build parks, and coordinate the construction of low-rent housing by limited-dividend developers.[86]

In 1931, Wood published the widely read *Recent Trends in American Housing*, which began with the assertion "that a substantial portion of the population cannot pay a commercial rent, much less a commercial purchase price, for a home fulfilling the minimum health and decency requirements." Moreover, she insisted that the situation was not due to the Depression. "It is universal and permanent,—to the extent, at least, that our economic system is universal and permanent."[87] By this time many people agreed, although no comprehensive policy proposal based on this analysis had yet been developed.

Conclusion

To many historians, the housing market of the 1920s has appeared robust, but contemporary participants and observers were often anxious and critical. Developers and financial institutions experienced problems such as cost increases of inputs and credit shortages that they found hard to understand and control. Consumers found higher levels of comfort and convenience in housing, but also higher prices. While new sources of credit allowed some families to support higher housing costs, rising foreclosure rates well before the crash suggest that housing costs were simply too high in relation to incomes for many families.[88] Reform-oriented professionals had been increasingly dissatisfied with the performance of the commercial market throughout the early twentieth century, in large part because of heightened expectations as to what constituted a good home. In the 1920s, many observers were disillusioned by the behavior of the market as they watched the building boom bypass the neighborhoods of industrial workers, whose low and unpredictable incomes would not support a move into newer and better areas of metropolitan regions.

Based on their various dissatisfactions, groups across the political spectrum put forward a variety of proposals. Certain themes recurred frequently. Many, from the founders of Forest Hills Gardens to Herbert Hoover, put their faith in the "gospel of efficiency" to overcome the failures they identified in the functioning of the American housing market. Others called for the government to subsidize residential development in some manner. Business groups wanted this strategy implemented through mechanisms such as tax exemptions and publicly organized secondary markets that left initiative, control, and profits with the private sector. Left-of-center critics also called for the government to support the housing sector with low-cost capital, but they usually suggested programs in which public authority took a clear role in defining the character of the housing produced and regulating its administration. These proposals generally envisioned noncommercial entities rather than government agencies doing the actual work of building and administering housing produced with public support. And, as shown, such plans sometimes included provisions for keeping the resulting housing out of the speculative market permanently.

Thus it is clear that well before the housing market faltered and the general economy went into depression, the idea of government entrance into the housing sector was on the national agenda. Much of the debate in these years was not about whether or not it should be involved, but how and for what purposes public authority should expand into this part of the economy. Ultimately, business proposals—supplemented by a miserly investment in public housing—won out, but this outcome emerged only after struggles with contesting visions for the future of American housing.

THREE

Catherine Bauer and the Plan for "Modern Housing"

F or those who accepted the more extreme critiques of the housing market that emerged in the 1920s, the development of a large noncommercial housing sector seemed the only practical solution. In the 1920s, Edith Elmer Wood was the best-known champion of this position. But Wood's focus was on economics, and she was more effective at demonstrating what was wrong with the existing housing situation than at putting forward appealing alternatives. In the early 1930s, Catherine Bauer, with her background in architecture and planning, took on this task and in so doing assumed leadership of the radical wing of the American housing reform movement. Through her writing, particularly her 1934 book *Modern Housing*, and her later work with the Labor Housing Conference, Bauer played a central role in developing and communicating a program for a new kind of American housing system.[1]

The approach Bauer publicized, which she termed "modern housing," connected Wood's concerns about the limitations of the market with new architectural and planning ideas that were circulating internationally in the interwar period. This program ultimately failed to shape the direction of American federal policy; however, it did influence many reform-oriented professionals and trade unionists in the 1930s and had considerable impact on the Housing Division of the Public Works Administration, the first of the New Deal housing agencies. In addition, the modern housing program suggested a way of designing a unified public policy with regard to housing issues as opposed to the usual two-tier approach, which generally isolates and stigmatizes the poor.

Bauer's career in the 1930s provides an excellent opportunity to examine the policy direction she championed, as well as the larger dynamics of federal policy creation in the New Deal era. Moreover, her experiences and ideas highlight the international context in which American housing debates and decisions took place.

The European Mass Housing Movement

Bauer's career exemplifies ways in which discussion and experimentation with regard to housing issues in the United States during the interwar period took place against the backdrop of dramatic events in Europe. Most Americans who participated in debates about housing between the wars drew on some kind of analysis of what had gone on in the other advanced industrial countries. For instance, as described previously, when the mortgage banker J. Willison Smith wanted to convince Congress in 1920 to approve tax exemptions for investments in mortgages, he warned that failure to aid the real estate industry could result in its collapse and necessitate costly public programs, as had happened in Britain.

Smith was alluding to the fact that after the First World War, national and municipal governments throughout Europe developed extensive programs to expand the supply of urban shelter. Through a conjunction of political and cultural trends, housing became a major public issue in most European nations in this period. This was a time of tremendous popular unrest, particularly immediately after the war. Revolutionary initiatives were defeated, except in Russia, but political authorities everywhere felt pressure for change. Governments at national and local levels launched programs to upgrade mass living standards, initiating a period of rich experimentation.[2] In the arts, the decade of the twenties was the high tide of what has been called "Utopian Modernism," a movement characterized by the conviction "that humanity and the environment could be improved through design."[3] Avant-garde architects aimed at creating not just more or cheaper dwellings, but better urban environments than capitalist development had provided thus far.

In Austria after the war, Social Democrats gained control of the city council of Vienna, where housing shortages were at emergency levels. Initially, the council responded to the situation with rent control, requisitioning underutilized apartments, and offering aid to families who were attempting to construct their own housing in the so-called wild settlements on open city-owned land. But these measures produced only a limited amount of new housing; meanwhile, private construction stayed moribund.

In 1923, the city instituted a steeply progressive housing tax on rents in order to finance an ambitious building program that rehoused approximately 10 percent of the city's population over the following decade. The tax meant that the city did not have to borrow to pay for construction, thus avoiding interest costs that would have sapped scarce funds from the program. Voters generally did not object, since rent control combined with inflation and kept rents lower than they had been before the war, even with a hefty tax payment tacked on. The large apartment complexes of "Red Vienna" featured extensive collective facilities, such as libraries, kindergartens, health centers, meeting halls, and recreation centers (see figure 3.1). These kinds of amenities reflected the Austromarxists' goal of creating a socialist alternative to bourgeois culture.[4]

Publicly supported housing programs in German cities were quantitatively

FIG. 3.1 Children at play in the wading pool at *Fuchsenfeldhof* in Vienna, built between 1922 and 1925. This large complex included 1,100 dwelling units and contained other interior courtyards. Besides the pool, group facilities included a children's playground, kindergarten, maternity care facility, gymnasium, and pharmacy, as well as central laundries and workshops. In the foreground, children are sitting on and touching large smooth statues of hippopotamuses. Photograph from *Modern Housing* by Catherine Bauer. Copyright 1934 by Catherine Bauer. Copyright (c) renewed 1962 by Catherine Bauer Wurster. Reprinted by permission of Houghton Mifflin Company. All rights reserved.

on a par with the Viennese achievement. In Germany, however, modernist movements in architecture and planning were stronger, and radical architects were given most of the commissions. Whereas Vienna's *Hof* developments were essentially refinements of conventional perimeter-block tenements that fit into the pre-existing street grid and were built using traditional methods, the Germans were more experimental. They tried novel architectural forms and employed new kinds of building materials and construction techniques.[5] In addition, much of the mass housing in the Weimar Republic was constructed in distinct residential districts, or *Siedlungen*, that featured innovative site plans created to increase amenities while also cutting costs. For example, buildings were often arranged in parallel rows called *Zeilenbau* to give all individual dwellings the best orientation for sunlight (see figure 3.2).[6] *Neues Bauen* became a popular term among architects and planners, an expression that signified not only a new approach to building and design, but also a commitment to creating a freer and more egalitarian society.[7]

German avant-garde architects in this period maintained that their ob-

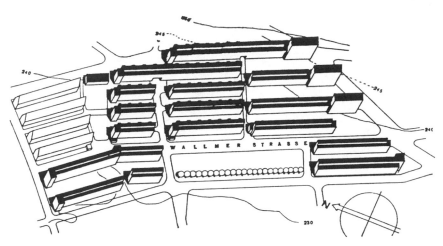

FIG. 3.2 *Zeilenbau*-style site plan for a portion of the Wallmer development in Stuttgart, by architect Richard Döcker. This kind of design evolved as a way of saving money while at the same time increasing livability. The rows of buildings are spaced so as not to cut off each other's sunlight (the rule of thumb was that they should be no less than twice their height apart). The three-story buildings in this drawing are only two rooms deep, with living rooms and kitchens on the southwestern side (that is, facing the bottom edge of this diagram) where they would receive maximum afternoon sunlight during winter and spring in Germany's northern latitudes. Bedrooms face east to obtain morning light. Note that much of the housing does not front a street, but is instead arranged at right angles to streets. This aspect of *Zeilenbau* planning allowed space for extensive landscaped grounds, cut down on noise, and saved money by reducing the cost of road-building. The long straight rows allowed for the use of machinery during construction, as did the technique used by Grosvenor Atterbury at Forest Hills Gardens (shown in figures 2.1 and 2.2.) From *Rehousing Urban America*, by Henry Wright. Copyright (c) 1935 by Columbia University Press. Reprinted with permission of the publisher.

jective was to create an architecture that would be "a pure representation of structure, function, and the means of its production" rather than to develop a particular "style." In fact, however, most coalesced around an idiom featuring simple rectangular shapes, no applied ornamentation, and generous window space (see figure 3.3). Of the various avant-garde design trends that existed in the early twentieth century, this rationalist approach seemed to offer the most hope for upgrading living standards for the majority of people, since its clean geometric shapes seemed most appropriate for mass production. Beyond its utilitarian potential, this aesthetic offered possibilities for exploring the qualities of abstract form, similar to the way cubism had functioned in painting. The consistency of the different buildings designed by architects from all over

Fig. 3.3 Small apartment houses and grounds built in Frankfurt, Germany, in the 1920s. This photograph, taken in 1990, shows how the precise geometric shapes and plain (often white) exterior walls characteristic of modernistic rationalism complement the lush gardening for which the Germans are famous. This strand of architectural modernism eventually won out over competing tendencies throughout the world and became known as the "International Style," in good part because its simple rectangular forms lent themselves to economies of production. Rationalism's proponents, however, prized it not merely or even chiefly for its utilitarian qualities, but rather for the abstract beauty of its forms and its connection to utopian social ideals.

she would not be later. The houses she described, were, after all, a set of expensive Parisian townhouses built for affluent clients. Even in this early piece, however, she noted that for Le Corbusier, the leading figure among experimental architects in France, the quest to achieve a new mode of building based on engineering and mass production principles was not motivated primarily by a desire to improve life for the privileged classes, but rather by an aspiration for "more and better and cheaper houses for the ordinary man."[16]

After her year in France, Bauer moved back to the United States. She took up residence in Greenwich Village in New York City, supporting herself, as she described later, with "miscellaneous boom-time jobs" related to advertising. In 1929, while working as advertising manager for the publisher Harcourt Brace in New York City, Bauer met Lewis Mumford. She was twenty-four; he was a decade older and already an established author, although he had not yet written any of the books on the city that would make him internationally famous. While in Paris, Bauer had read his 1926 book *The Golden Day*, in which he argued that the great American literature of the mid-nineteenth century provided hope that a less materialistic cultural tradition could be created in the United States. This book had helped convince her to return home, she told him after they met. The two developed an intense relationship based on their mutual passion for modern architecture and literature and, soon thereafter, for each other.[17]

In the fall of 1930, Mumford introduced Bauer to his colleagues in the Regional Planning Association of America (RPAA). Despite its formal name, the organization was essentially a discussion group that had been meeting regularly in and near New York City since 1923. Charles Harris Whitaker had introduced several of the key members to each other. Along with Mumford, core participants included the architects and planners Clarence Stein, Henry Wright, and Frederick L. Ackerman. Conservationist Benton McKaye, originator of the plan for the Appalachian Trail, was also involved. Over the years, other prominent intellectuals concerned with urban issues, including Edith Elmer Wood, economist Stuart Chase, and architect Robert D. Kohn, joined the group for limited periods. Bauer, although much younger than the others, was easily accepted into this circle and became the group's executive secretary in 1932.[18]

The Regional Planning Association of America is probably best remembered for its support of garden city planning ideas. Repelled by the trends toward massive metropolitan agglomerations, RPAA members tried to develop ideas for facilitating more humane physical environments in a society that was becoming predominantly urban. As an alternative to the uncontrolled incremental growth of gigantic "dinosaur cities," the RPAA proposed conscious planning of balanced development over large regions.[19]

Members of the group were particularly concerned with creating higher quality neighborhoods than either cities or suburbs typically provided Americans. A shared interest in housing issues had, as it happened, brought them together originally. As we have seen, Whitaker had been a leader in the successful drive for a government home building program during the war.[20] Ackerman had participated in this campaign by writing a detailed and favorable firsthand report on the British housing program for munitions workers. Whitaker published Ackerman's essay first in the AIA journal in 1917 and then as part of a book the following year.[21] After the U.S. wartime programs were underway, both Ackerman and Henry Wright did architectural and planning work under Robert D. Kohn, who was chief of production for the U.S. Shipping Board.[22] Mumford did not participate in the war programs, but he attributed his lifelong interest in housing issues to the policy discussions and reports of foreign initiatives Whitaker had published during the war.[23]

The RPAA initially formulated many of the ideas that Bauer would later promote as part of the "modern housing" program. Group members were sharply critical of the results of lightly regulated profit-driven development characteristic of American urban areas. Through their discussions, they developed alternatives to existing approaches both in terms of economics and spatial organization.

From the standpoint of economics, group members took the position that American housing was more expensive than necessary. Their analysis combined both of the major reformist perspectives articulated in the debates over the federal war programs. First, they believed large-scale modernized production techniques needed to be introduced. Second, they were convinced affordable urban shelter was not compatible with housing as a speculative commodity. The cost of housing was high because "our whole individualized process of home building at present is wasteful and extravagant," Henry Wright charged in an article in the *Survey* in 1925.[24] Mumford, writing in the *Nation* that same year, asserted that the high proportion of bad housing in the country was due to "the waste of speculative profits, which puts into the builders' and the financiers' pockets money which should have gone into the improvement of the house and land."[25]

The planning deficiencies of conventional practices constituted, if anything, an even more serious issue than the cost question from the RPAA's standpoint. The group directed its fire not primarily at the older sections of cities, such as the decrepit Chicago neighborhoods monitored by Edith Abbott over the years, but at the development standards of their own time. Most building in the 1920s took place on metropolitan fringes, both inside and outside of the legal limits of cities.[26] RPAA members criticized this suburban development for its lack of community amenities and its physical remoteness.

According to Wright, the flight from the central cities was a self-defeating cycle. Americans wanted to live on the outskirts of cities, as though they were "solitary Robinson Crusoes," because of the powerful ideal of the picturesque home in a rustic setting. But once families located far from the metropolitan core, they lost the "genuine advantages" of urban life. They often forfeited the advantages of solitude as well, he pointed out, given that likeminded others were soon building their own country homes in close proximity.[27]

The RPAA wanted to make radical changes in urban development practices, thinking that nothing less would make it possible to create affordable and appealing urban residential environments. The group energetically attacked the assumption, which was continually surfacing in the United States, that technology and administrative efficiency alone could solve the problem of high costs while leaving intact the larger framework of incremental, profit-based development.[28] Mumford was particularly acerbic on this point. He pointed out that while Americans continually experimented with techniques to cut the cost of the building's shell, the structure itself represented only about half of the cost of a contemporary house. Reducing the price of the building alone would not deal with the cost of land, site improvements, installation of utilities, and interest on borrowed money. Cutting interest rates would bring down the price of a home "far more drastically than the most ingenious cheese-paring on the structure," he insisted.[29] Solutions had to be sought, he argued, "not in terms of the "individual 'cell' but in terms of the larger unit," that is, not the house alone, but the entire neighborhood.[30]

With the support of wealthy real estate entrepreneur Alexander Bing, the RPAA formed a limited-profit company, called the City Housing Corporation (CHC), to put some of its ideas into practice. In 1924, the CHC acquired seventy-six acres in Queens, New York, and started building Sunnyside. Stein and Wright, who designed the project, had hoped to use the whole parcel flexibly to demonstrate the economic and physical advantages of free planning arrangements. Instead, they were forced to work within the confines of conventional city blocks, because municipal authorities refused to allow them to modify the previously established street pattern. Nevertheless, the Sunnyside development did break away from single lot planning, with its houses grouped in rows along the perimeters of blocks. Instead of dividing the remaining space into tiny individual backyards, Stein and Wright created large common lawns in the interiors of the blocks, thereby providing residents with something of the atmosphere of living at the border of a park.

While losing some projected economies because of being forced to work within a conventional street grid, the company did achieve savings from large-scale planning, purchasing, and a rapid construction schedule, coordinated by Bing, that minimized carrying charges on loans. Still, as with earlier efforts to produce superior housing for less through bigger, better organized operations, the results proved disappointing. Single row houses cost approximately $5,000, a price comparable with that of houses available from commercial builders, although the Sunnyside homes were smaller. According to Mumford, who lived at Sunnyside with his family for eleven years, the homes at Sunnyside were better planned and the outside areas had more "usable open space" than commercially produced houses, but they were not cheaper. The source of the problem, he believed, was that large development companies had overhead expenses that small-scale speculators did not face, which offset many advantages of scale.[31]

Three years later, the group began collaborating on a more ambitious effort called Radburn. The CHC acquired a one-square-mile tract of land in Fair Lawn, New Jersey, a rural area approximately seventeen miles from New York City. Here the RPAA hoped to demonstrate a clear alternative to contemporary commercial residential development: a comprehensively planned town combining the advantages of twentieth-century technology with access to nature—all in a setting that would foster face-to-face relationships. No longer inhibited by a rigid street grid, Stein and Wright organized the homes at Radburn on large thirty-to fifty-acre superblocks, grouping them away from automobile traffic and toward large open park spaces.

The depression doomed plans for a town of 25,000 to 30,000. When the CHC went bankrupt in 1934, only about 1,500 people lived in Radburn. Enough building had happened, however, to allow the community to concretely embody a number of the RPAA's innovative principles of site planning. But the RPAA's larger goal—its hope of demonstrating the superiority of nonspeculative, regionally planned land development—would certainly have proved impossible even if prosperity had continued. Even at its projected maximum size, Radburn was simply too small.[32]

Bauer Returns to Europe

Bauer's ideas related to housing issues clearly show the impact of RPAA theories, but she also benefitted from contact with European thinking. Stimulated by conversations with Mumford, she decided to educate herself more thoroughly about the new design trends emerging in Europe. The opportunity came when Harcourt Brace eliminated her job early in 1930 amidst the general economic downturn. Newly unemployed, she set off for several months of travel through Sweden, the Netherlands, France, and Germany.

The trip turned out to be a pivotal experience. "What I saw in Europe in 1930 was so exciting that it transformed me from an aesthete into a housing reformer," she wrote shortly before her death over thirty years later. Architectural modernism, later reduced to simply a "style," was initially, as she encountered it, a broad idealistic movement aimed at "improving human environment in a modern industrial society." The new tendencies in architecture were linked to movements to improve living standards for the whole population. Thus she experienced her own evolution from apprentice art critic to housing specialist and advocate as a natural progression.[33]

Among the places she visited, Bauer paid special attention to Frankfurt am Main, a city with the reputation as the "exemplar of the new architecture in Germany between the wars."[34] Mumford's friend Walter Curt Behrendt, editor of the influential German architectural and industrial design journal *Die Form*, gave her introductions in Frankfurt. In September 1930, she enrolled in a three-day seminar that the city sponsored to showcase its building program and educate people from other cities and countries about its principles and virtues. Approximately 150 architects and journalists from around the world participated in the lectures and bus tours, but Bauer was the only American.[35]

Since the end of the postwar inflation, Frankfurt had constructed approximately 160,000 new dwellings, enough to house about 10 percent of its population.[36] Several other German cities built roughly equivalent amounts, but Frankfurt's achievements were better known thanks to the inventive and tireless public relations efforts of Ernst May, the city's building director. An architect and planner, May dedicated himself to developing new forms appropriate for twentieth-century life. The seminar Bauer attended was just one example of how May disseminated his philosophy and advertised his city's accomplishments at the same time. *Das Neue Frankfurt*, the architectural magazine he edited, had subscribers from as far away as Japan.[37]

After returning to the United States in the fall of 1930, Bauer wrote about Frankfurt's housing program in an article she submitted to the *Fortune* magazine contest for the best essay on the theme "Art in Industry." The wealthy Pittsburgh department store owner Edgar Kaufmann had put up $1,000 in prize money for the competition. Kaufmann, an admirer of modern architecture who later in the decade commissioned Frank Lloyd Wright to design the famous Fallingwater house, served as one of the three judges. The other two were architect Joseph Urban and industrial designer Norman Bel Geddes. To everyone's surprise (probably Mumford's especially, since he too had submitted an article), Bauer won the competition.[38]

Bauer's thesis was that an aesthetic appropriate to modern life had not yet been achieved. Art and industry were not reconciled in the contemporary world, and "no commodity shows to greater disadvantage their present divorce than the contemporary small house." Yet, as difficult as the problem of the small dwelling was, efforts by the city of Frankfurt "to provide a twentieth-century solution for the problem of minimum-cost houses" were achieving noteworthy breakthroughs, not only for housing but for urban design generally.[39]

She explained how Frankfurt's housing program was part of a bold plan for the physical reorganization of the metropolitan region. May, who, early in his career, had worked for Raymond Unwin at Hamstead Garden Suburb in England, created a master plan in 1925 that projected metropolitan expansion through linking a series of suburban districts by rail and highway to the city core. In contrast to the usual pattern of urban growth through continuous expansion from the center, the plan called for concentrated development to take place in these decentralized nodes. Greenbelts would surround the new settlements, introducing large stretches of open countryside into the urbanized region. To be truly effective, the plan required that the whole metropolitan area be under a single administration, and in 1928 the city was able to annex large areas on its periphery.[40]

The jewel of May's efforts was the suburb of Römerstadt, a residential development northwest of the old city overlooking the Nidda River valley. Bauer, who had what one acquaintance described as a "religious passion" for modern architecture, found the suburb visually stunning.[41] Viewed from a distance, as a total composition, the neighborhood provided what seemed to her a new and appealing vision of modern life. From a distance, one had "a view of dazzling whiteness and the satisfactory geometry of clean lines, well-defined, largely conceived forms, and simple surfaces occasionally curved to conform to the topography" (figure 3.4). At close range, one saw "tiers of concrete and glass and gardens curving beyond the sheep-dotted valley of the Nidda—each house with a garden, each apartment with a terrace, half an hour from a city of 500,000 inhabitants."[42]

Of the homes themselves, Bauer explained that although May was convinced that "the one-family house can never have a worthy substitute," pressures for economy dictated some form of grouped units. The city had tried various kinds of low apartment buildings and row housing; her favorite solution was the two-story row unit topped by a one-story flat with a garden in the rear (figure 3.5). The units were small inside, but built-in furniture conserved space, as did the famous streamlined *Frankfurter Küche* (Frankfurt Kitchen) designed by the architect Grete Lihotzky. Each dwelling had hot and cold running water, an inside toilet, and a shower or small bathtub.[43]

Bauer did note that the residents were initially dismayed at the appearance of their new homes. She contended, however, that after moving in, they found their rowhouses and apartments "not only full of light, air, and modern convenience, but actually far handsomer than the unachievable cottage ideal they may have been lazily cherishing."[44] For proof of this conversion, however, she provided nothing but her own enthusiasm. Following the main line of the

71

European architectural avant-garde at this time, Bauer believed that the austere rationalism that characterized May's housing was the appropriate aesthetic for industrial society.

Bauer joked later that winning the *Fortune* contest had "inadvertently" transformed her into a "housing expert."[45] As she herself was well aware, however, she was still a talented beginner in the field of international housing policy at this point in her life. To illustrate this, she told the story of what happened to her when she went to Pittsburgh in the spring of 1931 to collect her prize money. Arriving in the city, she was treated like a minor celebrity, with write-ups in the *Pittsburgh Post-Gazette* and invitations to appear before several civic groups. Kaufmann held a formal luncheon in her honor, but the occasion turned into "one of her most embarrassing social moments" when her host began soliciting her opinions on housing policies in Vienna. Although Vienna was a major center of the housing movement, Bauer knew little about events there, while Kaufmann turned out to be very knowledgeable. The problem, she said in retrospect, was that "she had put all she knew into the essay."[46]

Four months of concentrated research in Europe during the following year would transform Bauer into an authentic expert. Mumford decided to travel in Europe during the summer of 1932 to do research for *Technics and Civilization*, the first of his major books. Although married, he was continuing the affair he had begun with Bauer two years earlier. His plan was for her as well as his wife to join him at different points in his travels. To help pay for Bauer's trip, he secured an advance from *Fortune* for a series on housing and used the money to hire her to do technical research. Bauer supplemented the *Fortune* stipend with a grant from the New Jersey State Federation of Women's Clubs and traveled throughout Europe doing what Mumford later described as "all of the legwork and not a little of the headwork" for the projected articles. Truthfully, if somewhat self-servingly, he characterized her work in this period as "a post-graduate course in housing and planning" that gave her a "special grasp of both social and architectural problems in relation to urban planning."[47]

While the research work that summer eventually did prove to be very valuable, in the short run Bauer found the trip professionally and personally frustrating. She and Mumford fought continually when they were together in Munich and Paris. Then, arriving back in New York, they discovered that, in Bauer's words, "*Fortune*, the bitch, has just decided that what they *really* want (and this is the exact opposite of what they told us in writing last spring) is just Lewis's personal impressions of architecture and such." The problem was that in their absence the magazine editors had decided to push for prefabrication of individual houses as the solution to the housing problem, a strategy

FIG. 3.4 A 1920s photograph of Ernst May's settlement of Römerstadt in Frankfurt, seen from across the Nidda River valley greenbelt. This image well conveys the dramatic possibilities of modern architecture. The development contained over 1,200 dwelling units (mostly in row-houses) in a compact but verdant setting, with various community amenities, including shops, daycare centers, communal laundries, and shared garden areas.

Fɪɢ. 3.5 This photograph, taken in 1990, shows the garden side of two-unit rowhousing at Praunheim, a settlement adjacent to Römerstadt. The first two floors form one dwelling, while the apartment at the top was designed as a rental unit for owners living below. As the apartments lacked direct access to the garden area, they were provided with open terraces at the rear. At Praunheim, May began using large precast concrete blocks to construct building shells, much like the ones Grosvenor Atterbury had used at Forest Hills Gardens. Eventually, May built just under 900 dwellings using this process.

articulated in the 1932 book *Housing America* sponsored by the magazine and written anonymously by Archibald MacLeish. *Housing America* railed that the "unorganized," even "reactionary," character of the building industry was to blame for high housing costs. Mumford's position was that there had to be "rationalization of *all* the factors involved," meaning reform of the financial as well as production aspects of residential building. Essentially, his call for eliminating what he called "speculative wastes in finance" amounted to a proposal for government coordination of low-interest loan programs to finance noncommercial housing developments. This perspective on the problem left the *Fortune* editors distinctly unenthusiastic, and they canceled the series after three installments, instead of publishing the projected five.[48]

The next period in Bauer's life was a difficult one. She told a friend that the exhausting months of travel and research in different countries had left her in a "slump." Although she wanted to do some writing on her own, she complained that it was difficult getting started, since she had absorbed "so many details and irreconcilable but nevertheless correct statistics, theories, policies, etc. that [she couldn't] make a single generalization off-hand."[49] Meanwhile her relationship with Mumford was deteriorating. She was growing restive with the three-corner relationship, but Mumford showed no inclination to choose between her and his wife. Things continued essentially on his terms for a while, although Mumford too was dissatisfied. Bauer no longer seemed the carefree woman with whom he had fallen in love. He complained, "I reach for you [now] and what do I touch? A housing expert. I call for you in the stillness of the night and what do I hear: The percentage of vacancies in *Laubengang* [garden] apartment houses in Germany as compared with cottages."[50]

Despite the pain both suffered as the relationship unraveled, their love affair was an enriching experience for each of them. With Bauer's encouragement, Mumford embarked on the more ambitious writing projects that would secure him a lasting reputation as an urban theorist. At the same time, he inspired her to acquire real expertise in the area of her interests and to believe in her potential as a writer. "You transformed an insufferable smart-y dilettante into a good semblance of a serious and responsible worker," she told him in a letter early in 1933.[51] Mumford's last important gift was his encouragement to use the masses of data she had collected for the ill-fated *Fortune* series to write her own book on housing.[52]

Bauer Proposes "Modern Housing"

Bauer took Mumford's suggestion and in the spring of 1933 began writing the manuscript that became *Modern Housing*, a description and interpretation of European housing programs for an American audience. It turned out to be a good time for such a book. Since the onset of the depression, housing had become a pressing public issue. No longer were shelter problems confined to low-income families. Builders and residential finance institutions were in trouble, as well as many formerly comfortable families. A quarter of a million homes had been foreclosed on in 1932, and in the first months of 1933 the rate climbed to over a thousand a day.[53] There was heightened interest in foreign programs, and the most recent booklength treatment of European policies was a decade out of date.[54]

Bauer's good timing was not initially obvious to her. She was dubious about her prospects when she set out to find a publisher. The obstacles were numerous, she told a friend, including "no book to show, no name, no libraries buying books, all architects in the breadline, etc." Despite her doubts, she secured a $1,000 grant from the Carnegie Foundation and a contract from Houghton Mifflin with a fair amount of ease. Ferris Greenslet, the editor she approached, had read her *Fortune* essay and been impressed with "its lucid and vigorous presentation of first-hand material." Convinced that her proposal had "great timeliness," he took it to his editorial committee, which readily approved it.[55]

The book took longer to write than first envisioned. Both the Carnegie Foundation and Houghton Mifflin had wanted it to come out in the fall of 1933, but the writing dragged into the following year. Finally in late April of 1934 Bauer shipped the completed manuscript to her publishers. "What a nuisance it is writing books!" she told her editor. "I feel as [if] I'd been in labour about six months, and trying to earn a living on the side as well."[56] The book appeared in December 1934 to wide and quite favorable reviews.

Bauer's thesis in *Modern Housing* was that the real achievement of the postwar European housing programs was not the quantity of dwellings produced. Instead, the significant breakthrough was the creation of an entirely new kind of shelter and a new framework for producing it. She termed this new kind of building "modern housing" and explained that it was distinguished from "the typical residential environment of the past century" in several ways. For one thing, modern housing was constructed for use rather than profit, which meant it did not enter the speculative market and was planned in such a way as to retain its quality for the long term. Another difference was that this kind of housing was built as part of comprehensively planned neighborhoods, with parks, schools, and other community facilities nearby. Since it was conceived of and constructed as a whole, she wrote, "a modern housing development does not, therefore, constitute a mere mechanical extension of streets and agglomeration of individual, competitive dwellings. It has a beginning and an end, and some sort of visible, organic form." Individual dwellings tended to be of modest size. However, designers strove to make the most of internal space and sited buildings so that individual units had good cross-ventilation, sunlight, pleasant views, and privacy. In addition, there were social and recreational opportunities close by that were not to be found in commercially produced residential neighborhoods. All this was available at rent levels affordable to people with average incomes or less.[57]

In the book, Bauer made her preference for architectural modernism clear. "It is not merely that the housing standard of one class of people has been hauled up a few notches nearer the next most privileged group, and the bill grudgingly underwritten by taxpayers," she told her readers. "The significant thing about it is that almost every one of the new houses is not only better, but completely different, from the general run of dwellings put up in the past century."[58] Of course, one cannot assume that residents saw things quite the same way as Bauer. While they presumably appreciated the improved amenities that these dwellings offered, it is not so clear that they had the same affection for designs that were "completely different" from what they were used to.

Bauer calculated that, since the war, European governments had aided in the construction of at least four and one-half million new housing units. State-assisted building since the war had accounted for approximately 70 percent of all residential building, providing shelter to around 16 percent of the population. She contended that this new housing would "not have been erected if there had not been an active public housing policy." This assertion was certainly correct in the sense that little would have been built at the same rent levels had it been done on a for-profit basis. She did not, however, bring out the fact that various aspects of the programs themselves sometimes inhibited private enterprise. While she emphasized that there was still need for many more housing units and that only about half of what had been built was affordable for the lowest-paid workers, she made it clear that she found the achievement impressive.[59]

In terms of its financial framework, most of the new housing had been produced on a not-for-profit basis and then kept out of the speculative market. Bauer estimated that about 30 percent of the total was erected directly by local governments and remained publicly owned. The least expensive housing was usually provided in this way, partly because municipalities often based rents on a family's ability to pay, rather than on actual costs. She noted that in Vienna, and sometimes in England, the actual construction was done directly by the government, cutting out the expense of profit margins for private contractors. Cooperatives or other private nonprofit groups were responsible for another 38 percent of state-aided domestic building. These building societies were often connected to trade union, religious, or political groups. One advantage of these organizations was that they provided a mechanism by which individuals could influence the design and administration of their housing. Private enterprise carried out the final 32 percent of state-supported work, although, as Bauer explained, these developers were not "private" in the sense that Americans understood the term, because "in addition to compulsory supervision of standards of layout and design, there are usually rental regulations and restrictions as to sale."[60]

Bauer thought there was a major difference between government coordination of housing programs and subsidized housing. As she saw it, the government could organize production without subsidies simply by providing loans to builders at lower rates than they could obtain through private capital markets and tying the loans to guidelines for quality and administration of the final product. Subsidies entered the picture only if further funds were used to make rents financially possible for lower-income groups, she claimed.[61] While there was clearly an important distinction to be made with regard to different kinds of public financial participation, Bauer's analysis of these economic questions is an example of the common illusion that passive and indirect forms of government intervention are cost-free. In reality, below-market loans are themselves a form of subsidy, favoring certain enterprises over others.

In addition to describing the financial arrangements of the programs, Bauer discussed the various architectural and planning elements of the new approach. She argued that designing large areas or "superblocks" allowed for flexibility and economy compared with working within conventional urban street patterns. By breaking away from preexisting urban grids, architects gained the freedom to site buildings so as to maximize sunshine, ventilation, and views within individual dwellings. She explained how designers had drawn on Le Corbusier's and Frank Lloyd Wright's rejection of special-purpose, boxlike rooms in favor of free-flowing interior space, which meant that small units did not seem cramped. Finally, she made the case that new building materials and methods, such as poured concrete and light steel framing, offered possibilities for economy.[62]

Bauer maintained that the American record during the 1920s was dismal compared with that of the Europeans. Even though most new housing in the United States was built for the top third of the market, she argued that in significant ways it was inferior in quality to the low-cost dwellings produced in Europe. Although new American housing generally had more technical amenities, she took the stance that features like electric refrigerators, tiled bathrooms, and (most extremely) central heating, were less fundamental to good living than maximum interior light and ventilation, pleasant views, and convenient recreation areas for children. Nor were American residential districts as well planned. "Even among the most luxurious, ample, and well-designed suburban houses," she maintained, "there are not many which are as well secured against neighboring blight as, for instance, the ten-dollar-a month houses in Frankfurt."[63]

Bauer did make a few exceptions to her general condemnation of American postwar housing. She cited developments such as Sunnyside in Queens; Radburn, New Jersey; and a few limited-dividend projects in New York City and Chicago as examples of well-planned, economical residential building. Quantitatively speaking, however, these efforts were infinitesimal, amounting to perhaps 10,000 dwelling units in all. "The contrast is only sharpened and given ironic point," she wrote, "if one remembers that during this period it was America, and not Europe, which was going through a New Era of Prosperity."[64]

The last section of the book was devoted to the question of how modern housing programs could be institutionalized in the United States. Her basic argument was that housing at its core was a political issue, not a technical one, and certainly not an area of life where gradual improvement could be expected to occur naturally in a capitalist society. She assumed that "'modern housing' and much of the framework of contemporary western society are mutually antipathetic." According to Bauer, "The premises underlying the most successful and forward-pointing housing developments are not the premises of capitalism, of inviolate private property, of entrenched nationalism, of class distinction, of governments bent on preserving old interests rather than creating new values."[65] Yet, European achievements demonstrated how "good low-cost modern housing has been done (however temporarily or incompletely, and whatever else may have been left undone) in . . . countries with governments more or less similar to our own."[66]

How had this come about? Her answer was: political pressure. Bauer explained that for many decades such pressure had not existed. Before World War I, efforts to improve the housing of low-income people in industrial nations had been initiated without their request or input. Certainly the nineteenth-century European urban proletariat never rose up to demand the model tenements or garden cities middle-class reformers were continually designing for them. As a result, she believed, these initiatives made almost no difference in improving mass living standards.[67]

While she took the position that Victorian housing reformers had had a negligible impact on the material conditions of their own time, she still credited them with making valuable long-run contributions. For example, it was philanthropists who invented the concept of the housing society, an organization set up to build and manage housing on a low-profit or not-for-profit basis. Trade union and consumer groups later used this kind of mechanism to secure housing for themselves. Also, philanthropic reformers originated the idea of large-scale development as a method both of cutting costs and securing a well-designed overall environment. Bauer argued that paternalistic employers, such as Krupp in Germany and Lever Brothers in England, pioneered important advances in physical planning, even if their model company towns provided an oppressively hierarchical social environment from her point of view. Thus, although she criticized the paternalistic, sometimes even authoritarian, aspects of many solutions put forward by middle-class reformers, she believed that their ideas provided a body of worthwhile planning theory and experimentation that was useful in shaping later demands for improvement.[68]

This legacy of ideas was particularly valuable given the dearth of proposals inherited from the revolutionary Left. Marxian socialists, she explained, had not put forward practical ideas for upgrading the physical environment, because they discounted possibilities for real improvement within the existing economic system. Friedrich Engels gave the classic formulation of this perspective in 1872 when he wrote that to solve the housing problem "there is only *one* means: to abolish altogether the exploitation and oppression of the working class by the ruling class."[69] Bauer complained that Engels was so averse to what he regarded as "utopian" thinking that he offered "not the slightest notion as to what new sort of environment the social revolutionists might be fighting for . . . other than the abstract notion that the 'contradiction' between the city and the country must eventually disappear."[70]

According to Bauer, the period after the First World War was a marked contrast to previous episodes of housing reform. For the first time, militancy and concrete proposals were combined. Bauer credited "the German trade-unionists who were prepared to carry out a large-scale housing program with government aid on their own initiative; the townspeople of England who elected Councillors on a housing platform; and everywhere, the workers who wanted not merely housing but revolution and a whole new social framework."[71] In her estimation, it was pressure from people who wanted to improve their own situation that had led to the large-scale building programs of the 1920s. "Housing was not bestowed from the top down in Europe any more than it ever will be in America," she maintained. "It had to be acquired by people who knew what they wanted, and how to get it."[72]

From this reading of recent European history Bauer drew her prescription for the United States. Even though "good, planned, community housing available to the average citizen [was] not a 'normal' product of a capitalist society," it seemed possible that it could be at least partially attained through "an active demand on the part of workers and consumers which is strong enough to overbalance the weight of real estate and allied interests on the other side."[73] Such a movement, she noted in a pointed reference to her associates in the RPAA, could never be made up only of "a handful of specialists—however admirable their intentions may be, however rational their proposals."[74]

Bauer was not dismissing the work of intellectuals and professionals. She believed that their inquiries over the decades had clarified the nature and extent of housing problems in urbanized industrial societies. Also, through technical research and artistry they had created "images and suggestions of a different world [that] inspired discontent with the old one."[75] These efforts had helped inform the content of working people's demands when they did mobilize for better living conditions.

But Bauer was becoming convinced that ideas alone were not enough. Changing the whole framework of American housing was going to require powerful pressure, and she warned that "unemployed architects and scattered idealists just do not supply that force." Large groups of people had to be inspired to want something else, so that demands for a new kind of housing could be backed by organized political pressure. She ended her book by stating her "firm opinion" that "there will never be any realistic housing movement in this country until the workers and the consumers—and the unemployed— themselves take a hand in the solution." She felt certain that "if the demand were there, most of the obstacles, now seemingly insurmountable, would melt away."[76]

The Critical Response

On the whole, reviewers reacted favorably to Bauer's book, although most expressed some unhappiness with her treatment of the American situation. Commentators were most impressed with the way she conceptualized housing issues as part of the larger question of urban development, and thus an issue of general concern, rather than focusing exclusively on the problems of the poor. Bernard J. Newman, writing in the *Annals of the American Academy of Political and Social Science*, was pleased to be spared "the usual sordid details that nauseate," and *Nation* reviewer Douglas Haskell remarked with evident relief that "the author is not socialworkerish, which in a book on housing is an unexpected blessing."[77]

Many reviewers, although they liked her fresh formulation of the topic, were unhappy with what they felt was a lack of attention to—even an alienation from—American realities. One stated rather petulantly that "instead of turning us into Europeans," housing theorists like Bauer should "try to take us as we are." Another described her as "somewhat embittered" by American capitalism.[78]

Indeed, it was true that Bauer did not address certain important features of the American situation. But this was not entirely because of differences between the European and American situation. In some respects, she misread what had happened in Europe. For example, Bauer implied that working-class groups in Europe had pushed directly for what she termed "modern housing." Yet, while there certainly was pressure from below for better living conditions, the particular artistic, economic, and political solution that emerged happened more circuitously than she implied. For example, many working-class people disliked the look of avant-garde architecture, a fact that she herself had noted in her *Fortune* article when she described the German families' dismay at the appearance of their austerely modern new homes in the Frankfurt suburb of Römerstadt. Given her strong democratic inclinations, Bauer had no adequate response to that resistance, so she simply did not acknowledge the contradiction.

While somewhat misinterpreting the role of popular political movements, Bauer's analysis suffered as well from underestimating the importance of institutional factors that had led to the creation of social housing sectors in European countries. For instance, she did not look at the way in which the structure of government affected the power of different groups. This meant that she did not recognize how little political power, compared with the United States, local real estate entrepreneurs wielded in most European nations where so many political decisions were made at the national level. Property investors were further disadvantaged in that they tended to be less integrated with other sectors of the economy than their counterparts in the United States. Thus, in periods of economic and social crisis, European industrialists and financiers proved willing to sacrifice private landlords to buy labor peace.[79] Bauer did not take these kinds of issues into account at this stage in her career. Her experiences in the 1930s, as she tried to get a modern housing approach adopted as federal policy in the United States, would teach her more about the importance of the institutional dimension.

Bauer Joins the Labor Housing Conference

As she made clear in the conclusion to her book, Bauer was moving away from Mumford politically as well as personally. She thought that the economic breakdown of the Depression, combined with the decisive repudiation of the Republican Party in 1932, provided an opportunity to move in a new direction in the housing field. Mumford and her other colleagues in the Regional Planning Association agreed, of course, but from her perspective they seemed to be doing little to take advantage of the situation. They and the whole country seemed to be listlessly waiting for some initiative from Washington.[80] By contrast, she felt restless and ready for some kind of action. Having become convinced that only a nationwide grassroots movement would be capable of significantly changing the American system of housing, she wanted to help bring such a movement into being.

Just at this moment, she found the opportunity she was looking for. "Having dashed off the last sub-section of my book, entitled, *Where Is the Demand?*, fate seems to have put me in the way of answering my own question," she told a friend.[81] Bauer was asked to become executive secretary for the Labor Housing Conference, an organization that had grown out of the experience of the Philadelphia-based Hosiery Workers union with a housing project it had sponsored through a new experimental federal housing program administered by the Public Works Administration. Over the next few years, Bauer would attempt to bring her vision of "modern housing" into being in the United States through her work with this organization. This phase of Bauer's career will be explored in chapter 7.

Conclusion

The ideas that Catherine Bauer presented for a new approach to housing were part of an international movement aimed at raising mass living standards throughout the industrialized world. These ideas drew on architectural modernism, new trends in city planning, emerging production technologies, critiques of the commercial housing market, and aspirations to improve personal and civic life in modern, urbanized society. The proposals she developed from these various elements aimed at creating large quantities of high quality, nonprofit urban housing, while curtailing urban sprawl.

Bauer did not single-handedly create the approach she propounded in her book. The ideas she described as "modern housing" were well known in Europe. Moreover, as the many American experimental projects and proposals reviewed thus far make clear, design professionals and urban theorists in the United States had already incorporated many aspects of this approach, albeit in piecemeal and implicit ways. Bauer's achievement consisted of pulling these ideas together into a coherent whole and articulating not just a critique but a constructive proposal for basic changes in the American system of housing provision.

FOUR

The PWA Housing Division

I n the 1920s, supporters of the new residential development ideas
later publicized by Catherine Bauer mounted a few experiments
using private capital. For example, the City Housing Corporation
developed Sunnyside and Radburn, and the Amalgamated Clothing Workers
Union built cooperative apartments in the Bronx and Manhattan.[1] These initiatives, however, were only small-scale demonstrations of particular aspects
of the approach Bauer advocated, which involved creating a large noncommercial housing sector, coordinated and assisted by the federal government. While labor unions or privately funded groups could mount small-scale
experiments, only the national government (and, to a more limited extent,
the states) had the resources and power to fundamentally alter the residential landscape.[2]

In Europe, many social democratic governments were developing noncommercial housing in the twenties. But the political balance of forces in
the United States was far different, particularly before the American economy
turned sour and the residential real estate market collapsed. Along with the
Depression came a political upsurge, sweeping into Washington not only Roosevelt, but the most urban-oriented Congress up to that time. These events
made possible the first direct federal intervention into the housing market in
the United States during peacetime. This was carried out by the Housing Division of the Federal Emergency Administration of Public Works, more commonly known as the Public Works Administration or PWA.

When the PWA housing program was established, Bauer and other advocates of the new housing theories thought it might be able to launch the vig-
orous noncommercial housing sector that they envisioned as the linchpin of
U.S. housing policy. Key to this strategy was the creation of a new type of
urban dwelling acceptable to the majority of Americans, rather than a second-
class alternative for the poor. Many of those who worked for the PWA Housing Division shared these hopes, and the agency produced much high-level,
and in some cases truly innovative work. As it happened, the PWA did not
bring what Bauer described as "modern housing" to America and, in later
years, the temporary, experimental PWA program was mostly forgotten. But
those who have studied the PWA residential developments see them as generally better designed and built than later public housing and, on certain dimen-

sions, better even than commercially developed properties. Why this program was so different from later publicly funded housing in the United States has to do with a variety of unique factors that came together in the early 1930s.

The Crisis in Residential Real Estate

In the spring of 1933, when the Roosevelt administration took office, the economy was in shambles. The housing sector was in particularly bad shape, as residential construction had been slumping for several years before the stock market crash in 1929. The building boom had peaked in 1925, setting an all-time record of 937,000 new nonfarm homes started in a single year. Each year thereafter housing starts were down, not only from the 1925 mark, but from the year before.[3] The continuing erosion of the market took its toll on the confidence as well as on the pocketbooks of groups connected to home-building. Even those not directly involved were worried, since the ripple effects of residential construction spread over many industries. In addition, the sector was economically important in and of itself. Between 1922 and 1926, the building of nonfarm dwellings accounted for 38 percent of net capital formation.[4]

The collapse of financial institutions that followed the stock market's crash exacerbated pre-existing problems in the housing industry, because builders were so dependent on lenders for capital. As one government official put it, credit operated as the industry's "throttle."[5] Moreover, the dependence went both ways, and the soaring rates of mortgage foreclosures threatened the entire financial structure of the country. Runs on banks and other lenders left them short of cash and unable to renew the short-term home mortgages common at the time. Even when families were lucky enough to hold onto mortgages, rapidly escalating unemployment threatened their ability to keep up payments. The result was that financial institutions rapidly acquired properties for which there were few buyers. Caught in the squeeze, lenders not only were unable to advance money for new construction, they also faced bankruptcy themselves.[6] In response to the increasingly grave situation, President Hoover called for a meeting of leaders in home finance and construction from all over the country.

This meeting, called the President's Conference on Home Building and Home Ownership, took place in Washington early in December of 1931. Almost four thousand people attended. Many were prominent industry figures. The atmosphere at the conference was charged with anxiety, since only 254,000 housing units were started in 1931, which was about one-third of the average for the 1920s as a whole.[7] Worried about the level of desperation, Hoover urged the delegates to consider the housing problem "in its long view rather than its emergency aspects."[8] The president wanted them not to lose sight of the importance of preserving private enterprise in housing, even though many of them faced personal financial ruin.

In his address to the conference, the president invoked what he termed the "immortal ballads" of "Home Sweet Home" and "My Old Kentucky Home" to demonstrate his allegiance to traditional values, but he simultaneously called for a major change in conventional practices.[9] Hoover proposed legislation to create a system of federally supervised banks for mortgage lenders as a way of expanding the supply of housing capital. Essentially, Hoover's Federal Home Loan Bank bill was the same plan first put forward after the war by the League of Building and Loans. A policy proposal that had seemed too extreme to make it out of committee a decade before was enthusiastically endorsed by the conference. Although the margin was narrow, the bill passed the following summer, becoming the first permanent piece of federal housing legislation.[10]

By the time of the President's Conference, residential construction was so depressed that many people, along with Hoover, were ready to experiment. Secretary of Commerce Robert Lamont, like his boss, was no wild-eyed radical. Indeed, so strongly did Lamont believe in the essential correctness of traditional real estate practices that he was at a loss to account for the crisis except to assume that working people had lost respect for the home. For Lamont, the cure to the problem was simple: Americans should buy homes even though they might seem too expensive, since "thrift is a virtue that can work miracles."[11]

Despite Lamont's seeming complacence, he was shocked by what he learned at the conference. The grimmest data had been compiled by the Committee on Negro Housing, which documented the ways in which segregation multiplied the deleterious effects of poverty on blacks. After reading this report, the Secretary of Commerce was moved to conclude that the terrible living conditions endured by African Americans stemmed from the "shortcomings of our individualistic theory of housing, and the failure which grows out of expecting each person in our highly complex industrial civilization to provide his own housing as best he may."[12] Such sentiments were startling enough coming from a cabinet-level official in a Republican administration, but they were all the more surprising given the particularly conservative assumptions with which Lamont started.

Liberal economist Richard Ely, who served on one of the conference's working committees, tried to ease the tension at the gathering by assuring the many businessmen in attendance that the people on his committee were "unanimous in their opposition to the construction of homes with public funds."[13] But just as Hoover feared, many of those in the real estate business seemed more preoccupied with their own survival than with supporting any particular political principle. The Republican Secretary of the Interior, Ray Lyman Wilber, turned out to be a better judge of the possibilities inherent in the situation than the more liberal Ely. Wilber predicted that if private capital did not soon respond to the challenge of housing for the majority by investing in technically innovative, large-scale residential building operations, then "housing by public authority is inevitable."[14]

Such heretical statements by important officials in a Republican administration and Hoover's willingness to initiate the first program of federal intervention into the housing sector during peacetime—limited though it was—signaled the degree to which confidence in the private market in real estate had deteriorated by 1931. The double messages of speakers such as Hoover, who paid tribute to the old verities while at the same time suggesting new policies, reflected a situation of fluidity created by the crisis.

Despite Hoover's legislative initiatives, which included, along with the Home Loan Bank Board System, authorization in 1932 for the Reconstruction Finance Corporation to make loans for low-rent housing and slum clearance, the market continued downward.[15] Housing starts in 1932 were only half of what they had been in the already bad year of 1931. By 1933, when Roosevelt began his first term, the situation had grown even more critical. Starts for the year were down again, by now to only 93,000, a sickening one-tenth of what they had been at the height of the boom in 1925, and only one-seventh of the average for the 1920s. In addition, half of all home mortgages were technically in default, and foreclosures were sweeping the country like a tidal wave. In Philadelphia alone, there were an average of 1,300 sheriff's sales a month during the first half of the year.[16]

These trends meant that when Franklin Roosevelt took office in March 1933, a large proportion of the middle class was facing the loss of its most important single investment, the family home. Meanwhile, mortgage lenders throughout the country were facing ruin, a possibility that threatened the entire financial system. It is against this background of catastrophe that we can begin to understand how it was that Congress supported a variety of federal interventions into the housing sector during the New Deal. More specifically, we can understand how, in the first spurt of emergency legislation, a program as previously off-limits as federal financing and even outright ownership of low-rent housing could be created. This temporary program, set up within the Public Works Administration, was significantly influenced by those who hoped to initiate a single, broad policy approach, aimed at the majority of Americans. Ultimately, the PWA disappointed the hopes of these reformers. Yet, at the same time, the activities of the PWA represented a more profound break from a market-based housing system than programs passed later in the

New Deal when private interests were stronger and able to exert more influence in Congress.

The Political Origins of the PWA Housing Program

As the new Democratic administration under Franklin Roosevelt scrambled to develop legislation to revive the collapsed economy, it encountered no powerful political coalition pushing for programs for low- and moderate-rent housing. Those who believed in the idea of federal support for residential building programs were relatively few in number, although highly articulate and committed. One was the prominent New York settlement worker Mary Kingsbury Simkhovitch, who headed the National Public Housing Conference. In the early days of the new administration, Simkhovitch traveled to Washington to visit New York Senator Robert Wagner, a principal architect of Roosevelt's key initial recovery measure, the National Industrial Recovery Act (NIRA). Along with Father John O'Grady, Secretary of the National Conference of Catholic Charities, Simkhovitch pleaded with Wagner to include a provision for urban housing in the legislation. The senator agreed and included a brief section on housing in the public works section of the bill.

The NIRA consisted of two main parts. Title I, the more controversial, aimed at halting the spiraling deflation by setting aside antitrust regulations and allowing business leaders to cooperate in organizing markets. With prices and wages stabilized by this program, the administration hoped to "prime the pump" with a large public works program. This is where the housing program fit in. Title II called for "a comprehensive program of public works," and specified a program of "construction, reconstruction, alteration, or repair under public regulation or control of low-cost housing and slum-clearance projects" to be included along with more traditional kinds of government building projects such as highways and public buildings. With the president's approval, states, municipalities, or other public bodies undertaking public works could be given capital grants. Congress appropriated $3.3 billion dollars to pay for the program.[17]

The NIRA, with its provision for a government housing program, was sent to a body very different than had previously gathered on Capitol Hill. Sentiment in the House of Representatives shifted quite sharply toward the concerns of working people in the nation's cities after the elections of 1932. Two factors explain the change: reapportionment and the political mobilization of previously inactive urban groups.

Reapportionment had a dramatic impact on the character of the Seventy-Third Congress, because none had occurred in two decades, during which time the population shifted dramatically. Throughout the 1920s the House and Senate bickered over the reapportionment issue. The process was never easy, but this was the first time since the initial census in 1790 that Congress had not been able to come to some agreement on a formula by which to reapportion representation in the House within two years. The unusual deadlock after 1920 occurred for a variety of reasons, but a large part of the problem was that whatever the specifics, any plan put forward would, in the words of Mississippi Representative John E. Rankin, "increase the power of the large alien-congested centers of this country by reducing the number of Representatives from agricultural sections of the United States." After years of wrangling, a compromise was finally reached in 1929 by which the House would be reapportioned on the basis of the 1930 census. Thus, the House of Representatives elected in November 1932 reflected twenty years of demographic change, rather than the usual ten, and this was the period during which the country had become predominantly urban.[18]

The second reason the Seventy-Third Congress was so different from its predecessors was that it included so many northern, urban, liberal Democrats. The children of the last great wave of immigrants were reaching voting age by the late 1920s, and they were overwhelmingly city dwellers. As they had begun to do in 1928, these new voters rallied behind the Democrats in 1932. The party gained ninety seats in the house and thirteen in the Senate. Even more significant, from the standpoint of potential support for urban programs, was that non-Southern Democrats represented a working majority in the House for the first of what would be only a few times in the twentieth century. Roosevelt's political instincts paralleled the mood of Congress, and he sought policies to tie the party's new urban supporters into a permanent majority coalition behind the Democratic Party. Federal urban housing was one such policy.[19]

When Roosevelt sent Congress his National Industrial Recovery bill with its provisions for a housing program in May 1933, he stressed that it should be passed immediately with no changes so he could move forward straightaway with his recovery program. Probably an even more compelling reason for insisting on no changes was that, since the NIRA was a complicated bundle of compromises, he knew it might totally unravel once Congress started tinkering. The deteriorating economic situation along with the new president's enormous popularity enabled him to achieve essentially what he wanted. The NIRA passed through both chambers virtually unchanged in less than a month.[20]

Since Congress was under great pressure to act quickly, there was little debate on the proposed legislation. Even in the crisis atmosphere of early 1933, direct government entrance into residential real estate was a radical step, so it is noteworthy that no one protested this portion of the bill, if only for the record. Previously, only the pressure of the wartime emergency had made this kind of policy acceptable and, even then, debates about building housing for defense workers turned emotional. In 1918, Senator Albert Fall characterized the effort to establish federal housing programs "an insidious, concerted effort" to "overturn the entire government of the United States."[21] That there were no comparable hysterical outbursts against the NIRA's provision for a housing program, and in fact no congressional opposition expressed at all, reflects the crisis mentality of the time. Quite likely, the different reaction was also due in part to the Congress itself having changed significantly from the body it had been in Senator Fall's days.

Despite the lack of drama, authorization for a federal housing program in 1933 was historically significant, as it can be argued that publicly built and owned low-rent housing was in some respects the most radical aspect of the New Deal. Except for the Tennessee Valley Authority, which mixed private with public enterprise, public housing was unique in involving actual government ownership, rather than merely intervention in the economy.[22] Thus, the usual interpretation of the creation of the PWA housing program that focuses almost completely on chance and effective legislative maneuvering by liberals, like Simkhovitch and Wagner, seems inadequate. While such factors were important, two others allow a fuller understanding of how and why the program was enacted. The first is the impact on Congress of the broad political mobilization of urban working-class constituencies. The second is the length and severity of the crisis in residential real estate, which so eroded the material and psychological resources of real estate entrepreneurs that they failed to oppose the housing section of the NIRA in the way they had previously tried to block direct federal entrance into the housing market. These two factors were significant in allowing some form of housing legislation to succeed in 1933. They were especially crucial in creating the opening that made it possible for the Housing Division to advance, albeit tentatively, a program that was far more challenging to private enterprise in the housing field than any previous or later federal policies.

After Roosevelt signed the NIRA into law in June 1933, the Public Works Administration was organized under Interior Secretary Harold Ickes. To implement the section of the bill pertaining to the construction of dwellings, Ickes established the Housing Division as a quasi-independent agency within the PWA. The division faced tremendous opposition over the four years of its existence but did manage to finance or directly build a total of fifty-eight housing developments containing approximately 25 thousand dwelling units around the country.[23] (Tables 4.1 and 4.2 give specific information on Housing Division projects.)

The First Months of the Housing Division

The Housing Division began its official life almost immediately after Ickes took over as administrator of the PWA in early July of 1933. To direct the agency, he appointed Robert Kohn, a distinguished New York architect. Kohn had been in charge of housing production for the Emergency Fleet Corporation during World War I and was therefore one of the few people in the country with any experience at running a government housing program. A past president of the American Institute of Architects and former head of the Building Congress of New York, he was also an influential figure in his profession. Kohn was strongly committed to the cause of direct federal support for low-rent housing. As a longtime friend of Clarence Stein, Henry Wright, and Lewis Mumford, he had participated in discussions with the Regional Planning Association of America, and he shared the general perspective on housing that Bauer publicized in her book.[24]

Shortly after the Housing Division was established, Ickes announced it would begin by expanding a program already established by Hoover's Reconstruction Finance Corporation (RFC). The RFC had offered loans to privately organized, state-regulated "limited-dividend" corporations, which were low-profit enterprises established to provide housing to people who could afford only modest rents. When Hoover started the RFC program, reformers had welcomed it as a step toward recognition of federal responsibility in the housing field, but when they tried to use it they found its stringent provisions "a legislative straight-jacket."[25] Before the RFC turned its housing files over to the PWA, the agency had approved only two housing loans in the thirteen months of its existence. One, for approximately $150,000, financed rural homes in Kansas. The other, for slightly over $8 million, went to Knickerbocker Village, a massive complex containing 1,593 apartments built on the infamous "lung block" of New York City's Lower East Side. Critics found the project depressingly dense. The apartments were small, the buildings were tall (twelve stories), and the land coverage was high. Even so, the financial setup was so stringent that rents were too high for former residents of the area to afford.[26]

Under the Housing Division, the RFC program was liberalized. Interest rates were lowered from five to four percent and the loan period lengthened from ten to thirty-five years. Loans could be secured for up to 85 percent of the estimated final cost of the project. Grants as well as loans were offered to local public entities legally empowered to build and own low-rent housing, but since no such bodies existed, this part of the program was only theoretical. Soon the new agency was inundated with applications, over 500 in all. The small technical staff worked past midnight seven days a week for months re-

TABLE 4.1 PWA LIMITED-DIVIDEND PROJECTS

City Name	Units	Kind*	Race	Site†	Funding‡
Altavista, VA					
[no name]	50	rows	white	vacant	$ 84
Bronx Borough, NY					
Hillside Homes	1,416	apts	white	vacant	$ 5,060
Euclid, OH					
[no name]	100	rows	white	vacant	$ 500
Philadelphia, PA					
Carl Mackley Houses	284	apts	white	vacant	$ 1,039
Queens Borough, NY					
Boulevard Gardens	967	apts	white	vacant	$ 3,071
Raleigh, NC					
Boyland	54	apts	white	vacant	$ 199
St. Louis, MO					
Neighborhood Gardens	252	apts	white	slum	$ 640
TOTAL	3,123				$10,593

* Rowhouses ("rows"), apartments, flats, or some combination.
† Slum, if slum clearance involved; vacant, if built on empty land.
‡ In $1,000 (thousands of dollars); this is the amount loaned for each project.
Note: This information is derived from Harold L. Ickes, "Activities of Housing Division of the Federal Emergency Administration of Public Works," report submitted to Senate Committee on Education and Labor, 75th. Cong., 1st Sess. (1937), Hearings on S. 1685 (Washington, DC: Government Printing Office, 1937).

viewing them. The work was fairly tedious, because few submissions merited serious consideration. Most fell in two predictable categories. The first, which were obviously not appropriate, comprised efforts by investors to salvage something from failed commercial ventures begun before the Depression. The second group came from organizations sincerely devoted to trying to expand the supply of good low-rent housing in their locales, but their plans, for the most part, were either poorly conceived or underfunded (often both). As a break from the monotony, the staff did encounter some entertainingly far-fetched proposals, such as a plan from a group of musicians requesting a loan to build themselves a clubhouse on the roof of a skyscraper. Ultimately, only seven limited-dividend projects were approved before the division made what Ickes termed "almost a right-about face" and turned to a program of direct development.[27] (Information about the limited-dividend developments can be found in table 4.1.)

Why was the initial PWA housing program abandoned? This is a question worth examining in some depth, because variations of this approach had been employed with success in Europe, where labor unions and building societies constructed shelter for their members with loans and other aid from the government. Moreover, advocates of affordable shelter in the United States have been pushing increasingly for this kind of policy since the 1970s.

In theory, working with local low-profit or completely noncommercial developers had a number of advantages. Projects sponsored by such organizations would have been more in keeping with the American ideology of grassroots initiative than ones originated and owned by a federal agency. At a practical rather than ideological level, the limited-dividend program allowed for groups with greater knowledge of potential tenants and local circumstances than the national government to develop housing in their locales. In addition, there was more possibility for residents to participate in the design and administration of the place in which they lived than if their housing was organized by a large professionally staffed bureaucracy based in Washington, DC. Despite these potential strengths, the strategy foundered in the 1930s. For different reasons, all of the major participants had problems with the limited-dividend program.

Ickes blamed the greed of commercial developers for the program's difficulties. "It quickly became obvious," he wrote in 1935, "that our much vaunted private initiative, as so often happens when the goal is a social good instead of private profit, was unable or unwilling to undertake the job." In fact, Ickes was probably always lukewarm about what he described as "fussing around with limited-dividend projects." Trying to carry out a housing program by responding to ad hoc plans from whatever groups around the country happened to get themselves organized was antithetical to his whole philosophy of public administration. Ickes was deeply committed to making decisions on the basis of a conception of long-run national purposes, as was illustrated by his creation of the National Planning Board as an agency to advise the PWA on public works. This was the first general planning operation ever set up in the executive branch. With regard to housing specifically, his actions indicate that he thought of the decentralized RFC program primarily as a stopgap measure to give himself time to develop his own program.[28]

A program that could be up and running immediately was extremely useful given the pressure for action that Ickes was under from the moment Roosevelt chose him to direct the Public Works Administration in July 1933. Particularly at the beginning, he lacked the administrative capacity to mount any kind of coherent program, even if he had had a clear plan in mind. Although he announced formation of the Housing Division almost immediately, in reality it was only a skeletal operation for some time. In February of 1934, six months after Ickes told the country the agency was up and running, *Fortune* magazine described the division's Washington headquarters as "a half-dozen devoted men sitting in small offices noisy with typewriters." Operating "without [a] waiting room, without secretarial space, without facilities of any kind," the agency was less organized than "the administrative offices of the country's smallest business," according to the business periodical.[29] Especially in the first weeks after it was formed, the PWA could not have handled a housing program that required more than responding to applications. By announcing that the Housing Division was continuing along the same lines as the RFC, Ickes gave himself time to work out his own approach and assemble a unit to implement it. Also, this strategy allowed him to maintain, in the words of his public relations office, that "the first decision of PWA in regard to exercising the authority of the housing provision in the act was that private enterprise should be given a chance to do everything it could." Thus, the limited-dividend program met a variety of needs, even though it did not generate very much housing.[30]

Unlike Ickes, Kohn and some of the other staff had greater expectations for the limited-dividend phase of the division's work. From their standpoint, the problems stemmed from there not being enough good applications on which to base a national program. They attributed the paucity of plausible proposals to the country not yet being "housing conscious."[31] The bulk of would-be "sponsors had no conception of the purpose of the housing program and no capacity to visualize it," according to Michael Straus and Talbot Wegg, two PWA employees who later wrote a history of the division.[32]

To rectify the perceived lack of knowledge, Housing Division representatives traveled around the country on "barnstorming trips" to "preach the gospel of housing" to civic groups, realtors, financial institutions, and architects.[33] In the words of Straus and Wegg, this gospel was that housing

> should not be regarded as an aggregation of houses but as complete neighborhoods, planned at one time and carried out to the mutual benefit of every neighbor. Homes should be located as to have adequate sun and air and plenty of protected play space for children. They should be isolated from and yet quickly available to transportation. They should be within easy and protected walking distance of schools and shops. Buildings should be low and well built and supplied with at least the minimum of mechanical equipment. These communities must be regarded as long term investments with wise and kindly management and not as speculative developments whose sponsors care only for quick sale and getting out from under.[34]

As this articulation of agency principles makes clear, division personnel were part of the same community of discourse as Catherine Bauer and the European planners and architects whose work she described, although the reference to "wise and kindly management" shows how ideas associated with the international mass housing movement were capable of being given a more paternalistic interpretation than Bauer gave them.

The Housing Division staff believed that comprehensively designed resi-dential districts—what they described as "complete communities"—would be superior living environments and at the same time more economical. As noted earlier, this had been a key tenet of the new housing ideas in America and Europe since before the First World War. Many of those affiliated with the program also believed that a more physically integrated residential en-vironment would encourage a livelier and more solidary local community. Straus and Wegg optimistically predicted that "the very nature of the large-scale housing project fosters natural group action, which in turn leads to com-munity strength."[35]

Later, these same architectural principles would be pursued solely for their economy, with the result that much American public housing had a bleak and immediately identifiable style. At this time, however, many design profession-als and others believed these concepts could be used to create something bet-ter than what the private real estate market offered even affluent families: neighborhoods that combined the lower densities, trees, and green spaces characteristic of the suburban fringe with the convenience of living near the metropolitan core. (May's garden suburbs of Römerstadt and Praunheim near Frankfurt, as shown in figures 3.4 and 3.5, embodied these same ideas.)

The division's publicity campaign did little to increase the pool of strong applications, because lack of money and inability to put together plausible financial plans were the critical barriers to participation. At the depth of the depression, few groups with the desire to sponsor low-rent housing develop-ments had the necessary 15 percent equity the PWA required. With returns capped at 6 percent and no guarantee as to the safety of capital, private invest-ors tended to shy away from the program, just as they had from earlier attempts to get them to put their money into model tenements. Normally, real estate investors expected a substantially higher amount to compensate for the con-siderable risks of investing in rental properties–18 percent or better, according to one authority.[36] Another problem related to financing was that little con-crete information existed about building and operating costs for good quality, low-rent residential properties that groups could use to develop convincing plans.[37]

Yet even a group with substantial resources and information would have faced almost insurmountable difficulties given the contradictions and ambigu-ities at the core of the program. One of these was the requirement that projects combine high-quality design and construction with low rents, all without any real subsidy except for low-interest loans. The inability of noncommercial local groups to submit proposals that inspired confidence within these guide-lines is hardly surprising. Speculative developers had never been able to pro-vide housing on this basis, and when Ickes later began direct building, he did not try to proceed within these limits. (Projects built by the Housing Division were subsidized with grants for 45 percent of construction costs.[38])

At a more general level, the housing program faced a basic tension found in all public works activity: the desire to construct things of long-term value while at the same time creating a great many jobs as quickly as possible.[39] When housing was defined as a public works activity, more difficulties arose, such as the thorny question of which groups would live in the housing built with public money.

In general, Ickes's strategy for coping with competing, sometimes inherently conflicting, objectives was to pledge to achieve them all. Thus, in response to the question of which groups were being targeted, the administrator said that the Housing Division was building for "those in the lowest income classes." This goal was the easiest to justify on humanitarian grounds as well as least threatening to real estate investors, since the very poor were not a lucrative market segment even in prosperous times.[40] The limited-dividend program failed, he told Congress, because "of the inability of limited-dividend companies to provide housing at rentals within the financial reach of families of low income."[41]

The problem with this line of reasoning was that providing shelter at rents the very poor could afford required deep subsidies, and such subsidies were not available. Ickes used the fact that rent levels at the limited-dividend projects were too high for the very poor to justify direct federal construction. But here, intentionally or not, he conflated two issues: the question of who would construct and own housing developments and the question of whether and how much to subsidize housing. It was expedient to argue that the PWA had to mount a more centralized program because that was the only way to provide for the very poor, since this was the direction that Ickes wanted to go anyway. The tactic had a downside, however, because the housing the PWA itself built—despite significant subsidies—was also too expensive for the very poor. By promising results that predictably could not be delivered, Ickes created expectations that later could be used to judge his programs as failures. Yet, without such promises, Ickes probably feared that he would not have the political support necessary to move ahead at all.

Kohn, the Housing Division's first director, was under less political pressure and was therefore in a position to be more candid with the public. In the fall of 1933, he readily acknowledged that the limited-dividend program was not even attempting to meet the needs of the very poor. He told the press that the Housing Division was aiming at the "middle third" of the market, not the most needy. For Kohn, this policy was not only realistic but desirable. Providing housing for the very poor was not in the cards, he explained, because it would require substantial subsidies, and the division did not have that kind of money at its disposal. Moreover, the director was not interested in supplying specialized housing for poor people. His objective, which he shared with his colleagues in the Regional Planning Association of America, was to upgrade the overall character of American housing. Trying to provide for the poor, without making more general changes in the larger patterns of physical development and financing, made no sense to him. In Kohn's mind, the value of the PWA housing program was as a laboratory for developing better and cheaper ways of building urban residential environments. The savings achieved could provide the resources to supply decent housing for those unable to afford it on their own. In this way, the least affluent could be aided without being isolated.[42]

The Attempt to Establish a Federal Housing Corporation

Ickes gave the first public indication that he planned to move the Housing Division in another direction in October 1933, when he filed a certificate of incorporation for a federal housing corporation under the laws of Delaware. The action was, he said, "an outgrowth of our recent experiences" that demonstrated "we may not depend upon private enterprises or limited-dividend corporations to initiate comprehensive low-cost housing and slum-clearance projects." He explained that the purpose of the corporation was to encourage the creation of state and local public housing authorities, but the fact that he largely ignored these entities after they came into existence suggests that his primary objective was gaining the ability to advance a program from Washington.[43]

Ickes was clearly anxious to mount an ambitious housing program. On one occasion he told the press that he saw PWA housing as comparable to government-run electric power facilities and indicated that he believed that public enterprise could legitimately compete with private capital in both fields.[44] He wanted to avoid trying to work through the Housing Division, because any construction work undertaken directly by the agency would be bound by the federal government's complex procedural rules. All bids for contracts and materials would be subject to review beyond the agency, and the already complicated task of land acquisition for large urban sites would become even more slow and unwieldy, with the Justice Department pulled into even the smallest legal detail.[45]

Ickes's attempt to create a public corporation through which to mount a national housing program was part of an ongoing search by the executive branch to develop new methods of wielding administrative authority that would prove acceptable within traditional conceptions of American government. Some of these innovations succeeded, as in the case of the Federal Land Banks in which the government held part of the stock. Established in 1916 and declared constitutional by the Supreme Court in 1921, the land banks served as the model for a myriad of other federal credit agencies, including the Federal Home Loan Banks, the Reconstruction Finance Corporation, and the Federal Deposit Insurance Corporation.[46] But other attempts to create new mechanisms—such as Roosevelt's Executive Reorganization Bill of 1937, with its provision for a permanent planning board—were perceived as too much of a break with traditions of American representative democracy.[47]

At first it looked as if Ickes's attempt to create a more flexible and efficient vehicle through which to work was going to succeed. Roosevelt agreed to order $100,000,000 of PWA funds transferred to the new corporation. However, the transfer was blocked by the rigidly conservative Comptroller General John Raymond McCarl, an appointee of President Warren Harding. McCarl refused to move the money on the grounds that the charter of the corporation gave it powers that went beyond the vaguely worded housing section of the National Industrial Recovery Act. Having a fixed term of office, the comptroller general was independent of the president. Furthermore, as one legal scholar observed, many members of Congress had the "jitters" when it came to corporations created by the administration. The political fallout seemed too high, and Roosevelt withdrew his support. Reluctantly, Ickes abandoned the plan.[48]

The Housing Division as a Direct Builder

In February of 1934, Ickes announced his decision to suspend the limited-dividend program and begin production through the Housing Division. This was the basis on which the PWA housing program operated for its remaining three years of existence. While previously the limited-dividend companies had functioned as developers, now the Housing Division itself undertook this role. The division used local architectural firms and building contractors, but closely supervised all phases of work. It acquired sites in its own name and retained title to land and structures after construction was completed. Under the terms of the National Industrial Recovery Act, the PWA could make capital grants to public bodies for 30 percent of the cost of a project. To public or private developers, it could offer loans for up to 70 percent of the cost of a project at 4 percent interest amortized over thirty-five years. (No outright grants were allowed to private developers, even if they were state-supervised limited-dividend corporations.) After careful analysis, Ickes and his staff decided that it was unrealistic to try to produce low-rent housing on this basis, and they successfully lobbied Congress for permission to raise the limit for grants to 45 percent, cut the interest rate to 3 percent, and lengthen the amortization period to sixty years.[49] When the Housing Division began operations, no public entities existed that were legally empowered to build, own, and operate low-rent housing, but as they came into existence, the Housing Division

Table 4.2 PWA Direct-Built Projects

City	Name	Units	Kind*	Race	Site†	Funding‡
Atlanta, GA	Techwood Homes	718	apts/rows	white	slum	$2,969
Atlanta, GA	University Homes	675	flats/rows	black	slum	$2,592
Atlantic City, NJ	Smithfield Court	277	flats/rows	black	slum	$1,550
Birmingham, AL	Stanley S. Holmes Village	544	rows	black	slum	$2,500
Boston, MA	Old Harbor Village	1,016	apts/rows	white	vacant	$6,636
Caguas, PR	Caserio La Granja	75	rows	native	vacant	$ 275
Cambridge, MA	New Towne Court	294	apts	white	slum	$2,500
Camden, NJ	Westfield Acres	515	apts	white	vacant	$3,176
Charleston, SC	Meeting St. Manor/ Cooper River Court	212	rows	both	vacant	$1,350
Chicago, IL	Jane Addams Houses (1st part)	723	apts	white	slum	$5,119
Chicago, IL	Jane Addams Houses (2d part)	304	apts/rows	white	vacant	$1,800
Chicago, IL	Julia C. Lathrop Homes	925	all	white	vacant	$5,942
Chicago, IL	Trumbull Park Homes	462	all	white	vacant	$3,038
Cincinnati, OH	Laurel Homes	1,039	apts	both	slum	$7,086
Cleveland, OH	Cedar-Central Apartments	650	apts	white	slum	$3,384
Cleveland, OH	Outhwaite Homes	579	all	black	slum	$3,564
Cleveland, OH	Lakeview Terrace	620	apts/rows	white	slum	$3,800
Columbia, SC	University Terrace	122	all	both	slum	$ 706
Dallas, TX	Cedar Springs Place	181	all	white	vacant	$1,020
Detroit, MI	Brewster	699	all	black	slum	$5,200
Detroit, MI	Parkside	779	all	white	vacant	$4,500
Enid, OK	Cherokee Terrace	80	rows	white	slum	$ 557
Evansville, IN	Lincoln Gardens	191	flats/rows	black	slum	$1,000
Indianapolis,IN	Lockfield Garden Apartments	748	apts/rows	black	slum	$3,207
Jacksonville, FL	Durkeeville	215	rows	black	vacant	$1,000
Lackawanna, NY	Baker Homes	268	rows	white	vacant	$1,500
Lexington, KY	Blue Grass Park/Aspen Dale	286	rows	both	vacant	$1,704
Louisville, KY	LaSalle Place	210	rows	white	vacant	$1,370
Louisville, KY	College Court	125	flats/rows	black	vacant	$ 758
Memphis, TN	Dixie Homes	633	flats/rows	black	slum	$3,400
Memphis, TN	Lauderdale Courts	449	apts/rows	white	slum	$3,128
Miami, FL	Liberty Square	243	rows	black	vacant	$ 970
Milwaukee, WI	Parklawn	518	apts/rows	white	vacant	$2,600
Minneapolis, MN	Sumner Field Homes	451	all	both	slum	$3,500
Montgomery, AL	Riverside Heights	100	rows	white	vacant	$ 403
Montgomery, AL	William B. Patterson Courts	156	rows	black	slum	$ 522
Nashville, TN	Cheatham Place	314	rows	white	slum	$2,000
Nashville, TN	Andrew Jackson Courts	398	flats/rows	black	slum	$1,500
New York, NY	Wiliamsburg Houses	1,622	apts	white	slum	$13,569
New York, NY	Harlem River Houses	574	apts	black	vacant	$4,219
Oklahoma City, OK	Will Rogers Courts	364	rows	white	vacant	$2,000
Omaha, NE	Logan Fontenelle Homes	284	flats/rows	both	slum	$2,000

TABLE 4.2 CONTINUED

City	Name	Units	Kind*	Race	Site†	Funding‡
Philadelphia, PA	Hill Creek	258	flats/rows	white	vacant	$2,110
San Juan, PR	Caserio Mirapalmeras	131	rows	native	vacant	$ 500
Schenectady, NY	Schonowee Village	219	apts	white	slum	$1,500
Stamford, CT	Fairfield Court	146	apts/rows	white	vacant	$ 929
Toledo, OH	Brand Witlock Homes	264	all	black	slum	$2,000
Virgin Islands	Bassin Triangle/Marley Homes/H. H. Berg Homes	141	rows	native	both	$ 250
Washington, DC	Langston	274	all	black	vacant	$1,842
Wayne, PA	Highland Homes	50	flats/rows	black	slum	$ 344
TOTAL		21,121				$129,089

* Rowhouses ("rows"), apartments, flats, or some combination.
† Slum, if slum clearance involved; vacant, if built on empty land.
‡ In $1,000 (thousands of dollars), as of 15 March 1937.
Note: This information is derived from Harold L. Ickes, "Activities of Housing Division of the Federal Emergency Administration of Public Works," report submitted to Senate Committee on Education and Labor, 75th. Cong., 1st Sess. (1937), Hearings on S. 1685 (Washington, DC: Government Printing Office, 1937).

worked with them. During this second phase of the program, the PWA constructed fifty-one projects in thirty-six cities in the continental United States, Puerto Rico, and the Virgin Islands. (See table 4.2 for information about the housing developments directly constructed by the PWA.)

Slum clearance became a controversial issue for the division during this period. Ickes, as he began outlining his plans for the Housing Corporation, described clearing slums as a central purpose. Bauer, Mumford, and other allies of Kohn protested this emphasis in a series of sharply critical magazine articles, arguing that resources should be used for producing new housing at the lowest cost rather than for the expensive and (from their perspective) less urgent process of urban redevelopment. Bauer maintained that undeveloped land was not only much cheaper, it was better because of the absence of already-established street patterns.

Mumford gloomily concluded that the turn toward slum clearance meant that "the government has temporarily given in completely to the demands of the financial and the realty interests and has no serious intention of lending money for any modern community housing whatever." Instead of making concessions that seriously compromised the creation of good housing in order to satisfy political opponents, Bauer believed that the government should aim high. A thoroughgoing solution to the American housing problem, which "goes so deep into the social and economic structure of the nation," was not in the cards in the near future, she argued. Therefore "a mere handful of examples of good modern planned housing would be more effective than any number of slum areas replaced at terrific expense by near or 'reform' slums."

Such examples might give "incipient radicals a more concrete idea of what they are fighting for." She proposed that "if we are going through our own experiment in social democracy—or even if we are not—let us at least use it to make clearer to ourselves what we really do want."[50]

Ickes was not persuaded by such arguments. Slum clearance was popular, and he was confident that he would be able to find ways to keep inner-city land costs down. Calling his critics "disappointed idealists," he charged that they wanted to use the PWA to experiment with "immature or ill-conceived ideas."[51] By the following summer, he had forced Kohn out. Although Ickes implied that the reason for the director's departure had to do with unspecified financial improprieties, it seemed clear that the actual problem was disagreements over policy.[52]

Ickes replaced Kohn with Colonel Horatio B. Hackett, an architect and administrator with the large Chicago architectural firm of Holabird and Root and an old friend. The two worked well together. Hackett, an able administrator with experience coordinating large building projects, was less theoretically oriented than his predecessor. Thus, he never opposed the general direction that Ickes set or expressed opinions at odds with those of his boss the way Kohn had. To carry out the new program, Hackett vastly expanded the staff and transformed the Housing Division into a large production office. Later he moved up in the administration of the PWA, and there were subsequently two more directors, but these personnel changes did not involve new policy directions.[53]

Land acquisition was the most difficult aspect of the direct-building program. To help resolve the conflict between the expense of clearing slums and pressure to keep development costs low, the agency periodically invoked the right of eminent domain. The federal government's power to condemn land for public purposes had been upheld by the courts since 1875, and it was specifically granted by the legislation that authorized the Public Works Administration. Nevertheless, Ickes knew that condemnation was politically risky, and he actively worked to keep public opinion on his side by talking about "recalcitrant owners who are unwilling to sell at a fair price" and the difficulties of land assembly in slum districts. Indeed, it was a daunting task to acquire the sometimes hundreds of small, individually owned parcels in deteriorated and largely abandoned urban areas that were required to make up large building sites. Many times it was a challenge just to locate owners, and even then titles were often defective. In Birmingham, Alabama, the division found that a key piece of property belonged to a branch of the Sons-and-Daughters-of-I-Will-Arise Lodge, a 200-member organization that had never been incorporated. No sale was possible without the approval of every member, and many members had moved away or simply disappeared.[54]

Ickes maintained that condemnation was used only "as a last resort," and even then mostly to save time by clearing titles rather than forcing down prices. Most transactions were achieved through what he described as "friendly negotiations" rather than condemnation. Of course, some owners undoubtedly felt less than friendly as they bargained with federal negotiators who could always fall back on condemning their property should the discussion reach an impasse. In other words, the very fact that the Housing Division was known to invoke eminent domain gave the agency enormous power vis-à-vis individual property owners even when it did not employ this legal mechanism.[55]

As it worked out, the agency was only able to use condemnation for a few months. In January of 1935, the U.S. District Court for Western Kentucky upheld the petition of a disgruntled Louisville landowner who maintained that it was unconstitutional for the Housing Division to use the power of eminent domain to take his property. The judge, an avid anti-New Dealer, agreed, declaring that the low-rent dwellings that the PWA proposed to construct were not going to be "devoted to a public use." He construed the idea of public use narrowly, as including only things available to all citizens on an equal basis, such as parks, roads, or government office buildings. Federally subsidized housing would not be public in the same way, he reasoned, because it would be available only to certain people. This ruling brought all land acquisition activities to a halt while the division's legal staff, together with the Justice Department, prepared an appeal. In July, the Circuit Court of Appeals in Cincinnati upheld the lower court's decision on a two to one vote. The division appealed to the Supreme Court, but at the last minute withdrew the case, presumably for fear of a decision that might have wide negative implications for the whole New Deal.[56]

The Louisville decision effectively blocked the use of condemnation, thus undermining the division's strategy of combining new building with slum clearance. Later site acquisition had to rely on willing sellers, which, in practice, meant buying undeveloped land on the urban periphery from property owners who owned large parcels. Of the PWA's fifty-one federal projects, twenty-seven were built on the sites of former slums and twenty-four on raw land. (One of the seven limited-dividend projects was constructed on the site of a former slum, while the other six used undeveloped land.)[57]

Just as Bauer and her allies had predicted, this change in policy made land assembly easier and cheaper. But as Ickes had seen from the beginning, the new focus cost the Housing Division significant political support. In the words of an agency publication, slum clearance, rather than housing, "had been the more dramatic and popular practice." Influential local business leaders liked slum clearance programs, because they rebuilt, at public expense, run-down parts of cities that often threatened their own property investments. Also, when slum clearance was linked to a building program, the total number of housing units available in a city often stayed in equilibrium. This pleased rental property owners, who regarded an expansion in the supply of rental housing as a threat, especially given the glut left over from the building boom of the 1920s. Arguments that federal housing would not siphon away potential tenants, because PWA developments were aimed at an entirely different market segment, were never completely reassuring (nor should they have been, since even the federal projects were not affordable to the poorest families).[58]

The Housing Division's Record on Race

The PWA allotted slightly more than one-third of its housing units to African Americans. Twenty-one developments were built for blacks only, and six others had both black and white tenants. Funding levels for construction were the same regardless of the intended occupants, and because of unpredictable factors like the talent of different architectural teams, some developments intended for blacks actually turned out better than ones built for whites (as was the case with the Harlem River Houses, discussed in chapter 6.)

With regard to employment opportunities for African Americans, Ickes was inclined to take an activist stance. At the point he had taken over as head of the nation's public works in the summer of 1933, he found only eleven blacks in a work force of over four thousand engaged in building Boulder Dam. Despite such occurrences, individual cases of discrimination were difficult to prove. Therefore, Ickes and his aide for Negro Affairs, Robert Weaver, were anxious for the Housing Division to move beyond the procedure of putting nondiscrimination clauses in contracts with private companies when it began its own building program. They came up with a plan for a minimum percentage quota system, by which contractors were required to pay skilled black workers a proportion of the total payroll amounting to at least half of their percentage in the local work force. The system worked well. In Birmingham, Alabama, for instance, blacks—who made up 23 percent of all skilled workers in the city—received 20 percent of the payroll that went to skilled workers who put up PWA housing. Reviewing the program in *Opportunity* magazine, Weaver concluded its success was due to the fact that it put the burden of proof on employers, rather than on blacks or the government. "Instead of the Government's having to establish the existence of discrimination," he wrote, "it is the contractor's obligation to establish the absence of discrimination."[59]

One important drawback to the Housing Division's record on race, however, was the agency's decision not to disrupt pre-existing racial patterns of neighborhoods. In effect, this meant building housing for African Americans in deteriorated sections of cities where they already lived. The purpose of the strategy was to avoid white backlash, but the practice reinforced existing patterns of residential segregation, sometimes even creating more highly concentrated racial ghettos than had previously existed.[60]

Controversy over Centralization

The PWA housing program was one of the most controversial innovations of the entire New Deal. Not surprisingly, it aroused hostility from anti-New Dealers and real estate owners, but it also provoked the ire of liberals and radicals who supported public housing. The emphasis on slum clearance disappointed Bauer and other advocates of the new housing theories. Local officials, whatever their policy preferences, generally felt ignored by the Housing Division. In general, supporters of public aid to low-rent housing deplored the "conflict, delay, and confusion" that marked the PWA program and were disappointed at how little was actually built. Many left-liberal critics concluded that these problems stemmed from too much centralization of power in Washington, which they attributed largely to Ickes's "ironhanded" style of administration.[61]

The critique had significant plausibility, because the PWA did not accept much outside advice. As the public exchange over slum clearance made clear, the strong-minded but personally sensitive Ickes set his own course and lashed out angrily when criticized. Even local housing authorities, formed originally at the urging of the Housing Division, had little impact on decisions in their own cities. Charles Abrams, who served as legal counsel to the New York City Housing Authority from 1934 to 1937, maintained that citizens lost interest in serving on the boards of local housing authorities as the role of these agencies "sank with successive PWA bulletins from entrepreneur to co-venturer, from co-venturer to adviser, from adviser to functionless entity."[62] In 1937, a Housing Division official conceded publicly that the PWA had in fact treated local housing authorities as though they were "intelligently interested bystanders," offering the rationale that it was the PWA that had been placed in charge of the controversial new program and therefore the federal agency had to assume final responsibility along with the "grief which accompanies any pioneering work."[63]

Nor did Ickes allow much latitude within the agency itself. Even his admirers described the internal workings of the division as overly rigid and centralized. Ickes, despite being responsible for running the entire Public Works Administration as well as the Department of Interior, still scrutinized "every detail of the Housing Division's operations." He insisted on making the final decision on every project and signed every contract the Housing Division made.[64]

In Ickes's defense, it needs to be emphasized that while his penchant for personal control was extreme, his fear of graft was not unwarranted. Real estate transactions had traditionally provided opportunities for corruption at every level of government. With his political roots in Progressive Era campaigns for clean government, Ickes knew that a scandal like Teapot Dome would undercut support for federal public works for years.[65] More important, his management style was not the fundamental cause of the "delay and red tape" decried by those who worked with the agency.[66] The "Old Curmudgeon" had far less power than liberals imagined and conservatives feared. Looking back, it becomes obvious that the Housing Division was a small, fragile operation trying to find ways to introduce new and threatening activities with few resources, little experience, widespread and powerful enemies, and no mobilized mass support. This larger reality, rather than specific problems with its bureaucratic structure or the personality of its administrator, goes furthest to explain the agency's slowness and inflexibility.[67]

When Ickes was first given responsibility for launching a national housing program in the summer of 1933, he inherited no pre-existing administrative apparatus beyond a few boxes of files from the RFC. Starting almost completely from scratch, he confronted both longstanding tendencies toward weak and easily permeated federal structures and almost a vacuum of experience with direct public intervention in the housing sector. Except for a few months in 1918, there had never been any kind of direct federal effort to stimulate residential construction, and only a very few programs had been attempted at the state or municipal level. This historical background meant a dearth of pre-existing institutional structures with which to work or experienced administrative talent to employ. Like other New Deal administrators, Ickes was forced to draw heavily from the private sector for his personnel. Although many of his appointments were, like Hackett, technically and administratively skilled, they had not been socialized into believing that they could analyze national economic and social problems and use government power to solve them.[68] In contrast, when European nations launched their ambitious housing initiatives after World War I, they built on decades of experimentation with direct programs at the local level and extensive legal precedents for public control of land use.[69]

Nor were the difficulties of a purely historic character. Pressures that had made for weak federal administrative structures in the past were still very much alive in the 1930s, as Ickes experienced when he tried to create the Housing Corporation as a way of freeing the housing program from the ponderous procedural rules under which federal agencies operated. In addition, the Housing Division was always uncertain about its funding, which significantly impeded efficiency. Roosevelt, who had been lukewarm from the first about large public works expenditures, continually used PWA funds for other emergencies. The biggest single financial shock to the Housing Division came in December 1934 when the president impounded $110 million for direct relief purposes out of the division's original allotment of slightly over $135 million. Practically all work in progress stopped and all long-range planning was disrupted until the following July when money started flowing to the division again.[70]

Thus, despite the always confident and sometimes blustering tone of its administrator, the PWA Housing Division was actually a frail operation. Indeed, it may have been Ickes's frustration with the lack of what Theda Skocpol has called "state capacity" as much as his legendary fear of corruption that led him to try to control so many of the details of the program himself.[71] Perhaps, possessing so few other resources, he thought he could advance some kind of coherent national housing program in good part through sheer force of personality. As scholars have noted in relation to other leading government figures in this era, such as Hugh Johnson, Jesse Jones, and Roosevelt himself, there were strong pressures to try to substitute "charismatic" or "heroic" styles of leadership for the weak administrative power that these leaders actually wielded.[72]

Conclusion

The crisis of the real estate industry in the early 1930s, the mobilization of urban voters behind the Democratic Party, and the passage of the National Industrial Recovery Act with its provision for a federal housing program created a political opening that made possible the first direct federal intervention into the housing sector during peacetime. While real, the opportunity was limited, given the absence of both government administrative machinery and a nationally organized constituency.

Despite the obstacles, the PWA Housing Division, with its faith in public enterprise and in the positive role that architecture could play socially, did manage to achieve some impressive results. Consistent with his stance on everything the Public Works Administration built, Ickes insisted on high quality work. While not himself particularly inspired by the new residential design theories, he nevertheless employed many architects who were and allowed them budgets generous enough to achieve handsome results. Most important, Ickes was skeptical about the ability of private enterprise alone to provide for the public welfare in fields like housing, and he had an expansive conception of the role government could play. In a fundamental sense, therefore, Ickes and Bauer were much closer than either of them probably ever realized. Under Ickes's guidance, the Housing Division's program represented the most thoroughgoing challenge to a market-based housing system ever attempted in the United States, showing what a broadly oriented federal program to aid noncommercial housing could look like.

In terms of architectural design, the work of the Housing Division was critically well received, and this positive assessment continues to the present. Architect Richard Plunz, writing in the 1970s, noted that: "In general apartment design standards were very high, with sizes, light, and ventilation equal to the best of the 1920s garden apartments." According to architectural historian Richard Pommer, "The early work of the PWA . . . remained for many decades the finest urban housing in America."[73]

Popular acceptance, not just critical success, greeted the agency's work. Ordinary citizens expressed their approval by moving into the federal developments—even when they might have afforded other accommodations. Senator David Walsh of Massachusetts drew attention to this fact when he complained in 1936 that "the houses which have been constructed [by the PWA] in New York, Cleveland, and Boston and elsewhere are really in competition with private property."[74]

That some moderate-income people not only found PWA housing appealing but were allowed to move in points to one of the best features of the PWA program in its first years: that it was not "means-tested." While using scarce public resources only for the most needy might seem fair and logical, programs limited to only the poorest turn out to have debilitating long-range problems. Their narrow constituency makes them more susceptible to budget cuts, and participants are often stigmatized. Only universal programs such as social security seem able to survive politically while not demeaning recipients.[75] Initially, PWA housing was open to anyone who cared to apply. This situation ended in 1936 when Congress passed the George-Healey Act, which retroactively set income ceilings for the PWA housing projects directly built and owned by the government. Where PWA apartment complexes did not become part of the housing stock of public authorities, and hence subject to income restrictions, white-collar workers were regular residents (as was the case of the Carl Mackley Houses in Philadelphia, which will be discussed in the next chapter).[76]

Although the Housing Division had a life span of only four years, it still proved a fruitful laboratory for the development of a new kind of urban shelter that might have been the basis for a majority-oriented noncommercial federal housing program. Architect Oskar Stonorov, who was involved with the design of two PWA complexes, articulated the objectives that he and other participants shared:

> . . . the purpose of low-cost housing is, at its present state of infancy in the United States, not only to house slum-dwellers or poor people but also to establish standards of living in a new mode . . . quite different from what individual speculative activity has created.[77]

With the resources of the Housing Division behind them, a number of vision-aries like Stonorov did make progress in developing a different kind of urban residential pattern. The next two chapters will investigate what these "stan-dards of living in a new mode," in Stonorov's words, meant for those who experienced them in two developments, each built in one of the two different phases of the Housing Division's work.

Fig. 5.1 The Carl Mackley Houses in Philadelphia. This development, built in 1934–35 by the Hosiery Workers' Union with the assistance of loans from the PWA, was designed by architects Oskar Stonorov and Alfred Kastner. This photograph, taken in the 1950s, shows the complex with its mature landscaping, planted by manager William Jeanes.

FIVE

The Hosiery Workers'
Model Development

The Housing Division of the Public Works Administration began operations in the summer of 1933 by offering loans to private companies organized to build and manage low-rent residential developments on a restricted-profit basis. As soon as the program was announced, the American Federation of Hosiery Workers, a Philadelphia-based labor union, came forward with plans for an apartment complex designed by architects conversant with the most recent European and American thinking on housing. Called the Carl Mackley Houses, after a union member killed in a bitter strike, the project received the first of the division's loans. To Catherine Bauer, the complex illustrated many of the principles of the modern housing idea. When it opened, she wrote that the development represented "the first successful effort of a group of workers to secure governmental aid toward bettering their housing conditions." She was optimistic that the building of the Mackley Houses would turn out to be "the first step in a movement which may sooner or later change the face of the country."[1]

The Hosiery Workers Union and Its Leaders

The Hosiery Workers were able to respond so quickly to the new federal housing program because the union had formulated its proposal before the New Deal was even announced. A key person in developing the plans was John Edelman, the union's director of research. Edelman was introduced to the new ideas about mass shelter by Leo Kryzski, Philadelphia organizer for the Amalgamated Clothing Workers. Kryzski was a dedicated radical who had served as sheriff under several socialist administrations in Milwaukee before coming to Philadelphia. In the late 1920s, he had visited "Red Vienna," which was famous for the numerous apartment blocks for working families that the city's Social Democratic administration had put up after the First World War. The Karl Marx Hof was the best known internationally of these large developments. Constructed around two courtyards and containing 1,382 apartments, the complex included all kinds of services, including a library, youth center, dental clinic, pharmacy, and kindergartens. Kryzski had taken many photographs of the complex, and, "at the drop of the word 'housing,' [he] would bring them out and deliver a spirited lecture on the feasibility of Americans emulating the Austrians."[2]

Edelman himself was no stranger to radical plans for social improvement. As a child, he had lived at a utopian commune in England, and as a young man in 1920 he followed Will Durant as director of the Modern School, an anarchist-sponsored experiment in progressive education based first in New York City and later in Stelton, New Jersey. Neither was he new to the world of architecture, as his father had been a colleague of the famous Chicago architect Louis Sullivan. Edelman's long career as a "labor skate," or in-house intellectual for the labor movement, began in 1924 when he accepted a job as Pennsylvania manager for Robert LaFollette's third-party presidential campaign. In Pennsylvania, the campaign was largely funded by unions, so Edelman was, in effect, an employee of the state labor council. After managing another electoral campaign effort underwritten by labor unions, this time for a slate of socialist candidates in Reading, he was hired in 1926 by the Hosiery Workers. Then called the American Federation of Full-Fashioned Hosiery Workers, the union was headquartered in Philadelphia.[3]

The leadership of the union that recruited Edelman was concerned with political and social questions as well as "bread-and-butter" issues. Emil Rieve, the Polish-born president of the union, was the most prominent example. After entering the mills as a boy of thirteen, he had worked his way up to become a skilled knitter, the highest-paying job in the silk hosiery industry. When he took over as head of the union in 1929, however, Rieve took a pay cut equal to half his former salary, because of a rule he himself had instituted mandating that officers and organizers would be paid no more than the industry average.

Rieve had little formal schooling, but he was nonetheless an intellectually sophisticated individual. He was, in the words of one colleague, "a devourer of books." During the twenties, Rieve was part of a circle of left-socialists in the Philadelphia area with ties to the union movement. He and his colleagues met regularly for discussions at the "soviet house," a home in the city's industrialized Northeast where several of them lived. While the group had ties to the Socialist Party rather than the Communist Party, the division between the two organizations was not very wide in Philadelphia at this time, as the nickname of their meeting place implied.[4]

Together with other leaders of the Hosiery Workers, Rieve tried unsuccessfully to build a labor party in the city, then controlled by a Republican machine. In 1931 he ran for county commissioner as part of a slate on both the Socialist Party and Independent Labor Party tickets. Alexander McKeown, head of the Philadelphia branch of the union, ran for mayor on the same ticket, as did Edelman, who ran for Congress in a special off-year election.

The slate lost badly; Edelman later joked: "I think we got the smallest vote of any Socialist candidates anywhere, ever, at any place in the United States, for public office." The Hosiery Workers were unable to enroll other local unions in their effort to start a third party in good part because of changes in the Democratic Party at the national level. Al Smith's presidential campaign and Franklin Roosevelt's New Deal sparked a rebuilding of the party in the city, siphoning potential energy from third-party politics.[5]

The late 1920s, when Rieve took over as president and Edelman came on staff, were the heyday of the union. Women's skirts had risen, and full-fashioned silk stockings, which were knitted to the proportions of the female leg, could not be produced fast enough. Seamless stockings, which were knitted as a tube, were cheaper but less desirable, because they sagged. Full-fashioned hosiery was constructed as a flat piece with curved edges (formed by dropping stitches), and then seamed at the back. Running a machine that produced these pieces meant constantly adjusting tiny loops of silk thread on complicated machines with close-set, fast moving needles. The men who did this work were among the highest paid of all blue-collar employees in the twenties, often commanding $75 a week compared with mean weekly earnings for all manufacturing workers that averaged $24 over the decade. In response to the seemingly inexhaustible demand, the industry mushroomed, with production increasing by a factor of sixteen from 1914 to 1929. An all-time high of 318 million pairs of silk stockings was produced in that same year, when supply outstripped demand for the first time.[6]

All through the 1920s, manufacturers behaved as though all the silk stockings that could be knitted would automatically find buyers. They bought more and more new machinery and continually opened new mills. In 1929 alone, productive capacity grew by 25 percent. Meanwhile, union leaders predicted that at some point a buying limit would be reached and the industry would crash. In 1926, the Hosiery Workers began gathering national statistics on hosiery production and consumption with an eye to developing a plan for maintaining high wage and profit levels in the industry. The union called its program "stabilization through unionization." A more conventional labor strategy would have been to focus on wages and hours and leave management decisions to the owners, but the union saw itself playing a more central role in guiding the industry.[7]

In 1929, the year buying capacity first weakened, the union pulled together the 30 percent of employers with whom it had contracts and negotiated the first of several national agreements. With the general depression compounding problems in the overexpanded hosiery industry, the union agreed to wage cuts and changes in work rules that intensified the pace of labor. On their side, the mill owners agreed to arbitration procedures, complete unionization of their workforces, and dues "check-off" (direct payment of dues to the union). Most striking of all, the owners promised to reveal their semi-annual profits to the union as the basis for future negotiations. Through this contract and the ones that followed the union was essentially allying itself with the unionized employers against nonunionized ones. The union promoted the alliance by distributing a "White List" of union-label hose to women's clubs, female trade union groups, YWCAs, and consumer organizations.[8]

This general pattern of action was similar to that pursued by the larger and better-known Amalgamated Clothing Workers of America (ACW), leader of the movement called "new unionism." Both unions were moving away from a craft-based organization, then the norm in the labor movement, and toward industrial unionism, which embraced everyone in a particular industry. Each visualized itself as the organizing force within a competitive and anarchic industry. Accordingly, the Amalgamated initiated (and the Hosiery Workers later followed) a pattern of union-sponsored research into industrywide conditions as the basis for a strategy of institutionalized negotiations. The strategy relied on arbitration with groups of employers, as opposed to threatening strike battles with individual concerns. In 1921, *New Republic* magazine, trying to convey the spirit of the Amalgamated approach, described the genteel tone of recent negotiations between union officers and clothing manufactures of Rochester. The owners met with union officials in one of the city's fashionable hotels, where they conferred across a long table, each side flanked by its corps of economists, engineering experts, and statisticians. Only partially in jest, the journal described the Amalgamated strategy as: "Class Struggle in a Ball-Room."[9]

Despite the respectable, even accommodationist tone of such tactics, the Amalgamated and the Hosiery Workers were militant and politically ambitious organizations. Both had informal ties to the Socialist Party, and the leadership of each employed rhetoric far to the left of the norm for that era. Both were actively involved in the electoral arena and supported third-party efforts. They sought alliances with liberal reformers beyond the labor movement and became institutional bases in their respective geographic strongholds for broad social reform initiatives.[10]

A dramatic example of the way the Hosiery Workers Union was able to mobilize people far beyond its own ranks was the massive funeral of Carl Mackley, a unionist killed in a bitter 1930 hosiery strike in Philadelphia. An estimated 1,500 cars followed the hearse as the funeral cortege moved through the streets of the city. Thousands of spectators lined the streets. Once the procession reached the cemetery, the union staged an elaborate ceremony, climaxed by a huge crowd pledging in unison:

> I will continue the struggle against low wages, poverty, and oppression, and I will not falter nor be intimidated by hired assassins, nor discouraged by a subservient and ofttimes tyrannical judiciary. If necessary, I, too, will lay down my life in order that all those who toil may be delivered from enslavement by un-American, avaricious, industrial despots.

The *New Republic* marveled that in such a difficult period for the labor movement, the union was able to stage one of "the most impressive and remarkable demonstration[s] ever held in Philadelphia." The magazine's editors were hopeful that the Hosiery Workers' combination of militancy and long-range strategy presaged a better period for the labor movement.[11]

The "New Unions" Confront the Housing Problem

Given their larger social and political ambitions (as well as their experience with economic sectors dominated by a multitude of small operators), it is not surprising that both the Amalgamated and the Hosiery Workers would turn their attention to the housing question. The larger and wealthier Amalgamated got started first, with an array of cooperative apartment buildings begun in the late 1920s.[12]

To some extent, the Amalgamated's housing program was a natural outgrowth of the general climate of experimentation within the labor movement in the 1920s. Led by the International Association of Machinists and the Brotherhood of Locomotive Engineers, unionists created a wide variety of alternative economic institutions in these years. The machinists got started first, founding their Mount Vernon Savings Bank in 1920, but the railway engineers, led by Warren Stone, were the most prolific. Stone, a leading sponsor of the 1920 All-American Farmer-Labor Co-operative Congress in Chicago, envisioned cooperative enterprise as a way of challenging capitalist organization of the economy. The railway union established a total of fourteen banks, eight investment companies, a printing company, two skyscrapers, and even its own model town in Florida. Laid out by a professional city planner, the Florida town was complete with houses for unionists, three tourist hotels, two farms, a nine-hole golf course and clubhouse. Other union efforts directed toward housing in the decade included eight home loan associations established by regional groups of labor unions: three of the loan companies were located in Ohio, two in Minnesota, and one each in Florida, Illinois, and Texas.[13]

Along with organizing mechanisms of financial assistance for home building or purchase, unionists in this period explored the possibility of being the direct providers of shelter. In 1925, a consortium of New York needle trades unions, including the International Ladies Garment Workers Union (ILGWU), began work on a cooperative apartment house in the Bronx complete with a gymnasium, an assembly room with kitchen facilities, and outdoor children's play areas. The architect for the 166-unit building was Andrew J. Thomas, a talented designer of moderate-cost garden apartments who often worked for John D. Rockefeller, Jr. When the unions ran into trouble with financing, Rockefeller took over the project. Calling it the Thomas Gardens Apartments, Rockefeller developed the complex on a low-profit basis, charging only 6 percent on the mortgage and taking no profit on the land and construction. He hoped that the apartment house would eventually become a cooperative, as the unions had initially envisioned, but this feature of the plan never worked out. At $6,000 to $9,000 apiece, the apartments turned out to be too expensive for the working-class families at whom they were aimed. More affluent families did not step forward as buyers, either, perhaps because the five- and six-story buildings had been constructed without elevators as a way of saving money so that community facilities could be provided.[14]

Such experiments by other trade unions influenced the leadership of the Amalgamated in the direction of organizing its own cooperative enterprises. In addition, the idea of economic cooperation had a lot of appeal for the union's many Jewish members. American working-class Jews were particularly drawn to the international consumer-cooperative movement that had originated in England in the mid-nineteenth century, in part because it reinforced traditions of ethnic solidarity.[15] During the twenties, Jewish groups established numerous housing cooperatives in the Bronx section of New York City. The United Workers, a communist-influenced union, moved into housing on a large scale after several successful years of operating a summer camp in Dutchess County and a small apartment house in Manhattan on a cooperative basis. In 1925, the group purchased land opposite Bronx Park and eventually constructed over 700 apartments. Other Jewish cooperative housing ventures in this period included the Shalom Aleichem Houses, sponsored by an organization devoted to the preservation of secular Jewish culture, and apartment buildings constructed by the Zionist-oriented Jewish National Workers Alliance, the (primarily Jewish) Typographical Union, and the Jewish Butchers Union.[16] Many of these ventures proved successful as physical and social environments, but almost none were financially stable for reasons similar to the problems that undermined Rockefeller's Thomas Gardens Apartments. The cost of good-quality, if modest, urban housing was simply very expensive in relation to working families' incomes, even when profit margins were cut down or eliminated entirely.

Encouraged by experiments by Jewish groups and other unions, Amalgamated conventions regularly passed motions on behalf of the cooperative movement. A typical resolution put the union on record favoring cooperative enterprise on the grounds that it would help "working people to free themselves from the exploitation of the capitalist class" and give them experience "managing industries for themselves."[17] Sidney Hillman and other ACW leaders were wary of overextending the union financially and moved cautiously to implement such principles. At first the impulse was channeled into organizing union-controlled financial institutions. These were extremely successful. The Amalgamated spawned seven banks and investment companies in addition to the Russian-American Industrial Corporation, which ran twenty-five clothing plants in the Soviet Union during the era of the New Economic Policy (NEP).[18]

One of these institutions, the Amalgamated's credit union in New York, was the seedbed for the union's residential activities. Abraham Kazan, secretary-treasurer for the union's New York Joint Board and a great enthusiast of cooperation, headed the credit union. In 1925, the cooperators began branching out from cooperative credit and formed a corporation to make bulk purchases of ice and coal. Next, the corporation moved into housing and bought a large plot of undeveloped land in the Bronx adjacent to Van Cortlandt Park. In 1926, after Governor Al Smith convinced the legislature to grant tax exemptions to state-supervised limited-dividend housing corporations (companies that limited their profits in order to hold rents down), the cooperative reorganized as the Amalgamated Housing Corporation and made plans to build. The corporation conceived an ambitious plan for 303 apartments in a group of six buildings, at a cost estimated at close to two million dollars.

Financing was complicated but ultimately possible because of the size and wealth of the union itself, the success of the numerous financial organizations it had spawned, and the fact that it had prosperous friends. One-third of the capital was to be obtained from the prospective residents, who were assessed $500 per room. This meant $1,500 to $2,000 per family, as most apartments consisted of three and four rooms. Since this sum was beyond the means of most garment workers, cooperators needed to borrow to pay even the one-third of the real cost that they were being assessed. The publisher of the *Jewish Daily Forward*, the major Yiddish-language newspaper in New York, aided the enterprise by depositing $150,000 in the Amalgamated's bank to be used as collateral for the cooperators to borrow against. For the mortgage, the Metropolitan Life Insurance Company put in over a million dollars, charging only 5 percent interest in accordance with the state's limited-dividend law. The rest was obtained from the *Forward*, the Amalgamated Bank, and other smaller financial institutions related to the union. Ground was broken on Thanksgiving Day, 1926; opening ceremonies were held on Christmas Day the following year.[19]

Housing expert Edith Elmer Wood hailed the Amalgamated's development as "the best and most successful cooperative housing thus far seen in the United States." Believing that cooperative housing had the potential to become an effective strategy for expanding the supply of modest-priced housing, she dealt with this form of tenure at length in her 1931 book *Recent Trends in American Housing*. While various kinds of what was called "cooperative housing" had become popular in the 1920s, the one Wood favored was an ownership structure in which participants did not reap profits from increases in property values. If real estate prices rose after they originally bought in, cooperators got back only the capital they had originally invested, with perhaps some additional money to account for inflation. Thus, later buyers would not have to pay more for their housing to cover the speculative gains that previous residents had taken. In Wood's view, people who participated in this kind of venture were "homeseekers, not profit seekers." She argued that housing cooperatives of the kind she favored should be publicly supported through low-interest government loans, as in Europe.[20]

For Abraham Kazan, who lived in the Amalgamated buildings and served as manager, "the social benefits" were even more important than the economic value of cooperative endeavors. He was convinced that people living in cooperative settings developed more personal responsibility, community spirit, and experience in democratic self-government.[21] At the Amalgamated apartments in the Bronx, which teemed with group activities of every description, this social dimension was much in evidence. A service corporation made bulk purchases of eggs directly from farmers and electricity from the Edison Company. School-aged children were transported to and from public school in a jointly owned bus, while younger ones attended a progressive-education nursery on the grounds. The complex boasted a library with several thousand volumes, a music room, and an indoor auditorium with seating for 500. Classes were held for both adults and children on subjects ranging from mandolin to Yiddish. A full-time education director worked with a committee of residents to plan these classes, along with forums, lectures, concerts, plays, and dances. Cooperative stores sold groceries, and tenants operated a tea room on a not-for-profit basis to provide a place for casual socializing in the evenings.[22]

The Amalgamated housing was a financial as well as a social success due to Kazan's skills as a financial manager, the high morale of the residents, and the tax exemptions (which were, in effect, public subsidies) allowed through the limited-dividend law. After the first buildings near Van Cortlandt Park opened, Kazan was swamped with applications. In 1929, the Amalgamated Housing Corporation began a number of new building operations, including the Grand Street Cooperative Apartments in lower Manhattan, which were financed by then Lieutenant-Governor Herbert Lehman and Aaron Rabinowitz, a wealthy real estate investor and member of the State Housing Board.

By 1931, the corporation was operating 856 apartments in the city. The next few years were very difficult, as cooperators suffered wage cuts and unemployment during the Depression. Kazan and the board of directors organized a variety of schemes to help residents, including a relief fund contributed to by those who had jobs, and the corporation was able to pull through. In 1940, the Amalgamated Housing Corporation started building again.[23]

The Housing Situation in Philadelphia

As with the Amalgamated, the Hosiery Workers put a high priority on developing an alternative to market provision of shelter. Unlike New York, Philadelphia had a reputation for affordable housing, but shelter costs were still high in relation to most working families' incomes. The widespread belief that the City of Brotherly Love was a city of affordable housing was based largely on the fact that only about 20 percent of families lived in multi-unit buildings. Also, Philadelphia had a significantly higher rate of homeownership than most other large cities. In 1930, 51 percent of families lived in homes they owned outright or were paying for through a mortgage, while the average rate of homeownership in the other twelve U.S. cities with a population of over a half-million was 36 percent.[24]

Philadelphia's higher rate of home ownership reflected a housing industry that produced more affordable homes for sale, but it also reflected the lack of good rental alternatives. The lower costs were partly due to the local tradition of rowhouse building, which brought construction costs down. (The pervasiveness of rowhousing similarly helps explain why Baltimore was the other large city with high homeownership rates.) Another important reason for lower costs was the easier and cheaper access to financing for both builders and buyers, because the city had one of the highest concentrations of building and loan associations in the country. The rockbottom price for a newly built Philadelphia rowhouse in the 1920s was $4,000, which represented a considerable savings compared with, for example, an economy-model new Chicago bungalow with its price tag of $5,500. Minimum-level new Philadelphia rowhouses were modest but not substandard dwellings. They had a living room, dining room, kitchen, bath, and two bedrooms, and they came equipped with central heating, gas cooking ranges, electric fixtures, standard plumbing, and hardwood floors. Builders marketed these homes for approximately $500 down and $30 a month.[25]

Yet, the high proportion of families who lived in Philadelphia's rowhousing reflected not only the relatively lower cost of this form of urban shelter, but also the lack of available choices. The city had no local tradition of small multifamily buildings, comparable to the Boston three-decker or the Chicago two-flat, and municipal building codes made large apartment buildings quite expensive to construct, which meant that developers only put them up for the luxury market. As a result, rowhouses originally built for a single family were often converted into units for two or three families. The dwellings created in this way were usually quite tiny and frequently lacked an independent water supply. Not only would toilet and bathing facilities have to be shared with one or two other families, but many times water for cooking would have to be drawn from the bathroom. Some observers believed that the lack of good alternatives pushed many families into buying their own homes when they might have preferred to rent.[26]

Whether Philadelphia's comparatively high proportion of homeowners resulted from families being pushed or pulled into the market, the number of foreclosures in the 1920s indicates that numerous families got in over their heads when they purchased. As in the rest of the country, a higher proportion of city families bought homes in the 1920s than previously. The rate of home-ownership in Philadelphia climbed from 39 percent in 1920 to 51 percent in 1930. But as home sales rose, so did foreclosures. In 1920, five sheriff's writs for foreclosures were issued for every 10,000 people in the city. By 1928, the rate had risen to almost 50 per 10,000. The director of the local Housing Association, who compiled statistics on forced sales, observed that local property owners showed signs of being "acutely distressed" as early as 1925. Thus, even in Philadelphia, where the private market in housing was operating at prob-ably its peak level of efficiency in the twenties, large segments of the popula-tion still experienced significant hardships.[27]

The Great Depression only exacerbated this situation. In part because so many residents were borrowing to purchase their homes, the Depression hit the city's property market with particular force. Philadelphia led the country in foreclosures, and the local lending industry practically collapsed. Less than half of the savings and loans operating in 1925 were still active eight years later. New construction halted almost completely: in 1933, less than 500 fam-ily accommodations were constructed in a city of close to two million people. This was only 6 percent of the yearly average for the first three decades of the century.[28] Yet, even with the severe drop-off in new construction, Univer-sity of Pennsylvania researchers found an overall vacancy rate of 35 percent. With incomes shrinking, more families doubled (or tripled) up into supposedly "single family" rowhouses.[29]

Within this larger situation, Philadelphia's hosiery workers were particu-larly hard hit. The city was the hub of the silk stocking industry nationally; consequently, it had the oldest, most obsolete machinery. This meant that local manufacturers had the most trouble competing when demand slackened, so the level of unemployment was high. The fall-off in wages was a particular problem for hosiery workers with regard to housing, because they had used their relatively high wages during the years of prosperity to purchase homes at higher rates than other workers. A 1931 survey conducted by the union with assistance from faculty at Bryn Mawr College revealed that 66 percent of the membership lived in homes they owned or were buying. Extended unemployment resulted in many members, especially younger ones who had not yet paid off mortgages, losing their homes. This was often a devastating financial catastrophe, since the overall deflation of prices meant that houses sold at sheriff's sales often brought less than what was still owed to the bank. Thus, even after losing their homes, many still had a debt that would follow them for years.[30] In his autobiography, John Edelman described how he dreaded visiting the families of hosiery workers who were being evicted after falling behind on their mortgage payments. "As union representative, I would steel myself to visit these families, for I knew I would find the kids crying, the mothers covering their faces with their aprons, the young fathers white-faced and lost." He recalled that "returning home from these heart-rending scenes, night after night, I grew more convinced that labor unions, labor people, simply couldn't allow such suffering to continue."[31]

The Hosiery Workers Plan Their Housing Demonstration

This was the context in which several individuals concerned with housing issues coalesced around the city's most innovative union. Oskar Stonorov was in many ways the key person in the group. A true cosmopolitan, Stonorov was ethnically Russian, but he grew up in Germany where his family had moved not long before his birth in 1905. As a young man, he traveled and studied throughout Europe, coming to the United States in 1929. Large and energetic, he was described by associates as a "bear" of a man. He was personally ambitious, but at the same time committed to the idealistic social ethos that Bauer described as the core of European architectural modernism. Throughout his life Stonorov maintained close ties with the American trade union movement. He died, in fact, in the same small plane crash that took the lives of Walter Reuther and his wife in 1970, while the three were on their way to inspect the progress of construction at the United Auto Workers' conference and education center at Black Lake, Michigan, which Stonorov had designed.

At the time he became involved with the Hosiery Workers, Stonorov and his German partner, Alfred Kastner, had recently become famous among the artistic avant-garde. The two took second place (over such formidable rivals as Le Corbusier and Walter Gropius) in the 1931 U.S.S.R.-sponsored international architectural competition for the Palace of the Soviets in Moscow. While this accomplishment won them prestige within the circle of architects and critics around the Museum of Modern Art, it made them decidedly unpopular with conservative mainstream architects. Both were fired from the

New York City architectural firms where they worked. With their $6,000 in prize money, the two relocated to Philadelphia and set up a joint practice.[32] Once in Philadelphia, they met John Edelman and became part of a group concerned with housing issues.

The group also included William Jeanes, a wealthy young Philadelphia Quaker who became a major investor in, and then manager of, the Hosiery Workers' housing. Younger than the others, Jeanes had only recently graduated from Harvard College and returned from a trip to Europe where he had toured low-rent housing developments. Years later, Jeanes recalled the stimulating, free-ranging discussions that the four had had concerning the housing question. "No subject was off limits: socialism, communism, none of the 'isms.'"[33] Like Catherine Bauer, the Philadelphia group drew on ideas developed by both American and European theorists, and like Bauer's modern housing program, their approach implied both financial and architectural innovation.

Not surprisingly, given the union's strategy with regard to the hosiery industry, the group's economic thinking centered on ways to transform the small-scale character of housing production and distribution. They hoped to demonstrate, as had so many other twentieth-century American housing reformers before them, that large operations could cut costs. But, in contrast to well-meaning developers of projects like Forest Hills Gardens, who attempted to deliver more for less, the Hosiery Workers group proposed spending an amount similar to what the speculative builder invested and producing a superior product. One of the first articles on housing issues that Edelman printed in the *Hosiery Worker*, the union newspaper, spelled out this position. The article stated that a typical Philadelphia block developed with rowhouses in the usual way would contain 182 homes, each with its own small backyard. The only large open space for children to play in would be the streets and alleys. If, however, the same block were developed as a four-story apartment house for 300 families, construction costs per individual unit could be cut in half. Large parts of the block would be left open for playgrounds and adult recreation facilities, which could then be constructed without spending more than the rowhouse builder.[34]

Despite the fact that their union was smaller and poorer than the Amalgamated and also that the economy had deteriorated drastically from the days when the ACW began its housing ventures, the Hosiery Workers' discussion group was in some ways more ambitious for their project. While the Amalgamated was oriented primarily toward improving the living situation of its own members, Stonorov and his discussion partners frankly aimed at upgrading urban housing nationally by influencing federal policy. They hoped to build a constituency for large-scale government loan programs to support noncommercial projects modeled on their development, in part to expand the supply of affordable housing and in part as a strategy for general economic expansion. According to one of the earliest discussions of housing Edelman ran in the *Hosiery Worker*, "the most effective single method of pulling the country out of its present slump would be to restore building activity." The article maintained that while an excess of commercial buildings and expensive homes was left over from the 1920s, there was still a real need for moderate-cost housing.[35]

Group members also agreed that the country needed to create more collective and less speculative forms of ownership for urban housing. Their first impulse was to follow the example of the Amalgamated and organize their venture along cooperative lines. They argued that moving away from individual ownership would benefit wage earners economically. When the first model of the project went on display in early 1932, Kastner told the *New York Times* that it was to be a

> cooperative apartment house project [which] will provide every possible facility for the convenience and amusement of the working man and his family on a wholesale scale which, as an individual, he could not afford.[36]

Along with the material advantages of collective ownership, they stressed the economic downside of private home ownership. In one of the *Hosiery Worker* housing articles, Edelman printed Clarence Stein's warning that the home buyer "gambled away his economic freedom." The group agreed with Stein's assessment that home ownership could be a high-risk proposition for working-class families. Their modest neighborhoods were more likely to become blighted than affluent residential sections, and buying a house put them at the mercy of a particular local job market.[37]

Despite such arguments, the group's real animus against homeownership was not based on an economic calculus. As Jeanes acknowledged in a planning report, homeowning was often a rational choice for the individual working-class family given existing alternatives. Paying off a mortgage meant building up a "retirement fund," and blue-collar families typically had no other comparable investment opportunities. While it was true that some lost money when their neighborhoods declined, others were able to make speculative gains.[38] The real problem with private ownership, from the group's perspective, was that it seemed to reinforce the privatism that characterized U.S. political culture.

The Hosiery Workers' housing discussion group believed that living in the physical separation of a single-family house and having to shoulder the complete financial responsibility for it encouraged individualistic modes of thinking. Stonorov called conventional houses "fortresses of individualism."[39] As he stated in a letter to federal officials in 1935, public support for low-rental housing was important not just as a way of providing affordable shelter but also "to establish standards of living in a new mode of living quite different from what individual speculative activity has created."[40] This new mode of living Stonorov spoke of had to do with the integration of park space, cultural programs, and recreational facilities into residential districts so as to encourage more social interaction and more interest in public life.

Stonorov and the others thought that people would experience more enjoyable and fulfilling lives in this kind of environment. In addition, they thought that the enhancement of personal opportunities and the pleasure of sociability would help bring a more solidaristic society into being. Before the construction of the Mackley Houses, Stonorov wrote that "community life is totally unknown" to families of union members. "Co-operation with each other is limited to mutual relief in extreme emergencies." But, he confidently predicted that living in a "community enterprise" would transform their outlook.

Thus it becomes clear that Stonorov and the others had far more ambitious goals than simply expanding affordable housing options. They wanted to create environments that would allow first-hand experience of what they viewed as the advantages of collective provision of goods. Then, as Americans began to enjoy more communal patterns of life, they might come to look favorably on expanding public programs of all kinds. For instance, there might be support for generous public pensions, which would serve to replace privately owned houses as bulwarks of security against the threat of insolvency in old age. (And this would, by way of return, affect housing politics, making nonmarket housing more acceptable.) In common with European social-democratic architects and planners such as Ernst May of Frankfurt, the Hosiery Workers' group saw new forms of housing as a step toward creating a better kind of modern industrial society—one able to diminish the power of the market over key spheres of life.[41]

Clearly, Stonorov's belief that life at the Carl Mackley Houses would by itself change individualistic attitudes into communal ones betrayed a somewhat naive faith in the power of the physical environment to overcome values with deep structural and historical roots. As noted, the tendency toward what might be termed "design determinism" was common among American reformers in the early twentieth century.[42] For instance, the social analysis of the architects and planners who had been involved in the federal housing programs during the First World War was rife with similar assumptions. Nor was this a peculiarly American way of thinking. As Bauer later explained, the modern movement in architecture that originated in Europe was infused with hopes that a better designed environment would improve society generally. In later years, such ideas would come to seem foolish, even destructive. Yet, perhaps the real problem with this approach to social change was not so much that it was wrong as that it was incomplete, paying insufficient attention not only to cultural factors but also to the economic and institutional context.

In terms of design, Stonorov and Kastner were committed modernists who aspired to create new physical forms for urban residential architecture. Traditionally, the source of ideas for housing was, in Kastner's words, the "old-fashioned, entrepreneur architect." This figure designed elaborate, personalized projects for wealthy individuals, which were then constructed through an expensive "piece-by-piece building process." According to Kastner, the unfortunate outcome was that the whole society's conception of shelter was based on these custom-built homes of the rich and, therefore, most residential development consisted of dreary streets of cheap, miniaturized replicas of mansions. This was particularly depressing and ironic in the same country that had pioneered production of so many kinds of well-made mass-produced objects, most obviously the modern automobile. Kastner joked that "if Mr. Ford's designers used the thought-process of traditional architecture we should undoubtedly be riding around today in small copies of King George's coronation coach."[43]

According to the two architects, a key step in developing a new kind of domestic architecture was to restructure architectural practice. Generally, when architects were involved with a commercial project, rather than working for a specific client, they proceeded on the basis of quite vague information about the ultimate users of their designs. To gain more familiarity with the kinds of people who would be living in the union housing complex, Stonorov and Kastner consulted with the officers and staff of the Hosiery Workers. In addition, they organized a survey to gather information from 1,400 union families. The research work was planned with help from faculty at Bryn Mawr College and directed by William Jeanes.

In his autobiography, Edelman remembered the survey as a channel for members to express their preferences on design questions. In fact, the main thrust of the research was aimed not at finding out what families wanted, but what they could afford, as practically all of the questions had to do with current housing expenses and income. As it turned out, the once-prosperous hosiery workers could no longer afford all that much. Twenty percent of families interviewed reported receiving no wages at all in the week before being questioned. Average income for the entire group at this time was $21.50 a week, less than half of the income necessary to cover monthly mortgage and ownership costs on a new rowhouse.[44]

In his influential 1978 article praising the design of the Mackley Houses, architectural historian Richard Pommer accused Stonorov of using the survey to justify his existing plans rather than "uncovering the workers' own wishes."[45] As proof, Pommer noted that the respondents were not asked whether they would prefer apartments or houses. Pommer's critique points to problematic issues regarding the role of professionals in a democratic society. Of course, he is correct that Stonorov and the others were not trying to translate the ideas of the union members into reality. Even if cost had not been an issue, the group clearly had no idea of constructing shelter according to prevailing American norms as to what constituted an ideal home. Edelman seems not to have been comfortable with this reality, imagining later that the survey had "provided us with answers to a lot of pragmatic questions," such as desirable room layouts. Actually, there were no questions on the survey instrument that asked for input on design.[46]

Stonorov, on the other hand, never thought of the survey as a tool to solicit the desires of the membership, and he never represented it as such. The introduction to the published report on the survey, which he seems to have co-written with Jeanes, talked about the need for the architect to know "the requirements" of those for whom he designs.[47] For Stonorov, the survey served that function. He saw himself as an expert working on behalf of the public good and, perhaps because of his upper-class European background, never seems to have felt uncomfortable about this role. "Housing must become a science to which the best minds . . . will be devoted," he told the Philadelphia *Public Ledger* in 1933.[48]

Despite the planners of the Mackley Houses having had a fairly clear idea about what they wanted to build before the survey, union members' preferences did affect at least one major decision. From the start, Stonorov and Kastner took for granted that tennis courts would be the major recreation facility; their first plan called for no less than three courts.[49] Yet when the union families were surveyed, 73 percent, which the planners considered an "amazing number," expressed a desire for a swimming pool. Baseball came in as the next most popular participatory sport, with 43 percent indicating an interest, while only 20 percent opted for tennis. In the end, the tennis courts were scrapped, and the development featured a 75-foot pool.[50]

At the outset, Stonorov conceived of the project as an aggressively avant-garde statement. A model created in the initial phase of planning was displayed with the famous Museum of Modern Art exhibition on modern architecture organized by Philip Johnson and Henry-Russell Hitchcock, when the show traveled to Philadelphia in the spring of 1932. Stonorov's model displayed three thin highrise buildings placed parallel to each other, in the *zeilenbau* pattern favored by German architects. (This design is shown in figure 5.2.) In this kind of arrangement, residential buildings no more than two rooms deep were built in rows running north and south. Such site plans maximized light and ventilation and also cut construction costs since there were fewer

FIG. 5.2 Model of Stonorov's original plan for the Carl Mackley Houses, created for the Museum of Modern Art show on Modern Architecture. In this first conception, the development was projected to be three high-rise slabs, arranged in *Zeilenbau* fashion. Stonorov probably envisaged the architectural avant-garde who came to see the exhibit, rather than the eventual residents, as the real audience for this design. In any case, the plan was vastly modified before the complex was built (see figure 5.3). Reproduced courtesy of the American Heritage Center, University of Wyoming.

streets per dwelling. At this stage of planning, each apartment had two stories, designed, as Stonorov explained, to be "vertical repetitions of the typical Philadelphia row house." But, in a radical departure from the local vernacular, each contained a double-height living room. As one architectural historian has suggested, Stonorov probably never regarded this "polemically modernist" plan as a serious proposal for the final project. Rather, it was a way to display his familiarity with the latest international trends for the sophisticated Museum of Modern Architecture audience.[51]

The Building of the Mackley Houses

Although Rieve and other union leaders were not involved in the initial discussions, they actively supported the plan for a housing project. The early 1930s, however, were not a good time for the union to try to assemble financing on its own, especially given the difficulties being encountered by the more affluent ACW, which had built in a far easier economic climate and had also received state aid. Edelman and the others concluded, based on their familiarity with practices in Europe, that low-interest federal loans were the only practical solution, even though the likelihood of such help seemed remote.

Yet, as we have seen, even before President Hoover left office, the slumping economy prompted him to agree to a bill allowing the Reconstruction Finance Corporation to make loans to limited-dividend housing corporations governed by state housing boards. When this legislation passed in the summer of 1932, only New York possessed the necessary state agency, so the first step for the Hosiery Workers was to get the legislature to organize a housing board in Pennsylvania. Governor Gifford Pinchot and his wife Cornelia were sympathetic to the union's plan. The two managed to get enabling legislation introduced into the state legislature, but the bill failed to pass, and plans stalled for another year. Then, in the first phase of New Deal, Congress passed the National Industrial Recovery Act (NIRA) with its provision for aid to low-cost housing.[52]

Soon after the NIRA became law in mid-June of 1933, Edelman was in Washington, DC, on union business and met Stonorov by chance late one night. Despite the hour, Edelman found his friend characteristically "bustling with energy." Stonorov explained how he had just gotten to know Robert Kohn, the new head of the Public Works Administration Housing Division, whom he described as "a fancy-pants New York architect but a good guy." This was their opportunity, Stonorov insisted; they had to approach Kohn immediately. As it was past eleven o'clock at night and Kohn was sleeping when they called, the new administrator was at first less than enthusiastic. But after some cajoling by Stonorov, Kohn responded that "for you bastards I'll get out of bed." The two made their pitch, and Kohn was impressed with the plan. With this head start, the union got the Housing Division's first loan, which eventually amounted to $1,039,000.[53]

Even after the federal money was approved, the union still faced serious obstacles. The first was land assembly. Financial help from Jeanes's family made possible the acquisition of a city block in the northeast part of the city. Northeast Philadelphia, while least developed overall, was still the city's most industrialized section, with over 2,000 factories in 1930. The location meant the housing would be near to manufacturing jobs.[54] The union's property was a 5.4 acre tract abutting Juniata Park and bordered by "M" Street and Castor Avenue to the west and east and Cayuga and Bristol Streets to the north and south. Before starting construction, the union needed permission from the City Council to close two streets (which existed only on paper) in order to create the superblock required for the project.

The request gave those groups in the city who regarded the plan as "not an American idea" the opportunity to try to block it. Leading the opposition was the North Philadelphia Realty Board, which took the position that a government-assisted residential development represented "unfair competition with private ownership." The realtors, together with the United Business Men's Association and the Philadelphia Company for Guaranteeing Mortgages, lobbied hard to get the City Council to reject the union's application to modify the street grid. No one at the council meetings seemed particularly surprised at charges by realty groups that the plan was "socialistic" and "communistic," but the press reported that one overwrought opponent did manage to startle council members and spectators with his prediction that the apartments would concentrate workers in such a way that "an inflamed mind might cause acts the police department could not cope with." Another argument leveled against the plan was that the high vacancy rates in the city proved that there was already more than enough rental property available, and expanding the housing stock would only serve to further deplete already slack demand. Property owners encouraged the council to seek federal money for rehabilitation, not new building.[55]

In response, the union mounted a spirited public relations counteroffensive. Members and officers attended council meetings and argued the merits of their plan with support from the head of Philadelphia's Building Trades Council. The union newspaper printed "Names of Foes of Decent Housing for Workers," a list that included all but one of the realtors of North Philadelphia, and advised readers not to patronize them. In addition, both Edelman and Stonorov gave newspaper interviews. Edelman told the press that the vacant houses available for rent in the Northeast were so decrepit that "no self-respecting tenant would occupy them." Stonorov made the case that rehabilitating blighted neighborhoods was a waste of time. "In twenty years they will revert to slums," he insisted, because the root of the problem was that these areas had originally been developed on the basis of poor land-use patterns. Outlining his vision of housing as a science, the architect argued that well-planned residential districts with plenty of parks and other amenities could be "the salvation of our urban civilization."[56]

By December 1933 the fight was won. Over the mayor's veto, the council sided unanimously with the union. It is likely, however, that the politicians were motivated to override local business interests less by the new planning theories Stonorov articulated than by the belief, as one councilman put it, that "it is a mighty poor time to throw all kinds of objections to the passage of legislation desired by public-spirited men and women in their commendable efforts to get employment for people."[57]

With the local opposition overcome, the union began building in February 1934 with a ceremony featuring Cornelia Bryce Pinchot. The governor's wife, a liberal Republican like her husband, hailed the effort as "an indication of the spirit of the New Deal" as she turned the first spadeful of earth.[58] By now, Stonorov's original modernist high-rise design had been changed by Kastner to four three-story buildings (figures 5.3 and 5.4). Kastner kept the original idea of narrow buildings aligned in relation to the sun rather than the street, but he bent them at the ends and indented them in the center, running passageways between. The design enclosed the site and opened up the interior of

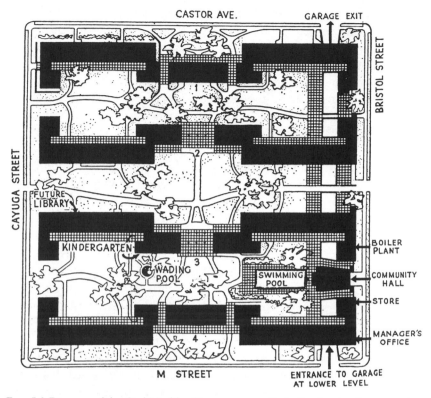

Fig. 5.3 Diagram of the Carl Mackley Houses as actually built, showing location of the community hall, cooperative store, swimming pool, children's wading pool, and kindergarten. The site is a "superblock" with automobile traffic excluded from the interior. A garage for residents' cars is provided below ground level. The three- and four-story buildings run roughly north and south (Cayuga Street is at the north end of the development), but the *Zeilenbau*-style design has been softened by turning the corners and indenting the centers of the parallel buildings. Reproduced with permission of the publisher from *Architectural Record* (November 1935), copyright (1935) by The McGraw-Hill Companies. All rights reserved.

the block. When completed, the complex contained nearly 300 apartments (most with porches), a pool, an auditorium, underground garages, a nursery school, basement rooms for tenant activities, and rooftop laundry facilities. For a while, because of costs and local construction codes, it looked like the buildings would have to be covered in very unmodern red brick. Then, at the last moment, Stonorov was able to locate a glazed industrial tile in shades of burnt yellow and orange, which gave the buildings a sleek yet not stark appearance.[59] Thus, the final realization of the project was significantly moderated from the original stylistically extreme conception. Its mix of European

CARL MACKLEY HOUSES

M & BRISTOL STS.   ::   PHILADELPHIA

JUNIATA PARK HOUSING CORPORATION

SPONSORED BY THE
AMERICAN FEDERATION
OF HOSIERY WORKERS

Fig. 5.4 The cover of the advertising brochure for the Carl Mackley Houses. The exterior walls were covered with burnt-orange ceramic tile. Many of the units had balconies, as shown here. Others had recessed porches where residents could sit outside in warm weather. On the top floor of the building segment shown on the right-hand side of the photograph are windows to one of the laundries. Women who used these laundries praised them as sunny, cheerful sites for sociability, but wished that the architects had thought to provide dumb waiters to transport baskets of clothes up the stairs between apartments and the roof level.

modernism and American suburban vernacular meant that the comple. had a contemporary appearance, but still blended with the residential neighborhood that grew up around it.

Arguing the merits of the complex, the union newspaper explained how the design was superior to the traditional working-class rowhouses of Philadelphia. The Hosiery Worker compared the thirty-foot-wide buildings, aligned north and south, with their large window areas on at least two (and sometimes three) sides, to "the superstructure of an ocean liner." More light and ventilation were possible than in conventional Philadelphia rowhouses, with their limited frontage and great depth. Another way in which the design was superior to standard local development patterns, according to the paper, lay in the availability of space away from the street where children could play. Rowhouses covered two-thirds of the block, "and the remaining one-third cannot be used to full advantage by children for play because the land is not concentrated enough." The Mackley, by comparison, left two-thirds of the land open, most of which was in the interior of the block and sheltered from traffic. The paper maintained that apartments, with their shared walls, were really no less private than row houses, while "an apartment creates more of a community feeling."[60] Thus, while the union newspaper argued for the development's superior physical amenities, it predicted that the biggest advantage over traditional living patterns would be intangible. The Hosiery Worker assured its readers that at the Mackley Houses "you will live with your friends where the spirit of unionism is strong and where there will be a real feeling of understanding between the families within the development."[61]

Life at the Mackley Houses

In January, 1935, the first apartments were completed and tenants began moving in. As it turned out, the Mackley Houses never became the stronghold of hosiery workers that some had anticipated with hope and others with dread. Before the complex ever opened, the union leadership determined not to let that happen, fearing that if most apartments were rented by hosiery workers, a strike in the industry would bankrupt the development. William Jeanes, who became manager, was instructed to lease at least two-thirds of the apartments to families not supported by a member of the union. As things worked out, no one was excluded by this rule, because the apartments turned out to be too expensive for many hosiery workers' families as well as many other working-class families. Around a quarter of those who moved in were white-collar workers, including several public school teachers.[62] Alfred Kastner, who believed that architects of residential developments should try living in places they designed, took his own advice and moved in with his wife Lenore in

February. The Kastners resided at the Mackley for almost two years until a new job took them to Washington, DC.[63]

The planners were unhappy about how expensive the complex turned out to be. To pay off the federal loan on the terms required by the PWA, rents had to be set approximately 20 percent higher than originally estimated. This meant that the largest apartments, which best corresponded in terms of interior space to a rowhouse, cost approximately $50 a month, instead of $40. The rent included services like heat, electricity, an electric range, and electric washers and dryers, in addition to amenities like the pool, so even critics of the project maintained that tenants got good value for their money. Nevertheless, costs were high in relation to incomes of hosiery workers and other blue-collar workers in this period, particularly considering that many were unemployed or working short hours. The costs were also high compared with what hosiery workers were accustomed to paying. The data Jeanes analyzed during the planning of the Mackley Houses indicated that union members in the early 1930s typically paid an average of $38 a month to rent and heat a rowhouse in a working-class neighborhood.[64]

Edelman and the others protested that their costs had been driven up unfairly, in part by the actions of the federal government itself. Therefore, they felt that the PWA should liberalize the terms of its loan. They maintained that rules in the National Industrial Recovery Act had forced them to pay higher than union-level wages during construction. Also, they pointed out that the staff was overwhelmed by the literally thousands of visitors who kept turning up wanting to tour the complex, because it was the first of the federal housing projects. In addition, they argued that the hostile city administration was levying unreasonably high property taxes.[65] These factors, combined with the more generous formula Ickes later used to finance the projects built by the PWA directly, led the Hosiery Workers to ask for a reduction in interest charges from four to three percent. They calculated that this would lower rents almost ten percent. The PWA never responded to these requests, however.[66]

Any assessment of the success of the Mackley Houses needs to take into account the hopes of the participants as well as the initiators. Most, it seems, did not particularly aspire to live in a socially active environment when they moved in, but many came to appreciate the communal atmosphere after they had been there for a while.[67] For example, Al Taffler, then a young hosiery worker, and his wife Nan, who took an apartment when the complex opened, recalled years later that for them the swimming pool was the main reason they

FIG. 5.5 The pool and community hall at the Carl Mackley Houses. In the background, one can see the dense rowhouse pattern of development that was filling up this working-class section of Philadelphia. (The empty areas in the photograph have now been filled in with the same kind of housing.) The community facilities, while built on a less lavish budget than those in Moorestown (shown in figure 2.6), were well regarded and heavily used by residents. Reproduced courtesy of the Historical Society of Pennsylvania.

took a lease (see figure 5.5 for the pool). After becoming residents, they enjoyed it tremendously, especially Nan, who talked about it as "really a Godsend to be able to get out there, at the pool, on those hot summer days." Still, by itself, the pool was not what prompted the couple to describe the Hosiery Workers' experiment as "a wonderful place to live." The facility was a magnet for socializing, and it was the friendships they formed that they remembered most fondly from their four years at the Mackley Houses. The Tafflers grew to value the possibilities for interaction with their neighbors, although their original aim seems to have been simply to secure an attractive dwelling which included appealing recreational facilities.[68]

Of course, people's precise motives are often hard to pin down. Jeanes re-

membered one man, a factory worker, who came in to inquire about an apartment. During the negotiations, the man asked Jeanes only about practical
matters, such as the amount of rent and the terms of the rental agreement.
After signing a lease, he said goodbye and walked toward the door. Then, just
as he was about to leave, the man turned and asked, "Have you ever read
Looking Backward?" To Jeanes this incident indicated that people sensed that
the Hosiery Workers' housing development was something other than a standard commercial apartment complex, even without being told so explicitly.[69]

Whatever the motives of the participants, a strong community ethos
was a major goal for the founders, as we have seen. Despite this, tenants were
not given any official introduction to communitarian ideas either before or
after they moved in. Larry Rogin, who replaced John Edelman in 1937 as the
union's research and education director, explained that conducting orientation programs at the Mackley would have been impossible, even if anyone had
wanted to do such a thing—and he remembered no one ever raising the issue.
According to Rogin, who lived at the complex with his family, the union was
pressed so hard fighting for its existence that most often he was deployed as
an organizer and was only intermittently able to do educational work within
the union. Thus, for him to have run programs at the union's housing development was clearly impossible.[70]

As manager, William Jeanes was hardly inclined to lecture residents about
how they should live. In keeping with his Quaker background, Jeanes's philosophy was highly voluntaristic. He took the position that the residents themselves should structure their life together. When asked by a federal official in
the 1930s about his approach to social activities, he joked that his philosophy
was to "just let [things] happen as you could not stop them anyway." That way
"you could not be shown to be wrong a few years later."[71] Despite Jeanes's
belief that it was not his place to advocate any particular pattern of behavior,
he was far from a passive administrator. The young manager worked energetically to support endeavors begun by tenants, somehow managing to scour up
an old printing press when a group of residents decided to start a newspaper,
for instance.

Rogin, who lived at Mackley between 1937 and 1941, affectionately discounted Jeanes's conception of himself as a neutral facilitator of the will of
the residents. Recalling life at the Mackley many years later, Rogin said,
"When Bill Jeanes says that he couldn't take the lead, I don't take it seriously."
Rogin explained that Jeanes was a Quaker, and "Quakers have a way of . . .
push[ing] very hard" for things without seeming to, and of "making you feel
like you're making up your own mind, but sometimes you don't." And yet,
the former union staffer concluded, "when you *do* make up your own mind, at

least you know why you're making it up; their way of working has that benefit."[72]

Jeanes's low-key encouragement of tenant activism was far from the norm in the PWA-assisted limited-dividend developments, according to reports by a representative of the Housing Division who traveled around the country in 1936 to observe day-to-day life in the new residential complexes. At Hillside Homes in the Bronx, management was so worried about maintaining control that "it was considered wise at the beginning to avoid any sense of strong organization, therefore no council or representative body was encouraged." There was a rule that no program whatsoever be initiated without a supervisor employed by management, and the only groups allowed to use the facilities were those that were "nonpolitical, nonsectarian and nonpropagandist in purpose and practice." The staff at Hillside had a highly professionalized conception of their role. Formal education was a necessity for staff, according to the recreation director, because it was through their "advice [that] the standards of the community life are created or influenced."[73] Meanwhile, at the limited-dividend project in the Queens section of New York City, the manager stated that "the only reason for any social activity at Boulevard Gardens is to develop a co-operative group rather than wait for the possible later organization of protest groups." In his view, the only purpose of organized recreation programs for children was to reduce damage to the grounds.[74]

At the Mackley Houses, in contrast, the open atmosphere allowed and even encouraged enterprising tenants to take the initiative. Many responded. One anonymous resident tried to motivate his or her neighbors with the following editorial in the first edition of the tenant newspaper, published in December 1935:

> The Carl Mackley Houses is primarily an experiment. Apathetic people don't make successes of experiments in workers' housing. Apathetic people are generally content to live and die in any little nook the social order shoves them into. It is obvious then that we cannot afford to be apathetic. It must also be obvious that we must cultivate a spirit of communal responsibility. For our community is not merely a new-fangled housing scheme benevolently bestowed by an allegedly friendly government. Rather, it represents the efforts of [a] progressive trade-union in conjunction with the non-profit taking effort of a few inspired individuals to exploit every possible method of improving the living standards of the great mass of workers and kindred groups. For this reason and for this reason alone it is a great experiment, and [d]eserving of the responsible co-operation of every social-minded person. The social, intellectual and even political potentialities of such a community as ours are enormous, and if they are properly developed[,] the power and the prestige of the Labor Movement will be greatly enhanced.[75]

Although the writer was concerned that not enough residents were taking responsibility for building community, the development quickly became the scene of a wide array of group activities.

Bernard and Irene Cohan, who moved in during 1935, are good examples of residents who became socially active. They were a young couple with a new baby, and Bernard had a job teaching elementary school in South Philadelphia. The Cohans joined the cooperative grocery store that was established on the premises. They sent their daughters to the nursery school and helped raise money to keep it going. In addition, they participated in the tenants' association. During the 1930s, Irene took drawing and piano lessons in the Mackley auditorium from Works Progress Administration (WPA) instructors. In addition, she drew on the help of WPA art and drama personnel when she produced children's plays and dance productions to raise money for the nursery school. After the WPA closed down, she and other art students formed a portrait drawing group and continued on their own. Asked years later why she became so involved in community life without any explicit urging, Irene explained that just seeing the available facilities was encouragement enough. Her first reaction to the complex was: "Here was this great opportunity . . . an *auditorium*, and *neighbors!*"[76]

Like Irene Cohan, many residents perceived the physical and social resources of the development as a "great opportunity." This was perhaps especially so for those with left-of-center political sympathies, since many of the activities had something of a radical tone. Years later, one former tenant recalled the high point of his five years at the Mackley during the 1930s as the time he spent putting on the play "Waiting for Lefty." When asked if he had done any of the acting, the energetic 78-year-old replied with relish: "My dear girl, *I* was Lefty."[77] Other evidence of left-wing sentiment on the part of active tenants includes editorials in the *Mackley Messenger*, the tenant newspaper, calling for such things as mandatory vacation time for industrial workers, mobilization against the Chamber of Commerce and the National Economy League in support of public education, and establishment of a congressional investigating committee to expose that "the capitalist class as a whole profits from war, and that conversely, the pursuit of profit leads inevitably to war."[78] In addition, there were fundraising dances to support the Loyalists during the Spanish Civil War, lectures on socialized medicine and the Farm Labor Party, a mock trial of newspaper magnate William Randolph Hearst, and the organization of a committee that traveled to the state capital to lobby the legislature for unemployment relief.

Pleased by the amount of tenant involvement, but a bit taken aback at the kind of political viewpoints expressed in much of what went on, one PWA official cautioned Jeanes that space in the project should be restricted to activities that were "nonpartisan, nonpolitical, nonpropagandist, and non-religious." Jeanes, however, with his strong commitment to resident self-determination, refused this advice, asserting that "the tenants would them-selves determine the right policy on these matters."[79]

Despite the extent of social activity in the early years, a significant portion of those who lived in the complex never became involved. One former resident characterized those who were active as the "like-minded people," meaning in general those people with connections to the Hosiery Union or to the Teachers Union.[80] There was a certain gulf, not necessarily hostile but definite, between, on the one hand, those who came in with a commitment to building social bonds beyond the family and getting involved in the public sphere and, on the other, people who rented because they wanted an attractive and convenient physical environment in which to live their lives along accustomed lines. For most of the latter, events such as forums on socialized medicine were not an effective way of converting them to a more communal vision. They simply did not attend.

In contrast, the nursery school did draw people into community participation. People like Irene Cohan were active in support of the school, but so were women who did not get involved in the political forums or even the co-op grocery. Ironically, the school had not been in the original plans formulated by Stonorov, Kastner, Edelman, and Jeanes. When the idea had been first suggested by Edelman's wife, they resisted it because of the expense and administrative difficulties it would entail.[81]

But Kate Edelman was not to be put off. A passionate proponent of progressive education who believed that "the children of workers [should] have the same kind of training that the children of the rich bitches had," she ultimately brought her husband and the others around. The architects added to their plans a rooftop play area complete with bathrooms and both indoor and out-door space. Ultimately, the school used an apartment on the ground floor in addition to the facilities on the roof, and another apartment was provided as a residence for the school's director.[82]

It took a few tries before the nursery school was operating smoothly. The first attempt, under the supervision of an inexperienced young woman, failed, as did the next effort, spearheaded by a group of mothers. After these false starts, the Edelmans secured a $1,500 grant from Pioneer Youth of America, an organization with ties to the Socialist Party. Finally able to pay at least a low professional salary (supplemented by a free apartment), the Edelmans were able to recruit Mildred Adams, a trained educator with a background in progressive methods of early childhood education and a decade's worth of teaching experience.[83]

In July 1935 the school opened with the new director. Adams turned out to be talented at both administration and teaching, and the school thrived. Enrollment was twenty children at the outset but reached fifty before the year was out. At first the staff consisted of Adams, a teacher and a cook paid by the WPA, and two regular volunteers, Lenore Kastner (who was married to Alfred Kastner) and Elizabeth Fox (Oskar Stonorov's fiancée).[84] By the 1940s, the staff had grown to three full-time paid teachers under the director, along with a cook. One parent (a teacher himself) credited Adams's success to her grasp of "parent psychology" in addition to her "keen knowledge of child psychology."[85]

Rather than thinking of nursery schools as primarily for the supervision and education of children whose mothers worked outside the home, Adams wanted her center to enrich and supplement the care already provided by mothers who did not hold outside jobs. Its purpose was to train children to be more self-reliant and more cooperative—to develop in children, according to a 1946 advertising brochure, "those constructive habits and attitudes which mark the intelligent, well-thinking adult of our American democracy." Mothers, with their children in school for a few hours, would "gain time for relaxation or completing their duties without worry or interruption." Adams believed that with such a break, "the mother is usually in a better psychological position to meet the demands of the child when he is at home."[86]

As the years went by, more mothers worked outside the home for longer periods, and there was pressure to keep the school open longer hours. By 1960, twenty of the twenty-eight children enrolled had mothers with outside jobs, all but one full-time. The director did keep the school open later, but she never liked the practice, believing that children suffered if they stayed on after midafternoon. In the opinion of a long-time close friend, Adams was always more sensitive to the needs of children than mothers.[87] This dedication to the welfare of children, together with her obvious abilities, clearly endeared her to parents, whatever tensions there may have been about such issues as school hours. One woman who worked part-time as a chemist in the late forties and early fifties while living at Mackley Houses explained how she and her husband had stayed at the complex specifically so their two sons could attend nursery school there. The school was not merely a custodial facility, she emphasized. It provided quality education. As proof, she pointed out that both of her sons had gone on to Ivy League schools and graduate education.[88]

Despite the school's success, it was never financially secure. The policy of charging low fees meant that, even with aid from outside individuals and organizations, volunteer labor was always a necessity. Mothers helped out in the daily operation with such tasks as washing linen for the children's nap cots. In addition, they organized dinners, put on bazaars, and staged entertainments to raise money. Paradoxically, the school's continually precarious financial situation may have been one key to its success—at least in its role as an agent of socialization and integration for parents. To keep it going, all of the mothers had to be involved. Their children's positive response to the school meant they had the motivation, and the tasks involved were ones that most women felt confident to take on, even if they lacked formal education or political experience.[89]

Looking back ruefully many years later at his initial resistance to the idea of a nursery school, William Jeanes commented that he was very glad he was overruled. In common with practically everyone who was interviewed, the former manager believed the school had been key to the cordial social atmosphere at the Mackley Houses. In his words: "It set the tone."[90]

After World War II, the level of activity at the Mackley Houses subsided. The nursery school continued, which meant that adults still came together at least periodically for events like fundraising bazaars. Also, the pool continued to serve as a setting for casual socializing. But the range and level of group activity that had characterized the earlier period no longer existed. According to one resident from the late forties and early fifties, "even while we were there [social life] began to decline as certain people moved away." His explanation for the change was the loss of particular individuals "who were very active and [took] real leadership in terms of trying to do things as a group" as opposed to others whom he characterized as not caring "a wit as to whether the Mackley apartment dwellers were together or not."[91] Of course, this difference in commitment to community had existed all along; the change was that the active core grew steadily smaller and the possibilities for tapping outside resources declined.

The underlying reasons for the loss of energy in the postwar era were related to events beyond the Mackley Houses. The activists there in the 1930s never could have imagined they were part of the American majority. Yet, during the years of the New Deal they probably did feel part of a larger search for fresh ways to approach the public issues of their time. After the war, the political climate in the country changed dramatically. One indication of the shift was the effort by the federal government to distance itself from a variety of innovative and experimental ventures begun in the 1930s. During the war, Congress defunded the Natural Resources Planning Board and mandated that the Farm Security Administration liquidate its community projects. Soon after the war ended, Congress directed that the three greenbelt towns built by Rexford Tugwell's Resettlement Administration be sold off. Washington also wanted to disengage itself from the PWA limited-dividend program. Federal officials began pressing the Hosiery Workers to pay off their loan early.[92]

Another indication of the changed atmosphere was the national crusade against suspected subversives. Anticommunism took a serious toll on the Mackley Houses, as several active residents were in fact associated in some way with the Communist Party. Some of the teachers belonged to the party-affiliated Teachers' Union, which in 1953 became the focus of a House Committee on Un-American Activities Committee investigation. The Philadelphia Schools superintendent suspended thirty of the forty union leaders called before the committee, including three who lived at the Mackley.[93]

The decline of the Hosiery Workers Union in the years after the Second World War also undermined the vitality of the Mackley experiment. The union became smaller and weaker for reasons both technical and political. Manufacturers replaced silk with rayon for making women's stockings. Rayon stretched, so hosiery no longer had to be made to fit the contours of a woman's leg. This meant that knitting hosiery became a less-skilled kind of work. In the meantime, production continued to shift to the South, where union organizing was notoriously difficult.

As time went by, the leadership of the union changed. During the 1930s, Rieve and Edelman moved to the Congress of Industrial Organizations (CIO). Rieve encouraged his old union to merge with the CIO Textile Workers Union. The new leadership resisted but failed to develop any long-range plan for survival as an independent unit. By the 1950s, the union's situation became desperate, as membership dropped from a prewar high of around 40,000 to somewhere in the neighborhood of 10,000. Meanwhile there was friction between the current officers of the Hosiery Workers and Jeanes. The long-time manager tried to buy the complex from the union, but his offer was refused. In 1957, the union refinanced the federal loan on the Mackley Houses with a private lender and bought Jeanes out. After this, he gave up his position as manager. No longer restricted by government regulations or Jeanes, union officers were then free to use revenues from the apartment complex to bolster their organization's faltering finances. Even so, the union was not able to survive for very much longer. With only slightly over 5,000 members in 1965, the American Federation of Hosiery Workers merged into the Textile Workers Union of America, making the Mackley Houses the property of the New York City-based union.[94]

By the time of the merger, the era of social experimentation at the complex was over. Mildred Adams's retirement in 1964 and the subsequent closure of the nursery school marked the end of any organized social programs. The Textile Workers, seeing no reason to administer what was in essence an ordinary apartment complex from their headquarters in another city, sold the Mackley Houses in 1968 to private investors who operated it as a moderate-rental commercial apartment complex.[95]

The Mackley Houses after Fifty Years

Even after the Mackley became a commercial operation, residents continued to be very positive about the complex. In 1985, tenants organized a celebration to mark the project's fifty years of operation. At this point, the development was still providing what residents perceived as a good environment. The pool had been filled in, but the trees that Jeanes and his friends had planted in the 1930s were mature, and the internal lawns were still safe places for children to play.

During the festivities, residents praised the friendliness of their neighbors and expressed contentment with the physical qualities of the complex. Yet, there was practically no awareness of the Mackley's origins as a union-sponsored and federally supported experiment in noncommercial housing. Margaret Traynor, an enthusiastic resident who had first lived at the Mackley Houses as a child in the 1950s and then moved back with her husband and children in the 1960s, stated at the anniversary party that she knew nothing about the Hosiery Workers Union. According to Traynor, Carl Mackley had built the complex. He had "built it and died for it," she said.[96]

Conclusion

The founders of the Mackley Houses had hoped to build a residential complex that would serve as a model for noncommercial housing development throughout the country. As Piero Santostefano points out in his study of the project's origins, there were two major goals involved: the complex was "to provide housing of the workers and for the workers, [plus it was] to be a model, and not just a single example, for reproduction on a national scale."[97] While the Mackley did succeed in providing a living environment that was much appreciated by residents for over a half-century, it failed to achieve its larger goal of changing the direction of residential development throughout the country by influencing national policy.

To be sure, such an aim was extraordinarily ambitious. It seems unlikely that any one demonstration by itself could hope to mold the direction of federal policy, but the project did manifest a strategy for making changes in the way American housing could be designed and provided. How should we assess this strategy?

The account of Margaret Traynor points to some of the weaknesses of this model. That a person who had lived in the Mackley as early as the 1950s and had so much allegiance to the complex would know nothing about its origins in radical unionism or its significance as an attempt to advance a new kind of housing suggests a serious failure to communicate and institutionalize the project's purposes even internally. Eleanor and Irving Fleet, two original residents, raised this issue when interviewed about their experiences and views. They complained that

> if you didn't know that it was sponsored by the Hosiery Workers you wouldn't ever find out. Most people moved in there because it was inexpensive and very attractive whether they were Hosiery workers or not, and they [the people in charge] didn't attempt in any way to make it a Mecca for hosiery workers or bring forth any of the principles of the Hosiery Workers' Union.

Irving concluded: "I think if they had tried to propagandize the idea of co-op living, [in] the full sense . . . including ownership [and] partnership, it might have been an idea that would have taken hold in future years."[98]

The Fleets' criticisms bring out an important ambiguity about the Mackley Houses, because, in fact, the development was not a cooperative. Although Stonorov and Kastner had initially assumed that the financial arrangement would be set up along the lines of the Amalgamated's apartments, where tenants were considered owners rather than renters, the terms of the PWA loan made a cooperative structure difficult and perhaps impossible. As former resident William Rafsky summed it up: the Mackley "wasn't a co-op in the real sense of the word, it was more an opportunity to be more neighborly than you might find in most apartment houses."[99] Given the powerful and legitimate desire that Americans have for control over their residential environment, this model has serious limitations for framing a housing policy that could achieve wide acceptance. The administration of the Mackley was more one of benevolent paternalism than of self-organization. And since paternalistic regimes are hard to legitimate within the dominant democratic ideology in the United States, the group responsible for design and management did not, and indeed could not, describe their model as universally applicable. At the same time, they did not articulate its weaknesses. Rather, they remained silent, so no particular perspective on how best to provide urban shelter was communicated to residents.

Another ambiguity concerns the relationship of the Mackley to left-wing trade unionism in the United States. The project was intended to advance the agenda of this movement, and yet it had only the most abstract connections with it, involving in the planning stages only a tiny elite group, many not even members or staff of the sponsoring union. For financial reasons described earlier, union officials did not even want very many union members as residents, and the relatively high rents in the complex meant that they got very few. Thus, the union and the Mackley Houses were largely disconnected in practice, and it is hard to imagine that the membership felt much commitment to the experiment. While a large amount of political activity went on at the Mackley Houses, it was carried on by groups of residents coming together for purposes they happened to have brought in with them. The activities were not related to housing issues *per se*, nor with purposes connected to the union, its political agenda, or the economic struggles with which it was involved.

A final weakness is that the project manifested some of the characteristic limitations of a longstanding tradition, going back to the dawn of European settlement, in American efforts at social reform. That tradition, of course, is of seeking social change through models, examples, cities set on hills. In the area of housing and community design, this tradition has been especially strong, manifested in utopian communities, company towns, model tenements, and the like. The impact of such models on large-scale social change has always been extremely hard to demonstrate and might fairly be said to be dubious.

On the positive side, the development was very successful as a physical environment, and it encouraged the growth of a rich array of social activities and services. Unabashedly modern in its site design and planning concepts, the Mackley nonetheless compromised significantly with vernacular conventions, with a result that residents found it familiar enough to seem appealing. Furthermore, as a social environment, the Mackley developed a degree of tenant-initiated activity almost unheard of in rental housing, whether public or commercial. One of the most critical features of the experiment, the presence of a rich array of social services on-site, proved beyond a doubt to be an important advantage in a variety of ways. The nursery school, for instance, clearly generated loyalty and solidarity by providing a place where residents became involved in the life of the complex on a practical level.

It is not clear how many Americans would have been willing to trade the privacy and control of a single family house for the superior recreational facilities, sociability, economy, and lack of individual maintenance responsibilities offered by a complex like the Mackley Houses if federal policies had not ended up giving significant financial advantages to homeownership. But the experience of the Mackley residents suggests that, on a level playing field, many Americans might have favored this kind of residential situation for at least some part of their lives.

Fig. 6.1 The Harlem River Houses in New York City. This complex, completed in 1937, was built directly by the PWA to serve African-American New Yorkers. The architectural team was headed by Archibald Manning Brown and included Will Rice Amon, Richard W. Buckley, Frank J. Forster, Charles F. Fuller, Horace Ginsbern, and John Lewis Wilson. This 1987 photograph shows the view looking north along the central courtyard. Vic Delucia / NYT Pictures.

SIX

The Harlem River Houses

T he Harlem River Houses, one of the most attractive apartment complexes in New York City, was constructed in the second phase of PWA housing work (in which the agency functioned as a direct developer). Like the Carl Mackley Houses of Philadelphia, Harlem River would never have come into existence except for the efforts of an active local constituency. African Americans in Manhattan had pursued a variety of strategies to improve their living conditions well before the Depression. At first, they worked for better treatment as tenants within the existing privately owned housing stock, but two events early in Roosevelt's administration encouraged the expansion of demands. These were the creation of the Housing Division as an agency within the PWA in the summer of 1933, and PWA administrator Harold Ickes's public promise to the new LaGuardia reform administration early in 1934 to earmark $25 million of federal housing money for New York City.[1] With the possibility of federal money for new construction on the horizon, black New Yorkers began pressing for building affordable good quality housing in their section of the city. The development that resulted turned out to be an exceptionally fine residential environment that might well have provided an appealing model for the kind of broadly targeted federal program proposed by Catherine Bauer and other advocates of the modern housing ideal.

To understand New York's African-American housing movement and its role in the creation of the Harlem River Houses, one must go back to the early real estate development of the Harlem section of Manhattan. Constituting a good part of the island above Central Park, the area was not typical of neighborhoods of the urban poor. Most poor people in American cities occupied worn-out and discarded dwellings left behind by affluent families who had moved on to more fashionable neighborhoods, or else they resided in buildings that had been initially constructed below the standards of the time, such as tenements. By contrast, in Harlem, due to an enormous speculative miscalculation, low-income families lived in relatively new accommodations originally constructed with wealthy occupants in mind.[2]

In the 1920s, the good physical condition of "Black Manhattan," along with the flowering of the arts dubbed the "Harlem Renaissance," fueled tremendous optimism. The very existence of this vibrant city within a city made it possible to look forward, in the words of NAACP Executive Secretary James Weldon Johnson, to a future of "greater and greater things" for Americans of African descent.[3] Yet the affluent face that Harlem's elegant buildings showed to the world was deceptive even before the Depression. Black intellectual and artistic achievements were real; economic prosperity was not. "Behind the inviting facades," many lived in "grim misery," according to poet Claude McKay.[4]

Harlem Becomes Manhattan's Black District

The explanation for the paradox of black people being forced by racial segregation into one of the city's better residential sections is to be found in the failure of a gigantic real estate gamble. Historian Gilbert Osofsky has traced this story in detail, explaining how the once out-of-the-way country village of Harlem, eight miles north of City Hall, was transformed by entrepreneurs who believed this part of Manhattan was destined to be the site of an elegant residential enclave for wealthy families. In the years after the Civil War, real estate prices in this part of the island shot up. Eager to profit from what was generally regarded as a sure thing, everyone from the Astors to small tradespeople in the slums briskly sold and resold Harlem property. Building began in the 1870s, just before elevated light rail service linked the district with downtown. A second wave of development was spurred by the construction of the Interborough Rapid Transit (IRT) subway, which opened in 1904. "Practically all the houses that stand in Harlem today," Osofsky explains, "were built in a long spurt of energy that lasted from the 1870s through the first decade of the twentieth century."[5]

In anticipation of an upscale clientele, builders erected apartments and rowhouses that were spacious, luxurious, and expensive. Typical rents in Harlem at the turn of the century were in the $35 to $45 range, compared with the $10 to $18 per month working-class families in the city paid. Top-of-the-line accommodations, such as the 1891 brownstones on 138th and 139th Streets designed by Stanford White, cost even more. The choicest of these rented for $142 a month at a time when urban families nationwide supported by a blue-collar or clerical worker lived on an average *income* of $48 a month.[6]

Initially, the area did appeal to affluent families, just as developers had hoped. Gilded Age New Yorkers were attracted not only by the gracious residences but also by the social amenities of the district, such as the Polo Grounds or the Opera House built by Oscar Hammerstein, Sr.[7] Visualizing a continuous stream of customers, investors poured money into the construction of high-class apartment houses, but after the turn of the century the expected volume of wealthy apartment-seekers failed to materialize. As whole buildings stood empty, it became clear that real estate speculators both large and small had seriously misjudged the size of the market for luxury dwellings in this part of the city. Just when a great many buildings were being finished to coincide with the opening of the new subway, the recession of 1902–4 further weakened demand.[8]

At the same time that so many apartments were sitting vacant in Harlem, African-American New Yorkers living further south on the island were desperate for housing. Construction of Pennsylvania Station (officially announced in 1901 and completed in 1910) attracted investment into Midtown, which was then a rundown redlight area of the city in which African Americans had been allowed to live.[9] At the same time as commercial development was pushing into their neighborhoods, black newcomers from the South and the Caribbean were arriving in the city at a rapid rate. In 1890, there had been 42,000 African Americans in New York City. Only a decade later, the number stood at 66,700, an increase of over 50 percent.[10] Thus, at the same time the black community was rapidly expanding, the already poor housing options available to this group were contracting.

While apartment-owners refused to rent to blacks in most areas of the city, the real estate bust in Harlem undermined such "principles" on the part of landlords there. Beginning in 1901, black realtor Philip A. Payton, Jr., convinced white owners to lease their buildings to him to fill with African-American tenants. Black congregations followed and also assisted the northward migration. The churches purchased Harlem apartment houses with the earnings from selling their midtown property, and they opened these buildings to black occupancy. As Harlem developed a reputation as a neighborhood where African Americans lived, white landlords there began to rent to blacks directly. By 1910, close to 28,000 African Americans were living in Harlem. In 1920, the number was over 83,000.[11]

The attractive neighborhood did offer improved conditions, but life was not easy for Harlem's new residents. The generously sized luxury dwellings, often designed to house live-in servants along with the renting family, were hardly the most suitable for New York's black community, given that around half of households consisted of one to two people.[12] The size and quality of the apartments meant that owners expected (and needed) relatively high rents. Moreover, the housing market was not race-blind, and landlords typically charged more and provided fewer services to blacks. Judge John Davies of the Seventh District Municipal Court located in Harlem told the 1925 Mayor's Committee on Rent Profiteering that it was "common for colored tenants in Harlem to pay twice as much as white tenants for the same apartments." High rents led to crowding within individual dwelling units and the neighborhood as a whole. Even so, housing costs were onerous. A New York Urban League survey in the 1920s reported close to half of black families paying over 40 percent of their small incomes for housing.[13]

Harlem's congestion was a sharp contrast to the situation in other parts of the city. During the 1920s, large numbers of modest-income white Manhattanites found better residential opportunities in the Bronx, Queens, and Brooklyn. Each year between 1920 and 1930 an average of 40,000 people moved out of Manhattan, resulting in an overall population decline of 18 percent by the end of the decade. The Lower East Side experienced the heaviest loss, with 40 percent of its residents leaving during the decade. Yet, at the same time whites were spreading out, blacks were becoming more concentrated at the center of the metropolis. African Americans migrated out of the American South in great numbers after the First World War, and many headed for what was in effect the capital of Black America. Harlem's black population grew from approximately 83,000 in 1920 to 204,000 in 1934—a 146 percent increase in just fourteen years.[14]

The Great Depression, not surprisingly, exacerbated the already serious economic pressures in Harlem. African Americans were the hardest hit by unemployment because theirs were the most marginal jobs. In 1933, the Urban League calculated that at least 66 percent of Harlem's workforce was unemployed. Income loss led to more extreme crowding. In the twenties, the population density in black sections of Manhattan was about 50 percent higher than for the rest of the island. By the mid-thirties, the Mayor's Commission on City Planning reported density levels in some African-American neighborhoods to be practically double what they had been ten years before. Not surprisingly, the death rate from tuberculosis in Harlem was approximately twice that of Manhattan as a whole, and the district had the highest infant mortality rate in the city.[15]

The Struggle to Improve Housing Conditions

The injustice of their housing situation was not lost on Harlem residents. Historian Mark Naison has described how Communist Party organizers were first able to attract attention and support within the black community beyond the intelligentsia when they took on housing issues. In the summer of 1929, membership in the Communist-led Harlem Tenants League grew to over five hundred during an attempted communitywide rent strike. While the strike itself failed, the campaign was a success in terms of building visibility and support for the party. Communists had failed dismally with previous efforts to organize in Harlem, but they attracted a wide audience once they took on the explosive housing question.[16]

A rent strike, of course, was a high-risk proposition for people with few housing options, and most of the time blacks in New York sought redress for grievances using more conventional tactics. Reinforcing this tendency was the fact that legal efforts did sometimes yield results. For example, community pressure led to passage of state legislation in 1930 giving tenants some protection against eviction if they could not find comparable quarters at a similar price. Also, African Americans knew they often could get a sympathetic hearing in one of the Municipal Courts located in Harlem (these were lower civil courts administered by the city). Judges in these courts, like John Davies quoted earlier, were well aware that landlords often charged blacks higher rents while providing fewer services than was usual for white tenants. These officials were willing to entertain questions as to the legitimacy of leases as valid contracts, given that they knew that the Harlem tenant was so demonstrably not an equal party to the bargain. Within this environment, talented and resourceful lawyers like Vernal Williams (who had defended Marcus Garvey) pioneered a legal defense of tenant rights using the new state statute in conjunction with a variety of other legal strategies and commonsense appeals. The result, according to Heinz Nordeen, leader of the City-Wide Tenant Council, was that "for the first time, tenants began to get a break in the courts."[17]

The possibility of success through legal avenues tended to channel tenant anger in this direction. An estimated 11,000 African Americans sought legal assistance from the major Harlem tenant organization between 1936 and 1941. In many of these instances, Harlem residents turned to the courts for more than just fending off rent increases. They also employed legal tactics offensively to secure better services. James Watson, the first black judge elected to the Tenth District Municipal Court in Harlem, observed that most suits to evict tenants for nonpayment of rent resulted from the tenants' "dissatisfaction with the condition of the premises or with services rather than . . . inability to pay."[18]

Two factors were important in influencing Harlemites to expand their political repertoire in the 1930s to include direct action. First, the deteriorating economic conditions undermined the black middle class's faith in progress within existing institutions. Second, African Americans observed the militancy of other urban groups and the concessions achieved by extralegal behavior, as in the large-scale Bronx rent strikes of 1932. By 1934, mass mobilizations were a regular feature of life in "Black Manhattan." Harlem residents used boycotts, picketing, rallies, and marches to achieve employment opportunities, fight discrimination in relief practices, and demonstrate support for the Scottsboro Boys. That summer tenants in the attractive residential section nicknamed "Sugar Hill" began fighting back against discriminatory housing treatment with rent strikes and picketing.[19]

On Sugar Hill, biased practices were particularly obvious, because it was an area of rapid racial turnover. When landlords admitted black tenants, they often hiked rents significantly, sometimes to as much as double the former level. At the same time, they cut back on maintenance and fired service personnel, like doormen and elevator operators. Resentment was so high among the neighborhood's heavily professional population that, after the first building organized, several others followed suit. Banding together beyond their individual buildings, the protesters formed the United Tenants League. By September, the new organization had won concessions from owners of all the buildings involved. Soon after, the group merged with another tenant organization in Harlem to become the Consolidated Tenants League (CTL).[20]

Middle-class professionals like Vernal Williams, influenced by Marcus Garvey's militant black nationalism, led the CTL, although Communists also participated. The organization specialized in fighting for tenant rights through the courts but was flexible with regard to tactics. When the landlord of the prominent Dr. Cyril H. Dolly, a black ophthalmologist on the staff of Harlem Hospital, tried to evict him from his apartment for leading a tenant protest in the fall of 1934, the CTL responded by ringing his building with pickets. When Dolly's case came to trial, fifty league members came with him to court.[21]

The league was particularly important in shaping public opinion with regard to housing issues after an outbreak of violence in March 1935 that became known as the Harlem Riot. The event started in response to reports (inaccurate as it turned out) that police had killed a teenage boy suspected of shoplifting in a department store on 125th Street, the district's main commercial thoroughfare. As rumors of the supposed murder began circulating, thousands of people poured out of their homes and began milling in the streets. Soon crowds began smashing store windows and looting. Mild in comparison with other urban racial violence in the twentieth century, the riot lasted less than twenty-four hours, fewer than a hundred people were arrested, and there were only two deaths. Nevertheless, the event shocked the city, and Mayor La Guardia established a biracial commission to investigate. CTL leaders played a major role at the commission's hearings, testifying personally and coordinating the appearance of numerous Harlem tenants who described in harrowing detail the profiteering of their landlords, the neglect of municipal agencies, and the dismal condition of their dwellings.[22]

Partly as a result of such work, the riot commission concluded that the disturbance was caused by the combination of severe economic distress and racism. The commission's report, which took over a year to research and write, was especially critical of government. For example, with respect to the district's filthy streets, the commission blamed the trash collection department rather than residents. The commissioners concluded that, in common with other municipal agencies, the staff of this agency seemed to be "more industrious about maintaining what they regard as the proper relations between the races than in seeing that the Negro receives his proper share of civic services."[23]

La Guardia, presumably fearing political repercussions given the tone of the commission's report, never officially released it. The report did become public, however, after it was leaked to the press and published in the summer of 1936 by the *Amsterdam News*, a black weekly. Also, at the request of Paul Kellogg, editor of the liberal *Survey Graphic* magazine, the mayor allowed journalist Dr. Alain Locke access to the complete findings. Locke's article on the report noted that the commission found housing to be "the most serious special community problem of Harlem."[24]

Harlem Activists Push for More Housing

Around the same time as the Harlem Riot, the Consolidated Tenants League and a variety of other local organizations started pressing for more housing—not just better treatment within the dwelling stock that already existed. As mentioned earlier, this demand was triggered by the creation of a federal housing program as part of the National Industrial Recovery Act of 1933. For the first time, Harlem residents could realistically imagine that it was possible to secure aid from the federal government.

Black New Yorkers worked to influence the city's response to the new federal program in a variety of ways. In December 1933, Lester Taylor, vice-president of the United Negro Progressive Association, wrote to LaGuardia's choice for Tenement House Commissioner, Langdon Post, expressing the expectation that East Harlem "be considered in the far-reaching plans of municipal housing improvement contemplated by the incoming city administration." Taylor enclosed a petition circulated by his organization and the Puerto Rican Service Center expressing the same sentiment. The petition explained that Puerto Ricans and Negroes who lived in the area were "making common cause in this demand."[25]

That same month, Francis Rivers, an African-American lawyer and former Republican State Assemblyman from Harlem, wrote to Richmond Shreve, the influential architect who had been put in charge of the privately financed but quasi-official Slum Clearance Committee. Composed of middle-class advocates of publicly financed low-rent housing and leading real estate investors in the city, the committee was undertaking an investigation of possible sites for locating PWA-funded developments. Rivers told Shreve that "a low-cost housing and slum clearance project in Harlem would be signally successful as an initial experiment." The former assemblyman urged Shreve to investigate possibilities for a site in the area. A few days later, Rivers met the architect at the Urban League Offices and, with the help of the prominent local realtor J. E. Nail, drove Shreve through the district pointing out possible locations.[26] Other community leaders, including the heads of the NAACP, the Urban League, and the North Harlem Community Council, also urged city officials to consider Harlem's urgent needs when drawing up plans to use the federal money.[27]

Despite such efforts and the obvious fact of need, months passed without any announcement of plans to build in Harlem. That summer Langdon Post, LaGuardia's Tenement House Commissioner, whom the mayor had also tapped to head the newly created New York City Housing Authority, told the press that rent levels in Harlem were higher than in any of the city's other slum areas.[28] Post asserted that "the Negro is known to be a good tenant and the records show that he has been squeezed more deliberately by the landlord than the inhabitants of any other slum area." He insisted that "we want to attack the low-cost housing problem in Harlem and before we have finished we will." The stumbling block, he explained, was the high asking-price of real estate in built-up sections of the city, even when lots contained only dilapidated structures.[29]

The problem of high-cost slum property put Post and the Housing Authority staff in a bind when it came to finding sites—and not just in Harlem. This was because, while building low-rental housing and doing slum clearance were virtually identical in the public's mind, in reality, the two endeavors were almost diametrically opposed because of the high prices owners wanted for inner-city land. Paying a lot for property drove up the final cost of any construction project, making it impossible for low rents to cover a significant portion of real costs. Despite the incompatibility of the two goals taken together, the idea of doing both at once had tremendous popular appeal as well as the fervent backing of real estate interests. Thus, even though good reasons could be given for vacant site development (and were, by Bauer and her colleagues), and cost calculations allowed little else, Post was in danger of encountering a political backlash if the authority did not seem to be tackling the problem of the slums.[30]

In truth, Post personally favored the idea of rebuilding at the core and would have proceeded on this course if financial considerations had not been at issue. In his mind, putting new construction at the fringe "drains the city at its very heart."[31] However, there was no easy way to finesse the land-cost factor if one wanted to get federal money out of Harold Ickes. The PWA administrator was fervently committed to private real-estate interests not taking advantage of government construction programs under his control, so Post knew Ickes would not approve any plan to pay more than rock-bottom prices for property. Essentially, this ruled out all of Manhattan, as assessments on even slum property on the island started at $10 per square foot. From Ickes's perspective, such prices were astronomical. The average price of all the land acquired by the Housing Division over the life of its program was 44 cents a square foot.[32]

The problem of finding land at price levels Ickes would approve was just one of the complexities city officials faced as they attempted to secure PWA housing. The whole relationship between the local level and the federal agency was undefined and ambiguous once the Housing Division became directly involved in building. Post and La Guardia struggled for as much control as possible, but the PWA was always the dominant partner, given that Ickes held the purse strings. (Even Ickes was not a free actor, since Roosevelt regularly redirected Housing Division appropriations to direct relief.) Adding to the already sizable difficulties of mounting an efficient operation, Ickes and Post heartily disliked each other. Ickes, often prickly around men from elite backgrounds, privately described the patrician Post as "a stuffed shirt without any stuffing." For his part, Post maintained that the rigid, suspicious Ickes "should have been Attorney General of the United States instead of Public Works Administrator."[33] Initially, the unpromising mix of personalities and strategies combined with real obstacles lead to inertia. Yet Post and La Guardia (and Ickes as well) could not let matters rest because they were personally committed to trying to improve housing conditions in New York City, as well as under political pressure to do so.

As 1934 dragged on with no funds forthcoming from the Housing Division, Post decided to launch a small-scale project financed with help from the Works Progress Administration (WPA), headed by the sympathetic former New Yorker Harry Hopkins. Vincent Astor, who had recently been identified by the press as the owner of rundown tenements on the Lower East Side, agreed to sell his property to the housing authority for $3.50 a square foot. Even at this modest price, the authority could not pay Astor directly, as its only source of revenue came from the sale of used bricks from buildings demolished by the city. The wealthy Astor, anxious to divest himself of the property (and the bad publicity), agreed to accept tax-free sixty-year bonds at 3.5 percent interest, in lieu of cash.

Astor's tenements were extremely old, some erected as early as 1846. In addition, they were densely built, which meant they had dark interiors. The city tore down every third building to make room for gardens and playgrounds, then joined and reconfigured the buildings that remained. Called First Houses, the project contained 122 reconditioned one-bedroom apartments. Prospective tenants found the complex appealing; over 3,000 New Yorkers requested applications.

First Houses proved to be a big public relations success for the Housing Authority. Nevertheless, the venture was not an altogether rational use of resources. Between the original cheap construction and the subsequent neglect, the buildings were so dilapidated that less than half had any parts worth saving. The others were reconstructed from scratch to look like rehabilitated old-law tenements. Thus the cost was in the same range as new construction, while the living quarters provided were constrained within a minimal building form that Post himself later described as "obsolete the day it was constructed."[34]

No other New Deal era housing programs followed First Houses' rehabilitation model, but one aspect of this venture did have a long-run impact on government housing programs. This was the successful use of the city's power of condemnation for the purpose of constructing low-rent housing. Mixed in with Astor's property were two parcels owned by landlord Andrew Müller. When Müller rejected the Housing Authority's offer for his property, the city condemned it. Müller went to court charging that the municipality did not have constitutional right to use eminent domain for land acquisition for public housing, as low-rent housing was not a public use. New York courts disagreed, however, taking a more liberal position than the PWA was encountering in the federal courts. In 1936, the Court of Appeals, the state's highest court, affirmed a lower court decision, ruling that "the menace of the slums" was "a matter of far-reaching public concern." The court stated that since regulations on private owners had failed to solve the problem, it was necessary to turn to "ownership and operation by or under the direct control of the public itself. . . ." The Müller decision would become particularly important after courts took the position that the federal government did not have the power to condemn land within the jurisdiction of states in a series of decisions starting in late 1934.[35]

While the authority was proceeding with First Houses, it also worked on obtaining land in the Williamsburg section of Brooklyn for a PWA-funded development. The reason for this location was spelled out in the authority's 1934 year-end report:

> For the first project, for which negotiations for a loan and a grant from PWA were opened, it was essential to find a site now encumbered with slum conditions with a dense population where at the same time land values were sufficiently low to permit the erection of apartments to rent at low figures.

The dilemma the authority faced was that there was political pressure to clear slums, but financially it could not afford to do so except in exceptional circumstances where developed land could be acquired relatively cheaply. Such circumstances existed in Williamsburg, and therefore this rundown section of Brooklyn—where the price of property per square foot, buildings included, averaged less than four dollars—was considered perfect. After acquiring a tract of suitable size, the authority made the site choice public in May 1934.[36]

No opportunities like Williamsburg existed on Manhattan. Planners and city officials recognized the legitimacy of the African-American community's claim for more low-rent accommodations in Harlem. In fact, the Slum Clearance Committee had identified Harlem as one of several prime locations in its first report to the Housing Division in December 1933.[37] The stumbling block was that market prices of land in Harlem, as in most other built-up sections of the city, were simply too high if buildings were to be operated on a paying basis but rents were to be kept low.

Theoretically, of course, the government could have subsidized construction and ongoing operating costs to the extent that there would be no need for rents to cover any significant proportion of costs. Neither Ickes nor Post saw this option as politically viable, however. Nor did either believe that it was politically feasible to encourage blacks to occupy the apartments in the large project projected for Williamsburg. In general, as we have seen, Ickes followed the policy of building for blacks only in neighborhoods where they already lived, and Post also shrank from the probable repercussions of integrating neighborhoods. An advisory committee to the housing authority did float a proposal to construct a complex earmarked for African Americans in an empty and remote part of the Bronx, but black civic leaders voiced united opposition, in part because they felt that population dispersal would undermine the vitality of institutions in their community.[38]

If one was willing to abandon the goal of slum clearance and concentrate solely on erecting residential units which would require only moderate rents, an attractive site did exist in Harlem. This was an open area above 151st Street bordering the East River. John D. Rockefeller, Jr., heir to the Standard Oil fortune, owned the property, and he was willing to sell it. Unfortunately his asking price was significantly higher than Ickes would countenance.

Rockefeller's Attempt to Improve Housing Conditions in Harlem

Rockefeller had acquired the tract in question at the time he was building his Paul Laurence Dunbar Apartments. An enthusiastic and ecumenical patron of architecture, the heir to the Rockefeller fortune backed construction endeavors as diverse as the art deco extravaganza of Rockefeller Center, the monument to American Georgian style at Colonial Williamsburg, and numerous innovative apartment buildings for people of modest incomes, such as the Dunbar. These last were designed by architect Andrew J. Thomas, for whom Rockefeller had named the Thomas Gardens Apartments in the Bronx.

Rockefeller hoped that both Thomas Gardens and the Dunbar would become self-sustaining cooperatives. He wanted these projects to prove that homeownership was possible in the city without government subsidies and that the private sector could provide good residential conditions even for African Americans.[39] In fact, so intent was Rockefeller on demonstrating his economic theories that he refused state and city tax abatements for which the Dunbar, as a low-profit venture, qualified under the State Housing Act of 1926. Accepting tax exemptions would have lowered costs for the residents, but according to Rockefeller's advertising brochure: "The Dunbar Cooperative Community rejoices that it has not been called on to sacrifice its own civic self-respect by foisting upon others its due proportion of the burden of taxation." This assertion that the hard-pressed black residents were so anxious to uphold the principle of unaided private enterprise that they were pleased to pay more for their living quarters sounded unlikely to housing analyst Edith Elmer Wood. In response to the advertisement's claim, she commented dryly: "one may be pardoned for a certain amount of skepticism as to the amount of the rejoicing."[40]

As it turned out, the private enterprise system, which had worked so well for Rockefeller's family, was not particularly successful for the residents of the Dunbar. After the economy went bad, wage levels in Harlem—for those who had jobs at all—were so depressed that residents were unable to continue purchasing their units by installment, even on Rockefeller's liberal terms. The development had to be converted to a rental operation, and even then the occupants had trouble making their payments. In the words of one historian, the situation indicated "the hopelessly weak economic position of the city Negro," given that Dunbar residents were a carefully screened group consisting of some of the most affluent families in Harlem.[41] With the initial phase of his Harlem housing program foundering, Rockefeller put the plans for expansion on his property to the north on indefinite hold.

Given his enormous wealth, of course, Rockefeller could have easily underwritten a total loss on the $3,300,000 endeavor. His personal fortune was estimated at approximately a half-billion dollars, and in some instances he did make outright philanthropic gifts. For example, he donated a quarter of a million dollars to build the Harlem YMCA, and his effort to restore Williamsburg, Virginia, as a shrine to the taste of the Southern planter aristocracy cost him $79 million by the mid–1930s. Rockefeller felt differently about the Dunbar, however. The Standard Oil heir wanted his Harlem apartment complex to demonstrate his conviction that good housing for low-income people could be provided entirely though the private sector. When this proved impossible, he lost interest.[42]

Post first approached Rockefeller to buy the vacant Harlem land early in June of 1934. The family's real estate business agent countered that the authority should take the open land and the financially ailing Dunbar complex as a package deal. From the city's perspective there were serious problems with this offer. Rentals at the Dunbar would have to be higher than the authority wanted to charge, while the apartments there were of a lower standard than the new PWA-funded project would be. Most important, the asking price was far higher than the city wanted to pay. Post's offer was $2 million for the apartment buildings and $3.25 per square foot for the vacant land. Rockefeller wanted $3 million for the Dunbar and $6 per square foot for the land.[43]

Apparently, when Rockefeller refused to agree to terms the city could accept, hopes for securing the site were abandoned, since the list of possible sites in the authority's 1934 year-end report did not include one in Harlem.[44] In private correspondence with the mayor, Post referred to "reluctance" at the federal level as the reason no move had been initiated to take the Rockefeller property by condemnation.[45] Yet, city leaders must also have been hesitant to take legal action against this powerful local family. Post specifically was in a difficult position, because the Rockefeller Foundation was a major source of support for local and national housing research. The foundation had provided financial backing for the Slum Clearance Committee, for example. A few months after negotiations over the Harlem property broke down, Post wrote the foundation requesting a grant on behalf of the National Public Housing Conference, an advocacy group for government-sponsored low-rent housing.[46]

The Community Campaign Intensifies

Meanwhile, with no word about a Harlem site coming from the authorities, the Consolidated Tenants League began to press for action. On May 23, 1935, the league sponsored what the *Amsterdam News* correctly predicted would be a "monster housing mass meeting," drawing a crowd of 1,500. The rally was preceded by a well-organized publicity campaign of letters to President Roosevelt, Governor Lehman, Mayor La Guardia, and Chairman Post decrying the fact that no commitment had yet been made to a Harlem site. All four took the trouble to send a reply.[47] Probably not coincidentally, La Guardia picked the day before the CTL mass meeting to tour Harlem with members of the Housing Authority, taking the occasion to promise that federal housing would be built in the district despite the high land values, which he called "just crazy."[48]

On July 2, Ickes made the first official announcement of PWA plans to build a residential development in Harlem. In reporting the story, the *Amster-*

dam News credited the "persistent campaign conducted by the Consolidated Tenants League," noting as well "stimulation by the events of the night of 19 March [the time of the riot]."[49] Ickes's statement was not a final commitment, however. The plan depended on the city securing the Rockefeller property through condemnation by the end of the month. In response to the news, the Consolidated hit the streets with flyers urging: "TENANTS OF HARLEM, WAKE UP!!! $7,000,000 from the Federal Government is knocking at your door to build houses to rent from $5 to $7 a room, per month, but the monied interests won't sell the land."[50] The Consolidated urged supporters to march on City Hall together with the Unemployed Council and called a mass meeting for the 18th of July.

Post attended this gathering. Clearly on the spot, he told the crowd that "he was afraid the League had heard him promise action so many times and he had not been to Harlem for such a long time, perhaps they felt he was stalling."[51] In fact, Post was sincere about wanting to improve living conditions in Harlem. From a privileged background (at Harvard he had been a member of the same social club as Franklin Roosevelt), Post had a long record of working for reform causes. Nevertheless, he believed that slum dwellers needed to do more than rely on sympathetic people in positions of authority like himself. Dr. Dolly, the Harlem tenant leader, reported that Post told him that "only by bringing mass pressure to bear, could housing be made a live political issue." With regard to the discontent expressed by city tenant unions in the early thirties, Post later wrote: "I am proud of the part I played in encouraging this uprising. . . ."[52] At the Consolidated's July demonstration, he told the crowd: "We won't get the land without a fight, but we'll get it."[53] A few days later he was proved correct. On July 24th the city was awarded title to the property by the courts.[54]

The Design Solution

Ever since the Harlem River Houses were completed they have been praised for their design. A committee of architects that studied the development several years after it was built called it an "outstandingly excellent job of planning."[55] To some extent, this outcome was the lucky result of a particular mix of talented architects who were given significant funding. But it was also important that these designers worked within a local environment where people were asserting their right to good housing and within a national and international climate of opinion among design professionals favorable to the artistic and social ideas Bauer called "modern housing." The design solution at Harlem River clearly indicates an attempt to create shelter that would appeal to the broad center of the population. As John Lewis Wilson, one of the architects, explained later, the designers were "interested in housing, *not* housing for the poor." The team's purpose, he maintained, was to create a residential complex which "could have been built for anybody, anywhere."[56]

The unlikely person to whom the Housing Authority gave creative control was Archibald Manning Brown, a wealthy, polo-playing society architect. Elected president of the Architectural League of New York in 1935, Brown had the professional prominence appropriate for the lead role, but his specialty was estates and country clubs.[57] The authority assigned six associates to work under Brown. Only one, Horace Ginsbern, had any significant experience designing multi-unit buildings. Luckily, Ginsbern was "one of the ablest and most prolific apartment house designers in New York City (and therefore in the United States) during the 1920s and 1930s." Other members of the team were Frank J. Forster, Charles F. Fuller, Will Rice Amon, Richard W. Buckley, and John Lewis Wilson, the first black graduate of Columbia University's school of architecture. Wilson was hired by the city after Ickes objected to initial plans for an all-white group.[58]

The strength of the team lay partly in its mix of expertise. As a result, Harlem River Houses combined in creative tension quite different, almost contradictory, planning styles, achieving advantages from each. On the one hand, the design blended the American garden apartment tradition with European-derived classicism. On the other, it combined superblock planning with a traditional orientation toward city streets.

The team's orientation toward classicism is not hard to explain. Before the 1930s, nearly all academically trained American architects were schooled in the classical tradition. This was certainly the case for the affluent Brown, who had gone on from Groton and Harvard to the École des Beaux Arts in Paris, but it was also the case for Wilson, the Columbia graduate. Wilson, as a black architect, initially found only small jobs and remodeling work after finishing school in 1928. With regard to the discontinuities between his classical training and the limited opportunities available to him, he later joked: "My training at Columbia had been in Beaux Arts methods, and I suppose I did a Beaux Arts boiler room."[59]

The self-taught Ginsbern was an expert in the American garden apartment style. This building type consisted of low-rise structures set around the perimeter of a lot, enclosing a landscaped interior. Apartment houses built in this fashion were extremely popular with the public in the 1920s and 1930s. While the garden area offered a pleasant break from the concrete and stone of the city, the interiors of apartments in such buildings were more cheerful as well. Arranged within thin buildings, the units were able to offer their inhabitants all of Henry Wright's basic criteria for a good dwelling: light, ventilation, and

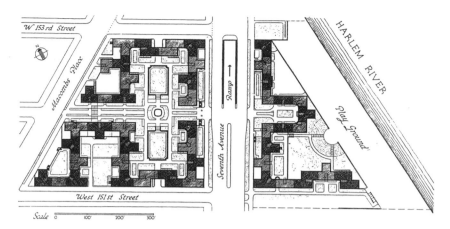

Fig. 6.2 Site plan for the Harlem River Houses, organized around two perpendicular axes. These were a large central courtyard running north and south in the main (west) section of the development and an east-west walkway on what had originally been 152nd Street. The walkway continues on the smaller plot of land to the east, visually integrating the two parts of the development. The amphitheater and play-ground at the east edge were later lost when Harlem River Drive was constructed. Reprinted with permission of *Progressive Architecture*, Penton Publishing.

view.[60] Writing in 1980, architectural historian Richard Plunz stated that this type of residential building "set a standard of urban housing for middle-class families which has not since been matched."[61]

While the site was generous in size, with 8.5 acres suitable for building, it was a difficult shape. The former Rockefeller land parcel consisted of two differently sized trapezoids cut through by a busy street (see figures 6.2 and 6.3). The property was bounded by 151st Street at the south and 153rd Street to the north. The western edge was formed by Macombs Place, and the Harlem River was the eastern boundary. The designers were allowed to close the stretch of 152nd Street that crossed the parcel, but not Seventh Avenue.[62]

To organize the buildings on the site, the architects used a simplified but elegant Beaux Arts approach based on two perpendicular axes. The horizontal element of the design was the portion of 152nd street that had been closed to traffic. The former street became a pedestrian mall on the western section of the plot. Crosscutting it, as the vertical axis of the scheme, was a long rectangular courtyard, which formed the center of the development. The horizontal axis extended across Seventh Avenue, becoming a court on the eastern section, thus pulling together the two separate pieces of the composition. After construction, one prominent architectural critic commented that even though the formal pattern of the layout was clearly apparent, "the impression

Fig. 6.3 Architect's rendering of the Harlem River Houses and the surrounding neighborhood, facing north. At the top is the Macombs Dam Bridge that crosses the Harlem River from Manhattan to the Bronx. The buildings look consistent with the size, shape, and texture of the apartment houses in this part of the city. At the same time, the arrangement conveys the sense of a unified whole. Note the higher density of land use in the pre-existing commercial housing to the west and south.

is never of any overpowering or imposed formality; it all seems merely gracious, natural, and designed."[63]

The central court on the west side was the heart of the project. With its cobblestone paving, London plane trees, and park benches, the space was serene and urbane. While away from the street, the courtyard was not isolated from the surrounding community, as it could be entered easily from the west and east via the pedestrian mall that replaced 152nd Street and also from two large passages running through the buildings to the north and south.

The complex worked as an integrated and independent design, yet it also related to the larger neighborhood. In this way, the development combined the advantages of superblock planning with conventional urban building patterns. The continuity with existing expectations as to what residential buildings should look like was important to the success of the project. In 1939, *Harper's Bazaar* published an article on New York's new public housing, written by journalist Katharine Hamill and illustrated by documentary photographer Walker Evans. Hamill compared Harlem River favorably with the larger Williamsburg development built for whites. Williamsburg, with its freestanding buildings set within large superblocks and unrelated to the surrounding

FIG. 6.4 Architect's model of the Williamsburg Houses in Brooklyn, designed by William Lescaze. This was Harlem River's sister project, intended for white residents. The off-grid parallel design is superficially reminiscent of *Zeilenbau* style but did not provide its practical advantages. The prevailing winds in this area turned the courts into wind tunnels, and many of the rooms were not properly oriented for receiving good sunlight. The Carl Mackley Houses, though they had a more traditional appearance and fit into their environment more comfortably, did provide many of the advantages of *Zeilenbau* planning. The Harlem River Houses looked like commercial New York apartment buildings of the era, but they were designed on superblocks containing extensive landscaped grounds (a core modern housing idea). AP/Wide World Photos.

streets, was a harbinger of what was to become the stereotypical United States "housing project" (see figure 6.4). While Hamill praised the interior design of the apartments, she was clearly put off by the "huge set of blocks placed in irregular regularity along the long stretch of concrete walks. . . ." In contrast, she noted approvingly that at Harlem River "the whole mass and substance of the buildings are more what-we-are-accustomed-to—set squarely, conservatively, straight with the streets."[64] Hamill was responding to the fact that the architects, while taking advantage of the increased possibilities inherent in plots larger than city blocks, still observed enough of the city's traditional design conventions that their creation fit comfortably into the neighborhood around it. Another way in which the design was familiar was that it provided apartments in a city of apartment dwellers. By the 1930s, the habit of apartment living had "filtered up" to even the most affluent of New York City's residents.[65]

At Harlem River Houses there were 574 units of varying sizes. The smallest consisted of a living room combined with a small kitchen (called a "kitchen-ette"), one bedroom, and a bathroom. The largest had three bedrooms, an eat-in kitchen, living room, and bathroom. The interior dwelling space, although small, was well laid out. A committee of the New York Chapter of the American Institute of Architects (AIA) that evaluated public housing in the city in 1949 commended the apartments for their high standards of livability, since they were well arranged from the standpoint of room privacy, flexibility for furniture placement, ventilation, and outlook.[66]

Although the overall design of Harlem River Houses was physically similar to (if more handsome than) typical market-produced New York apartment complexes of the time, it differed significantly from a commercial operation in the services it offered. The development included a nursery school with an attached outdoor play area, a tuberculosis diagnostic clinic, a baby welfare clinic, a branch of the New York Public Library, social rooms, and, on the river side, a large athletic field (destroyed when Harlem River Drive was built in 1957).[67]

As it turned out, the seemingly anomalous choice of Archibald Manning Brown, the prestigious society architect, to lead a team of designers in charge of a large-scale housing project for black New Yorkers was an auspicious decision. While Ginsbern seems to have been primarily responsible for key design decisions, Brown's self-assurance must have been important in creating a high level of morale within the work group he administered. His inclusive attitude toward African Americans must also have been a positive factor. Wilson later described how Brown welcomed him to the team, treating him from the first with an easy friendliness and later offering him work on other projects.[68] The AIA committee mentioned earlier concluded that, with few exceptions such as Harlem River, the city's subsidized housing stock was of a lower quality than necessary, even taking into account the budgetary stringencies. It censured the authority and its architects for succumbing to "psychological obstacles to the realization of aesthetic values, which, in general, are avoided not because they add to costs so much as in deference to hostile public opinion, which still thinks of public housing in terms of minimum provision for the amenities of living."[69] According to Wilson, the group of architects he joined were "proud people," intent on producing something good and confident enough not to fear criticism for achieving it.[70]

Life at the Harlem River Houses

Harlem River Houses were ready for occupancy in mid-October of 1937, and response from the housing-hungry community was overwhelming. Over 14,000 families applied for admission to the 574 apartments, almost twice the ratio of applicants to apartments that occurred at the development's sister project in Williamsburg, which was slated for white occupancy. The New York City Housing Authority had the task of dealing with the avalanche of applications.[71]

To cope with the problem of tremendous demand but limited supply, the authority attempted to construct a procedure of "mathematical impartiality" to rate applicants by "need and merit." Interviewers made home visits to prospects who looked promising on paper and awarded them points based on the condition of the places where they were then living. The worst situations rated the highest scores. Post explained that "this method of selection was our answer to the claims that the people who needed housing would not get it, that politics, discrimination, and an inability properly to investigate would militate against a fair and equitable selection."[72]

Although the rating system seems to have been administered with admirable impartiality, the procedure did include noneconomic criteria that would be open to question in later years. At the same time as an applicant's current living quarters were being evaluated, the Housing Authority investigator assigned the candidate points on the basis of "good character" and "cleanliness." As one public relations pamphlet put it: "Tidiness raised the score considerably. . . ." Also, it was taken for granted that applicants should live in what was then regarded as an optimal family unit consisting of mother, father, and children—no more and no less. Lorinda Johnson, an early tenant, described years later how she believed that she hurt her chances for selection when the development opened by applying for accommodations large enough to share with her brother-in-law who lived with her family.[73] By the time she tried again for admission, she understood the assumption that apartments were intended for nuclear families only, and she asked for quarters just large enough for her husband, her child, and herself. This time she gained admission.[74] Thus, the point system not only favored families that fit a particular image, it actively shaped ones like Johnson's.

Looking back, the noneconomic criteria the authority used might be seen as culturally exclusive, but there is no evidence of objections being made to them by the black community at the time. Even Lorinda Johnson, who lost her second child to pneumonia in a cold apartment after she was initially turned down for not conforming to the authority's definition of a proper family, did not question the legitimacy of the conception. Given the huge ratio of applicants to apartments, it was not hard to fill the complex with those who did or would fit.

By themselves, however, even high levels of "merit" and need were not sufficient to get people into Harlem River Houses. One also had to possess enough income, although not too much. Again, the size of the applicant pool made it possible to employ very specific criteria. Minimum income was based on the rent required to generate enough money to pay back fifty-five percent of the capital costs of the development to the federal government over sixty years (the other forty-five percent was written off as a grant from the PWA) and cover operating expenses. To achieve the required level of income, rents at Harlem River were initially set from $19.16 to $31.35 per month, depending on the size of the apartment. (These charges covered heat and water but excluded the cost of fuel for light and cooking.) The Housing Authority expected not only that tenants would have incomes sufficient to cover such rents, but also that their earnings would be high enough to ensure that their shelter costs would consume only about twenty percent of their income. This was the rent-to-income ratio endorsed by social work authorities of the time, who believed that if low-income families spent more than this on shelter they would have to cut back on consumption of basic necessities. The maximum income allowed was set by the 1936 George-Healy Act, which mandated that PWA tenants could earn no more than five times the maximum rent plus utility charges.[75] Given that the minimum income set by the authority was almost the same as the federally specified maximum, the range of acceptable earnings was obviously rather narrow. Again, however, the immense pressure for housing meant that there were more than enough qualified applicants, although a significant amount of administrative work was needed to verify and constantly monitor earnings. After World War II, when incomes rose, the limits would cause significant disruptions in the lives of residents, because many were forced to move out.

In the 1930s, the authority's financial criteria meant that residents of Harlem River Houses were a comparatively well-off group. Average yearly earnings were $1,312.50 at a time when median income for black families in New York was $837. Yet even though family earnings at the complex were higher than typical for black New Yorkers, in general residents did not hold prestigious jobs. Like many African Americans in this period, a significant proportion worked below their skill level because of racial prejudice in the workplace. Miriam Burns, who grew up at Harlem River, described how her mother, a college graduate, was only able to find work as a live-in maid when she came to New York City from Texas in the early 1930s. After marriage and throughout her life, she worked cleaning people's houses. Like Burns's mother, over 60 percent of the residents who held jobs outside the home worked in occupations commonly classified as unskilled, such as elevator operator, waiter, porter, or house cleaner. Only 4.5 percent held professional jobs. The reason that the Harlem River residents' earning power compared so favorably with that of black New Yorkers generally was that each family had at least one wage-earner and close to one-fourth had two, at a time when unemployment was at least 40 percent in Harlem.[76]

Once settled in, the new residents could choose to participate in a wide range of social and educational activities. A 1939 management report noted that residents had organized a tenants' association, community newspaper, women's club, mothers' group to support the work of the WPA recreational programs for children, men's club, parent-teachers association of the nursery school, and Boy Scout troop. These groups met in the buildings' large basement rooms, which had been designated for community use. In addition to activities organized by the tenants themselves, some programs were run by staff provided by outside agencies. WPA personnel conducted afternoon and evening recreation programs for school-age children, including classes in dancing, puppetry, and dramatics. The city's Recreation Department provided supervisors for the municipal tennis and handball courts located on the river side of the complex. Although most staff supplied by outside organizations worked with children, the WPA did send personnel from the Federal Theater program to coach an adult drama class and provided teachers for other adult educational programs.[77]

The nursery school was the major social program at the development (figure 6.5). The architects had designed a large, well-organized space of interconnecting rooms with kitchen facilities and an attached outdoor play area specifically for a school. The New York Kindergarten Association, a private organization, managed the operation. In 1939, 140 children between the ages of two and five attended either in the morning or afternoon. Some lived at Harlem River Houses, while others came from the surrounding neighborhood. The association provided the full-time professional staff, and the National Youth Administration and local teacher-training schools sent assistant teachers. As at the Carl Mackley Houses, the nursery school promoted adult participation. Nixcola Ramsay, an original tenant who remembered attending Harlem River's dedication ceremony, which featured Mayor LaGuardia, first worked at the school as a volunteer and eventually joined the paid staff. After almost fifty years of residence, Ramsay described herself as a "flag waver for Harlem River Houses."[78]

Formal group activity in the early years was largely confined to the spheres of recreation and education. Residents did not vie for administrative prerogatives. Even those who were active in the tenants' association seemed to conceive of their group as an adjunct to the Housing Authority administration rather than as a vehicle for representing interests that might at times diverge from those of management. According to one early resident, the purpose of the association was: "to take up any difficulties the tenants were having or things that they didn't understand, [such as] certain policies of the housing office. [The tenants' association] would help to interpret it to them."[79]

The low level of apparent tension between residents and management at

Fig. 6.5 A nursery school at Harlem River Houses. This photograph shows a class from 1938. As at the Mackley Houses, the nursery school was one of the most successful aspects of the development, functioning to integrate adults into the community as well as providing a service for children.

Harlem River was not characteristic of all of the city's housing in the 1930s and 1940s. At Williamsburg Houses, some tenants attempted to influence tenant selection procedures not long after they themselves had moved in. The Williamsburg tenant activists also tried to get income rules modified so that families whose earnings increased would not have to move out immediately.[80] Nothing similar occurred at Harlem River. Different explanations were advanced to explain why. One journalist maintained that most public housing tenants did "not seem to resent what kindly institutionalism exists in the projects." She assured her readers that "only the fractious and the supersensitive tenants complain."[81] Another view was offered by a WPA researcher who suggested that the giant waiting list for housing in Harlem made tenants wary of "making trouble."[82]

Fear may have played a role in suppressing criticism at Harlem River, but the development was also well run. Long-time manager Roger Flood described his administrative philosophy as an effort "at all times to maintain a sympathetic approach." Flood combined tact with experience at running a large residential property. An African American, he had studied architecture at New York University and worked for apartment designer Andrew J. Thomas. For eight years, Flood supervised maintenance at Rockefeller's Dunbar development, briefly serving as manager there before accepting his position with the city. At Harlem River, Flood won the respect of children as well as adults. Vincent Hammond, who lived in the complex as a child and went on to become director of planning for a suburban bus authority, described Flood as a "role model."[83]

Despite competent and diplomatic management, at least one administrative procedure seemed designed to grate on more than the "supersensitive." This was the combination rent collection and apartment inspection that occurred each week. Social worker Miriam Burns, who lived at Harlem River as a child, explained: "In the olden days, in terms of collecting rent, we had a white woman, I guess she was a manager, and she came to the house and collected the rent." Burns observed that even though it would seem "unbelievable" now, while the housing official was in the apartment "she was not averse to looking in the refrigerator or whatever." When questioned as to whether her mother resented such behavior, Burns insisted that her mother never seemed to mind. She speculated that her mother, like many African Americans prior to the civil rights movement of the 1950s, was simply not that assertive. Also, Burns wondered if her mother might actually have enjoyed the regular opportunity to display her meticulous housekeeping.[84]

To a certain extent, it may have been that tenants at Harlem River were so relieved to be free of the many assaults on their dignity that slum living entailed, that having their apartments examined struck them as trivial in comparison. Melvin Ford, a resident interviewed for a magazine article in 1939 commented: "We're lucky to be here. We're sure lucky. It's a lot better than where we were or than where most folks live."[85] Whatever the true feelings of residents regarding paternalistic management procedures such as apartment inspections, their lack of resistance must have pleased Housing Authority administrators. In this period, the authority's philosophy was that recreational activities were the only appropriate form of resident participation—as opposed to involvement with actual administrative decisions.[86]

With regard to the physical and social aspects of their environment, most residents seem to have been very contented. Priscilla Reed, who served as tenant association president during the 1980s, commented that in the fifties when she moved in, "I thought I was in a new world, it was so beautiful."[87] The complex was particularly appealing to children. David Scott, who lived at Harlem River as a boy in the thirties and forties and went on to become a precinct police chief in New York City, described living at Harlem River as "almost like a status symbol."[88] He and others who grew up there remember a great range of activities in which they participated, recalling with special fondness such highlights as ice skating in the winter in the sunken court in the central plaza and watching movies projected onto the backboards of the handball courts on hot summer nights. Many youthful friendships started there continued into adult life, and adults likewise got to know each other. In the words of Edward McClendon, who moved in as a boy of six with his parents when Harlem River opened and went on to become Director of Community Affairs for the New York City Housing Authority, "It was like living in a small town."[89] Vincent Hammond related that, like all kids, they got into their share of trouble, but "all the parents knew us, so we could only get into so much devilmaking." Along with the advantages, however, went a certain amount of pressure. In Hammond's words, "It was, as we looked at it, the great experiment: to see how our generation would do given decent housing."[90] Like him, many went on to professional careers. Robert Moses, one member of this first generation of children at Harlem River, gained national prominence as the Director of SNCC's 1964 Mississippi Summer voter registration project.[91]

People who have lived at Harlem River consistently attribute its tranquility and neighborliness in great part to the development's design. The low-rise four and five story buildings wrap around small courtyards, making it possible for parents to look out of apartment windows and supervise children playing outside (figure 6.6). The possibility of playing within sight of one's parents made Harlem River, in the words of a person who grew up there, "a homey kind of place."[92] The central court was another popular feature. In the 1980s, long-time resident Nixcola Ramsay was a widow who was living by herself. Explaining why she thought the courtyard was the best part of the complex, she said, "In the summer it's delightful. You can sit out in the court and you won't feel lonesome, because if you're alone you'll have someone to talk to."[93]

The prosperity that followed the Second World War proved a double-edged sword for many at Harlem River Houses, as their incomes rose above what was allowed by the authority's rigid guidelines. The city offered openings in its middle-income apartment buildings to the over-income families, but these developments were high rises with apartment layouts inferior to Harlem River. Rather than take this option, a number of families bought their own homes in Queens. In the opinion of their children, the adults would not have left had they not been compelled. They liked Harlem River and had close friends there.[94]

Harlem River after a Half-Century

Contemporary conditions at Harlem River Houses are characterized by continuing high morale and affection for the complex. The condition of the buildings and landscaping, while not what it once was, does compare favorably to that of publicly and privately owned low-rent housing in other American cities. Of the many social programs from the early years, the one that contin-

Fig. 6.6 Children at play in the wading pool at Harlem River Houses in the 1940s. This photograph conveys the intimate scale of the courts and the child-friendly atmosphere.

ues into the present is the one for young children. In the same facilities that the architects originally designed for a children's center, a large and well orga- nized nursery school continues to function.

Since the 1970s, however, there has been significant tenant activism. By contrast with the first decades, residents now organize around issues that are not exclusively recreational and social. Grievances related to security and maintenance have led them to challenge the Housing Authority at the high- est levels. (Apartment inspections are not a source of friction, as these were discontinued in the 1960s.) Probably the single biggest source of conflict in recent years has concerned admissions policy. Two recent heads of the tenants' association, Priscilla Reed and William Booker, disagree with the Housing Authority's current willingness to allow people with no jobs to move in, ar- guing that the long-term unemployed often have a host of problems that make them difficult neighbors. Reed and Booker believe the complex would func- tion better if there were regulations in place restricting residency to low- income working people.[95]

Val Coleman, Director of Information for the Housing Authority during the 1980s, disagreed with this perspective. Responding to the position of the tenants' association, Coleman asked: if only the working poor can move into public housing, where are the very poor to go? In his opinion, public housing should be the refuge of the poor, but it cannot serve this function if tenants of public projects refuse to admit poor people. This issue, in Coleman's view, exposes a key pitfall of the current enthusiasm for tenant management.[96]

Like the Carl Mackley Houses, in the late 1980s the Harlem River Houses celebrated its fiftieth anniversary.[97] The Harlem River event made it clear how much (despite some conflicts with management) residents continue to appreciate the development. As tenants' association President Priscilla Reed stated in her address at the fiftieth anniversary celebration in September 1987:

> For fifty years [Harlem River Houses] has worked. Not always perfectly! As president of the Tenants Association these many years, I've had my share of differences with the landlord. The Housing Authority and I have tangled more than once . . . but that's what it's all about . . . making life better . . . in a living, breathing community.[98]

In line with Reed's interpretation that resident assertiveness represents engagement, not alienation, the decade of the 1970s saw tenants take a more active role in a variety of ways. For instance, former and current residents took the initiative in obtaining landmark status for Harlem River Houses in 1975. Also, past and present tenants began to organize reunions, drawing people from around the country. Both the landmark designation and the reunions represent an effort to celebrate and preserve the special physical and social amenities of the development.[99]

Reed's anniversary address also makes it clear that some of the ideas associated with the modern housing approach continue to live on. According to Reed:

> When the first tenants moved into Harlem River Houses in 1937 it was an experiment. The idea was to bring together the best of the best: the best architects, the best building materials, plenty of land and plenty of sunlight, great art, the latest developments in electric lighting and refrigeration, a health care center, a place for children and this beautiful courtyard where we could grow up and grow old . . . in peace.[100]

In terms of the development's actual history, Reed's appraisal is obviously somewhat romanticized. It does, however, accurately reflect currents of thinking about housing that were circulating internationally in the interwar period and that Catherine Bauer articulated as the modern housing program. Reed did not seem to have learned these ideas through reading but, instead, through living in a place where they were implemented under favorable circumstances. In a rare twist on "separate but equal" policies, African Americans in Harlem obtained in this complex some of the most attractive low-rental housing ever produced in the United States.

Conclusion

In a number of ways, the history of the Harlem River Houses parallels the Mackley experience. Both developments originated in strong local social movements that were able to overcome serious obstacles. Talented and committed architects attached themselves to both projects and, for each enterprise, came up with plans that combined beauty with livability. In both cases, the designs were influenced by modernist currents in architecture but still provided aesthetic continuity with residents' previous experience of the built environment. The Harlem River Houses may be the most successful aesthetically, but both developments were excellent by the standards not just of public or subsidized housing, but of any kind of housing. Both provided a wide range of social services and programs on-site. They were, in short, quite successful incarnations of what Bauer articulated as the modern housing ideal.[101]

Possibly it is just a coincidence that two projects of such high quality both originated partly as a result of social movements rather than merely from decisions of philanthropists or government agencies. It is also possible, however, that, at least in the American context, issues of democracy and power can be separated from issues about how to provide social welfare programs only at significant peril to the chances of success for liberal or social-democratic political purposes.

Accordingly, it is not surprising that the major limitations of both projects have to do with issues of control. Each may have come into existence to a significant extent as a result of grassroots initiatives, but each was administered in a benevolently paternalistic fashion. The higher level of self-organization and activity at the Mackley can be explained by the fact that many of the people who came to live there were already political activists, in contrast to the original tenants at Harlem River, who were more focused on living coherent family lives and making the most of their opportunities. The Civil Rights Movement and the tumults of the 1960s changed the climate, so that by the 1970s some of the spirit that had animated Harlem's tenant struggles of the 1930s characterized residents' attitudes at the Harlem River Houses.

Admissions policy has become the most contested issue between residents and management in recent years at Harlem River. The antagonism generated by this issue seems somewhat predictable, given that it concerns a basic axis of control. The nature of one's neighbors in a relatively dense environment of an apartment complex is probably the single most important determinant of the livability of one's housing, and lack of any voice in choosing these neighbors is a critical form of disempowerment. Americans in general desire this kind of control. Middle-class people living in suburban communities, for instance, use a variety of techniques to ensure that they will not be surrounded by those whom they consider undesirable. But the institutional structure of both Mackley (when it was still owned by the union) and Harlem River made this kind of control unlikely.

Basic decisions were made from above at each of these housing developments, but both were run by capable, honest, and committed managers, and they provided humane and livable environments. In many ways, the atmosphere was not entirely different from that created by some of the Europeans Bauer admired. Ernst May's housing, for example, was and continues to be managed along benevolently paternalistic lines. But in a different political and social situation, this kind of administrative structure has provided more liveable environments than similar regimes created in the United States. The difference is not just that the European projects receive more funding, although that matters a great deal, but also that tenants there are in a very different legal position. They benefit from security of tenure and a variety of other rights that greatly narrow the gap between renting and owning. Accordingly, tenants in May's Frankfurt projects routinely remodel their apartments; in many ways, they are not very different from owners in condominium associations in the United States who turn over most management rights and responsibilities to a professional firm. If anything, the European tenants are likely to feel more attached to their homes and be more residentially stable, since they do not accumulate equity they can realize upon exit. In the United States, however, such paternalism, however benign, is unlikely to meet with much acclaim since American aspirations for democracy and self-determination are so intense.

One significant difference between the Harlem River Houses and the Mackley is that at the New York complex there is more consciousness among residents of the experimental significance of the housing they live in. The contrast between the remarks Priscilla Reed made at Harlem River's 50th anniversary and the comments by Margaret Traynor on the parallel occasion at Mackley is striking. Perhaps the fact that the Philadelphia complex is now fully within the for-profit housing market means that more historical imagination is required to recall the original purposes of the development. Probably another factor is that Mackley residents never organized around their common concerns as tenants whereas Harlem River residents did.

Finally, the financial structure of the Harlem River Houses is important. Unlike either Mackley or the Amalgamated co-ops, and unlike the experiments and demonstration projects described in earlier chapters, Harlem River succeeded in providing modest but appealing housing to people who had very low incomes relative to other Americans. The complex did so, of course, on the basis of major subsidies: a capital grant covering almost half of construction costs, extremely generous financing terms for the remainder of the costs, and other subsidies since. Of course, other forms of American housing (including privately owned homes) have also benefited from a variety of public subsidies, so this kind of aid is not unique. What *is* unusual is that, compared with other directly subsidized American housing, Harlem River Houses provided an environment that might well have appealed to a broad spectrum of Americans.

SEVEN

The Struggle to Shape
Permanent Policy

J ust as the first PWA housing developments were getting started, crucial battles over the direction of federal housing policy were being fought out in Congress. While a number of important pieces of legislation related to the housing sector were passed during the 1930s, whether and how the federal government would support a national stock of noncommercial housing was in many respects the key issue. The decision would define not only what Americans would come to think of as "public housing," but also the overall pattern of government activity in the housing sector for decades to come. Senator Robert Wagner began introducing bills that would mandate permanent direct government involvement in 1935, and two years later, a much-amended version of his bill became law. At the time and since, the 1937 Wagner Public Housing Act has been viewed as a progressive measure, but it could equally well be interpreted as an important brake on the social democratic possibilities of the New Deal.

While modern housing advocates hoped that permanent federal policy would support the development of a broadly acceptable new kind of urban dwelling, as it turned out, the 1937 legislation mandated a weaker program with significantly cheaper construction compared with that of the PWA Housing Division. Some of the PWA housing developments were physically similar to commercial middle-income apartment complexes of their day, and they did prove appealing to people with options, as at the Mackley and at Harlem River after the war. By contrast, the housing produced under the Wagner Act usually looked unambiguously like the poor peoples' housing that it was in fact meant to be. Thus, passage of the Wagner Public Housing Act marked the institutionalization of a two-tier framework for federal intervention into the housing market.

The Variety of Early New Deal Housing Programs

In the early summer of 1933, when the Public Works Administration was setting up a federal housing agency in accordance with the National Industrial Recovery Act, normally vigilant private real estate interests were moribund at the national level. Not only did industry groups raise no clamor in Washington at the time the NIRA was passed, no serious objections were made in the months following. In November, the head of the Home Builders and Land

Developers National Committee did try to rouse his members to action with a proposal for a march on Washington to protest government competition, but nothing came of the plan.[1]

Real estate interests typically rallied somewhat when the Housing Division began work in their own city, but by this stage they were restricted to localized and defensive struggles. For instance, the Atlanta Real Estate Board and the Atlanta Apartment Homeowners Association, arguing that they already faced a 25 percent vacancy rate, opposed PWA plans for Techwood Homes, an apartment complex to be built adjacent to Georgia Institute of Technology. Not only were these groups unable to enroll public support for their position, but they also faced organized opposition from important elements of Atlanta's business community and from influential local organizations. In fact, the Housing Division was encouraged to move forward on the project by a group that included the president of the Atlanta Chamber of Commerce, the publisher of the *Atlanta Constitution*, the president of Georgia Tech, a representative from the city's unions, and the mayor. As Charles F. Palmer, the Atlanta business executive who promoted the development, candidly admitted, many local interests stood to gain if the PWA went forward. The proposed site was a derelict area close to the central business district. Property values would be stabilized if the PWA cleared the area and built on it. In addition, the local economy would be stimulated by the contracts, jobs, and materials procurement that federal construction would stimulate.[2]

The Atlanta situation illustrates how significant support was often forthcoming for PWA housing endeavors. Nevertheless, this program represented only one kind of federal intervention into the housing arena in the early years of the New Deal. As the government groped for methods of stimulating the economy and responded to the demands of various constituencies, it launched a variety of initiatives. Many of these were aimed at resuscitating commercial real estate activity, most frequently through attempts to increase liquidity in mortgage markets. Due in good part to the success of these efforts, the resources and morale of real estate entrepreneurs began improving, and by mid-decade they were able to respond more energetically and effectively to the threat posed by publicly aided noncommercial housing.

As described in chapter 4, the first piece of permanent federal housing legislation predated the New Deal. Hoover's Federal Home Loan Bank Act of 1932 linked mortgage lenders throughout the country into a federally regulated network with a common credit pool. Though useful to the mortgage industry and still in effect today, this initial federal involvement, by itself, was insufficient to stop the financial free fall of residential real estate. By 1933, approximately half of the twenty billion dollars of national mortgage debt was in default, with foreclosures still on the rise.[3]

To deal with this crisis, Roosevelt, soon after taking office, urged creation of the Home Owners Loan Corporation (HOLC) to refinance personal mortgages. In its first year of operation, the HOLC loaned more than three billion dollars on over one million mortgages, helping to save 10 percent of all owner-occupied nonfarm residences. Politically, it was a brilliant move. Historian Arthur Schlesinger, Jr., believes that "probably no single measure consolidated so much middle-class support for the New Deal" as the HOLC. Roosevelt wanted to support homeownership for more than opportunistic reasons, however. Like Hoover before him, FDR thought that "the broad interest of the nation requires [that] special safeguards be thrown around homeownership as a guarantee of economic and social stability." Here Roosevelt was expressing both a cultural preference for homeownership and an intention to use it to maintain political equilibrium.[4]

Although the HOLC did contain the national foreclosure crisis, it was not successful at restoring the real estate market to health, much less at reinflating the general economy. Toward the end of 1933, Roosevelt started casting around for measures by which the government could stimulate residential construction, which he regarded as "the wheel within the wheel to move the whole economic engine." He asked some of the major figures connected with his administration to advise him on a long-term program, including Harry Hopkins, Henry Wallace, Frances Perkins, Rexford Tugwell, John Fahey, and Averell Harriman. The majority initially favored some kind of large-scale, publicly financed construction program, but Roosevelt's growing unease about budget deficits convinced him to back a plan involving little direct federal spending. This became the National Housing Act of 1934.[5]

Marriner Eccles, then special assistant to Treasury Secretary Henry Morgenthau, Jr., played a key role in drafting the legislation. As Eccles recounted in his memoirs, he was committed to making sure that the housing program "be private in character." The act created the Federal Housing Administration (FHA), which provided federal insurance for home rehabilitation loans and mortgages for newly purchased homes. Privately operated financial institutions were to make these loans based on specified criteria. Mortgages had to be fully amortizing, meaning that the borrower paid off both principal and interest in equal-sized installments over the life of the loan. This kind of mortgage allowed a much higher percentage of the home value to be financed than had previously been the convention. For buyers, this meant lower down payments and less necessity for expensive second loans. By making homeownership easier to swing financially, the guidelines aimed at expanding the market. At the same time, the insurance lowered risks for the mortgage industry. Eccles described the mechanism of federal guarantees for private loans as a device that "avoided any direct encroachment by the government on the domain of private business, but which used the power of government to establish the conditions under which private initiative could feed itself and multiply its own benefits." (A better statement of the principles of indirect government intervention in support of business could hardly be found.) Evidence for the success of the FHA policies in increasing investor confidence was provided by the movement of private capital back into residential building business. In 1934, housing starts were up for the first time in eight years. They continued to climb until the war.[6]

Success for the private market, however, hardly translated into good news for those seeking to expand the PWA housing program. Housing economist Paul Wendt, in his comparative analysis of housing policy in industrial nations, concludes that by the later stages of the New Deal the success of the Federal Home Loan Banks, the HOLC, and the FHA was such that "the ambitious housing programs of the PWA and the Resettlement Administration during the mid-depression years were looked upon as unnecessary and visionary."[7]

The shift that Wendt describes did not happen without conflict. Better times emboldened private operators to oppose any role in which the government might operate as a competitor (although not activities that served to support business). Yet, because the PWA was defined from the beginning as a temporary agency, the struggle over how much of the market the government would enter directly did not occur in relation to the PWA's Housing Division. Instead, the fight took place over whether there would be a permanent federal program of directly assisted housing construction at all and, if so, how it would function.

The Labor Housing Conference

The FHA foreshadowed the general orientation of federal public policy related to housing, but before the overall structure of the New Deal housing reforms crystallized, the Labor Housing Conference (LHC) urged a very different approach. The organization was started by officials and supporters of the Hosiery Workers and other trade unionists in the Philadelphia region who wanted to secure a large-scale program of worker-initiated housing developments along the lines of the Carl Mackley Houses and European projects. The LHC was formally established at the annual convention of the Pennsylvania Federation of Labor in May 1934. Speakers at the kickoff meeting included John A. Phillips, president of the Pennsylvania Federal of Labor; a sprinkling of federal officials from such agencies as the Federal Emergency Relief Administration; Mrs. Cornelia Bryce Pinchot, wife of the Republican governor of Pennsylvania; Abraham Kazan, administrator of the Amalgamated Clothing Workers co-operative housing in New York City; Edith Elmer Wood, the housing analyst and reform advocate who had recently been appointed to the New Jersey Housing Authority; Charles Hollopeter of the Central Labor Union in Camden, New Jersey; and Oskar Stonorov, one of the two architects who designed the Carl Mackley Houses. James J. McDevitt, president of the Building Trades Council of Philadelphia, agreed to head the group, and Catherine Bauer accepted the invitation to become executive secretary.[8]

In the words of a 1934 resolution to the American Federation of Labor (AFL) submitted by the president of the Pennsylvania Federation, the Labor Housing Conference proposed federal, state, and municipal financing of "large-scale planned housing developments on a non-profit basis, designed, constructed and administered in direct collaboration with bona fide groups of workers and consumers."[9] The group's strategy was to organize union members around the country into local housing committees and to convince the AFL to endorse and put resources into pushing its program. As was described in chapter 2, the AFL had supported federal involvement in building for working-class families during World War I and throughout the immediate postwar period. In the years following, however, its position shifted. The *American Federationist*, the AFL's official journal, concluded in 1932 that government-sponsored housing programs on the European model ran counter to American "ideals of individual initiative and rights." The journal asserted that "since the American working man revolts against direct government intervention in providing his home, the government can encourage him only by loans or tax exemptions."[10]

Early in 1934, as the Labor Housing Conference was first developing, Bauer was in the last stages of finishing *Modern Housing*. Her affair with Lewis Mumford was winding down and, at the same time, she was losing patience with his approach to politics. Mumford and the other socially concerned planners and architects who formed her professional circle behaved as though major political change could be effected through rational appeals to efficiency and justice. Although keenly dissatisfied with the pace and direction of the PWA's housing work, they simply went on writing articles and making speeches. Frustrated, she observed that the "energy used up on talking, writing and designing 'low-cost housing' during the past few years in this country would probably, in a simpler society, have served to carve an entire city out of the wilderness."[11]

Years later, Bauer concluded that the behavior of many of her associates in the 1930s sprang from assumptions pervasive in this period as to the sources of social change. Writing shortly before her death in 1964, she stated that during the interwar period, "quite apart from one's political belief, it seemed inevitable to almost every sophisticated person that collective ways of living would result from modern technology." It was taken for granted that the future held "good mass produced meals, in great apartment complexes where all the services were done for us." As it turned out, technological development did not automatically usher in the cooperative commonwealth. In fact, it did just the opposite. Within the institutional context that existed, machines had been used "to make ourselves freer and more self-sufficient in the house rather than less."[12]

In contrast to her associates, Bauer was not temperamentally suited to waiting for the emergence of what Mumford assumed to be the "basic communism which is latent in the emerging economic order."[13] She reasoned that any effort to substantially restructure the field of residential real estate would face "bitter and organized opposition" from powerful interests throughout the country.[14] Where was pressure sufficient to overturn the status quo to come from? Certainly not, she decided, from a small group of "unemployed architects and scattered idealists," nor "a handful of trained specialists hired by the Government."[15] Based on her analysis of the conditions that produced the European housing programs, she concluded that drastic changes in American housing would be possible only through a militant grassroots housing movement composed of "those who are the most directly and vitally *interested*, families who need better houses to live in and workers who need work building those houses." She advocated democratic self-determination in how housing would come into existence and also in how it would be run. Not only did ordinary people have to demand better homes for themselves, "workers' and consumers' representatives must be delegated real power and responsibility in every department of the housing operation, from surveys and policies straight through to administration." When she was offered the position of executive secretary to the Labor Housing Conference, Bauer saw her chance to be part of organizing the kind of grassroots movement she deemed essential. Trade unions had to take the lead in the housing movement, she believed, since "the only large body of organized consumers today is organized labor."[16]

Working with the Labor Housing Conference, Bauer ultimately reached a wide audience. At the beginning, however, the LHC was a shoestring operation. Bauer worked out of a corner of Stonorov's and Alfred Kastner's architectural offices in Philadelphia and had to devote much of her time to soliciting donations. Even so, there was very little money. She wisecracked to her mother that the dreary room she took in downtown Philadelphia when she moved to the city gave her a chance "to learn about the slums firsthand."[17]

By summer 1934, the organization was gaining momentum. Central labor councils in New York City, and in Boston and Lawrence, Massachusetts, established housing committees that became affiliates. In June, over 800 union delegates from the greater New York City region gathered to consider the housing question. The unionists listened to Bauer's presentation, as well as addresses by Mayor La Guardia, Tenement House Commissioner Langdon

Post, George Meany of the Building Trades Council, James C. Quinn, president of the Central Trades and Labor Council, and Charney Vladeck, a member of the New York City Housing Authority and editor of the *Jewish Daily Forward*. Participants established a housing committee to be affiliated with the LHC and endorsed a resolution calling on government authorities to treat housing as a "public utility" similar to roads and education.[18] Two months later, the Massachusetts Federation of Labor passed resolutions at its annual meeting endorsing the concept of a government-supported housing program organized outside of the commercial market and also established a committee to be affiliated with the Labor Housing Conference.[19]

That same summer the LHC gained national exposure for its platform when it issued a joint statement with the Housing Study Guild of New York and the Philadelphia Chapter of the Federation of Architects, Engineers, Chemists and Technicians condemning the direction the Roosevelt Administration was taking with regard to housing policy. The statement blamed the slow pace of the PWA Housing Division on lack of administration support and characterized the National Housing Act, which established the Federal Housing Administration (FHA), as a "thoroughly bogus measure, which will be of no immediate service either to workers or consumers, and which may work to their eventual harm." Daily newspapers around the country, including the *New York Herald Tribune*, picked up the story, and the *New Republic* ran a supportive editorial.[20]

By fall 1934, the Labor Housing Conference had organized support in New Jersey, Connecticut, and North Carolina, as well as in New York, Massachusetts, and Pennsylvania.[21] Bauer and her colleagues felt confident of an endorsement from the American Federation of Labor when it met for its annual national convention in San Francisco in October. At the convention, John Phillips, head of the Pennsylvania Federation, introduced a resolution calling on the federal government to make an immediate $500 million allocation to a low-rent housing program, to initiate demonstration projects in every industrial center, and to support groups of union members and consumers who wanted to initiate nonprofit housing projects. But neither this nor the more moderate resolution submitted on behalf of the LHC by M. J. McDonough of the Building Trades Department passed. Instead, the convention adopted only a vague recommendation instructing the Executive Council "to continue its efforts to have a practical and far-reaching Housing Program put into effect." Despite this setback, the group gained exposure for its platform within the labor movement nationally, and Bauer, Edelman, and McDevitt were soon meeting with the leadership of the AFL in Washington.[22]

The group built strength over the next year. Local labor housing committees formed around the country, many of them established in response to a well-received speaking tour Bauer took in early 1935. With an unexpected windfall contribution of $500 from two wealthy supporters, Bauer embarked on a six-week trip, speaking to unionists in Pittsburgh, Cleveland, Toledo, Detroit, Chicago, Kenosha, Milwaukee, Madison, Minneapolis, St. Paul, St. Louis, Indianapolis, Cincinnati, and Columbus. She talked to small groups and also gave slide-illustrated formal lectures that described achievements of the European housing movement and presented the program of the Labor Housing Conference.[23]

In order to stretch her funds as far as possible, Bauer often stayed with old friends from Vassar, which invariably involved a certain amount of tedious socializing with "their highly conservative husbands & fathers" in the midst of her packed schedule.[24] Although Bauer struck her former classmates as the same entertaining, lighthearted sophisticate they remembered from college days in the twenties, working within the labor movement had actually changed her considerably. She observed to a friend during this period, "My old Arty self of 1927-Paris would commit suicide at the spectacle [of my present life]—if she were not so thoroughly dead."[25]

Somewhat surprisingly given her background and gender, Bauer turned out to be extremely effective at working within the labor movement. By all accounts a magnetic personality, with a quick wit and a keen intellect, Bauer was able to develop an easy rapport with conservative leaders of the building trades unions, as well as with unionists who were politically on the left. John Edelman commented later that "it was really quite a feat for an 'intellectual'— and a young woman at that—to find her way into the confidence of an important segment of the trade union movement; to persuade it to move into a new field; to begin to think along new lines."[26]

As she traveled around the country, Bauer encountered what she described as an "extraordinary" level of enthusiasm among union members and leaders for a program of government-aided housing organized with significant input from labor. But she found little real sophistication on the subject. She wrote to a friend that "the local labor leaders, however sincerely interested they may be, do not as a rule know what steps to take."[27] Given the Labor Housing Conference's scanty resources, it was difficult to do much to develop the new local groups.

In the spring of 1935, Senator Robert Wagner introduced a public housing bill into Congress.[28] The bill was written by Mary Simkhovitch, Helen Alfred, Louis Pink, and Ira Robbins, who had been working together in a small group called the National Public Housing Conference (NPHC). This group, centered in New York, had organized in 1931 to promote a permanent public housing program. Their bill would have terminated the PWA Housing Division, replacing it with a Housing Division in the Department of Interior and funding it with an initial allocation of $800 million. Local public authorities would carry out the actual building of low-rent housing, specifically targeted to low-income tenants, with the help of grants covering up to 30 percent of construction costs. The purposes of the bill were defined in terms of slum clearance, providing housing for the poor, and promoting industrial recovery. Wagner was too involved with pushing social security and labor relations legislation through Congress to make the bill a priority, but he was willing to introduce it, given that his allies in New York reform circles wanted to start getting publicity for their program.[29]

Labor Housing Conference leaders were skeptical of the Wagner bill, believing that it turned over too much initiative to local housing authorities. Also, they disliked the decision to place the program in the Department of Interior, because they found it difficult to work with Harold Ickes. Bauer and Edelman, together with Stonorov and William Jeanes, manager of the Carl Mackley Houses, decided to draw up what they regarded as a better piece of legislation as a way of influencing Wagner and others. Henry Ellenbogen, a sympathetic congressman from Pittsburgh who had been born and educated in Vienna, agreed to work with them and submit the bill.[30]

The Ellenbogen bill called for replacing the PWA Housing Division with a freestanding United States Housing Authority. The purpose of this entity would be "to construct, and aid in the construction, of modern large-scale housing, available to those families who in good as well as bad times cannot afford to pay the price which will induce the ordinary and usual channels of private enterprise to build such housing." The authority would build directly where that seemed advisable, make grants and loans to regional, state, or municipal housing agencies, and (a critical point) make grants and loans to nongovernmental housing agencies such as cooperatives and other types of noncommercial housing organizations. Its grants were to be limited to 30 percent of costs, although low-interest loans for the entire cost of a project were allowed. In place of a direct allocation from Congress for expenses, the federal authority would issue bonds.[31]

Thus, the Ellenbogen bill placed more authority at the federal level, but simultaneously allowed for more nongovernmental participation through its provision for nonprofit, limited-dividend, and cooperative building societies to develop housing. Labor Housing Conference supporters believed that a variety of mechanisms had to be available so that citizens who wanted to create housing for themselves might have a real opportunity to succeed against predictable resistance from locally powerful real estate investors. The LHC took the possibility of hostility from real estate groups very seriously, because, unlike the NPHC leaders, who stressed slum clearance and provision of housing for the very poor, the labor group wanted to pave the way for moderate-priced housing development. This kind of program would indeed pose a threat to commercial interests.[32]

The following fall the Labor Housing Conference received the official backing of the American Federation of Labor. Meeting in Atlantic City in October for its annual convention in 1935, the AFL approved a resolution condemning "the long-standing inability of private enterprise to supply new or modern dwellings at a price within the reach of the average worker" and concluding that the government should undertake a long-range policy of "public aid and initiative" for "planned neighborhoods." According to the resolution, local labor committees needed to take the lead in initiating the building of "low and medium rental housing." It specified that "sponsoring and management committees of all specific projects must include a majority of representatives from the groups for whom the housing is intended." Thus, concerns for democratic management processes were central to the resolution.

An AFL housing committee, consisting of the presidents of the Bricklayers, Masons and Plasterers' Union, the Plumbers and Steam Fitters United Association, and the Operative Plasterers International Organization, was established to work directly with the Labor Housing Conference.[33] Following the convention, the AFL began providing financial support for Bauer's group. The LHC then moved its headquarters to Washington, where economist Boris Shishkin joined Bauer on the staff.[34]

By this time, the Labor Housing Conference was working directly with Senator Wagner. Impressed by their critique of his original public housing bill, Wagner asked Bauer and Ellenbogen to help him rewrite the legislation for the 1936 session of Congress. The relationship continued after his housing bill failed to pass the second time around. In 1937, Wagner introduced a public housing bill for the third time. During the hearings in 1936 and 1937, the AFL threw its lobbying weight behind Wagner's bill, and Bauer was joined by national labor leaders in testifying for an expansive program of direct federal intervention into the housing field.

Labor-affiliated witnesses made four basic points in their testimony to congressional committees during the three years that public housing bills were under consideration. First, they argued that direct federal involvement should not be aimed solely at the poor. Moderate-priced shelter was also a problem area. Even during periods of prosperity, the commercial market had not consistently been able to supply the broad middle of the market in urban areas with new or used homes that were in good condition and located in pleasant neighborhoods. Harry C. Bates, chairman of the AFL Housing Committee and president of the Bricklayers, Masons, and Plasterers International Union, maintained that although union workers had better than average incomes, very few had been able to achieve the "famous 'American standard of living,'" which he described as a "modern kitchen and bathrooms, central heat, a sunny garden and a quiet neighborhood for the children to grow up in."[35] Bauer told the committee that "the real problem is not nearly so much the existing slums as it is the incapacity of private enterprise to meet the great need for new housing in the near future."[36]

Second, labor representatives insisted on an active role for future residents of government-aided housing. Bauer argued for mechanisms to allow for "effective participation of wage-earner and consumer groups who want to go after some housing for themselves. . . ." She warned that relying totally on local housing authorities implied "a fantastic degree of optimism" with regard to the energy with which municipalities could be expected to pursue housing development programs. Without the profit motive to spur activity, some other "spark" needed to be found. Such a spark would be provided "by setting up machinery whereby groups of people who desire to secure better housing for themselves may participate directly in the program—without waiting for the uncertainties of local authorities."[37] Bates outlined a plan whereby groups of families would form housing societies and initiate the planning of developments. These would be built by local housing authorities, but then leased to the societies, which would manage them. This possibility for control by the people who would be living in government-aided housing, Bates argued, would be "a safeguard against bureaucratic or paternalistic management."[38]

Third, labor witnesses justified their program with what in later years would be termed "industrial policy" arguments. Bauer argued that "residential construction is a highly speculative and fluctuating luxury trade—the first to fall off at even the smell of depression—instead of being what it obviously should be, a basic staple of production."[39] Michael J. Colleran, president of the Operative Plasterers and Cement Finishers International Association and member of the AFL Housing Committee, pointed out that ever since Herbert Hoover's commission on unemployment in the early 1920s, federal policymakers had acknowledged the need for a long-range program of planned public works to be used to counterbalance the effects of swings in the business cycle. In Colleran's opinion, low-rent housing was a perfect field in which to develop a countercyclical program. On the one hand, the need was "almost limitless," but when the economy was overheating, "the construction of publicly assisted housing for low-income families can be temporarily curtailed."[40]

Fourth, labor witnesses were adamant that they wanted a program with "ideals and standards diametrically opposed to the policies of [the] FHA." After an initial period of openness, organized labor had become disillusioned with the strategy of responding to problems in the housing sector by increasing the flow of credit to mortgage markets. Bates told Wagner's Senate committee in 1936 that although the Home Owners Loan Corporation (which refinanced mortgages of people unable to meet their payments because of Depression conditions) had been "necessary and valuable" as an emergency response, "its chief result [had] been to bail out insurance companies and banks," rather than to increase the stock of housing available to families with low incomes.[41] By early 1936, the AFL was castigating the Federal Housing Administration for making credit more available to "those very subdividers and small speculative builders who have always tended to be chiselers of labor" (a charge based on the tendency of small operators to pay less than prevailing union wage rates). In addition, the AFL charged that the housing produced with FHA help was much too expensive for most union families.[42] Core supporters of the Labor Housing Conference had raised these kinds of objections to the FHA from the time the agency was established. In print they labeled the National Housing Act the "Anti-Housing Act." And in private, they often referred to the F-H-A as "F—— Housing Altogether."[43]

Opposition to Permanent Public Housing Legislation

The organizations that mobilized against Wagner's legislation for directly funded, publicly owned housing were the U.S. Chamber of Commerce, the National Association of Real Estate Boards (NAREB), the U.S. League of Building and Loans, and the National Retail Lumber Dealers Association.[44] Strikingly, it was only business organizations immediately involved with residential real estate that worked to prevent passage of these bills. (In the case of the Chamber of Commerce, it was a Housing Committee composed of representatives from construction and real estate firms that took the lead.)[45] One explanation for this pattern may be that, even though taking shelter out of the market posed an ideological threat to all forms of private capital, many business groups—as in Atlanta—saw advantages in federal development of housing. On the other hand, it is also possible that other business groups were simply too distracted by their own problems to devote much attention to this controversy.

Of those who opposed the legislation, it was the lumber dealers who most explicitly articulated their own material stake in the battle. They stated for the record that they were against a federal residential building program on the grounds that it would utilize new construction materials such as concrete and steel. Such innovations were extremely threatening to lumber suppliers, since wood constituted the largest single cost factor in conventional home construction.[46] Not surprisingly, this argument failed to win broad-based support, and the Lumber Dealers Association was increasingly marginalized as the debate proceeded.[47]

Much more politically effective were arguments that linked private homeownership and laissez-faire economics to the public good. NAREB President

Walter Schmidt worried that renting from the government might prove such an attractive option that "the urge to buy one's own home will be diminished." This, of course, was precisely what Labor Housing Conference supporters hoped, but in Schmidt's mind such an outcome would undermine the nation. Alluding to venerable traditions in American culture linking economically independent small holders with political virtue, he maintained that "widespread ownership of land . . . is the bulwark of a democratic form of government."[48] Thus, private ownership of houses supplied along business lines was connected to themes of freedom and democracy.

Even though representatives of real estate groups argued that state-provided shelter was tantamount to communism or socialism, they never questioned federal support for the activities of their own members. NAREB lobbyist Herbert U. Nelson, for instance, relentlessly opposed publicly subsidized dwellings. Yet, like Eccles, Nelson was happy to see indirect intervention in support of business, stating that "public credit can be properly used to help sustain homeownership and private enterprise."[49]

In light of what ultimately happened, the alarm expressed by people like Nelson and Schmidt might seem out of proportion to the threat that public housing actually posed to their well-being, either ideologically or financially. It should be kept in mind, however, that what was at issue at this time was not public housing as Americans came to know it. Rather, the issue was the possibility of having an expansive program of the kind advocated by the Labor Housing Conference, and to some extent modeled by the PWA program, that would be potentially attractive to a large segment of the population.

Passage of the Wagner Public Housing Act

Over vociferous objections, Wagner's legislation finally passed Congress the third year it was introduced and was signed into law by Roosevelt in September 1937 as the United States Housing Act. While passage of the bill did represent a defeat for the business groups that had lobbied against it, it was not a major one, since important elements of the proposed legislation had been compromised away. Indeed, historian James T. Patterson pinpoints the evisceration of Wagner's housing bill as the first big victory for the conservative coalition in the Senate.[50]

The section on nonprofits and cooperatives was quickly killed, followed by the provision for demonstration projects directed from Washington. These changes left all location decisions, and even the decision as to whether to build at all, entirely at the local level, where many of the most politically powerful groups greeted the idea of public housing with, in the words of one commentator, "the same enthusiasm as they might have greeted the introduction of bubonic plague." Other changes included amendments that kept construction costs minimal, specifically excluded all but the lowest income groups, and mandated elimination of slum property in a quantity equal to new dwelling units constructed.

This last, the so-called "equivalent elimination" clause, formally linked public housing to slum clearance. It meant that private developers would not face significant competition for choice land parcels on the fringes of developed areas while, at the same time, commercial landlords would be protected from publicly supported increases in the supply of available apartment units (which might force down rent levels at the bottom end of the market). A focus on slum clearance also meant that the increased expenditures required to purchase already-developed property would consume more of the limited resources allocated to public housing.

Proponents were distressed, but supported the final version as the best they were likely to get. As it turned out, some later regretted their decision. Charles Abrams, a long-time advocate of public housing who had initially been positive about the Wagner Act, wrote in the 1960s that "in retrospect, I believe that the compromises that were made in the 1937 debate on the public housing measure lastingly impaired it and will ultimately contribute to its demise."[51]

Of all of the alterations made to Wagner's proposed bill, the cost limitation amendment added by Senator Harry Byrd was most devastating to the hope that government building programs might eventually develop a widely appealing new architectural design for urban residences—one of the most radical possibilities contained within the program advocated by the Labor Housing Conference. Senator Byrd, perturbed by what he regarded as the excessive costs and threatening social implications of the cooperative farms the Resettlement Administration had organized in his home state of Virginia, was determined to minimize federal spending on subsidized housing. His amendment to the Senate version of the bill capped costs at $4,000 per family unit and $1,000 per room. Backers of the legislation argued against specific cost ceilings, since construction costs varied so much in different parts of the country. If there had to be limits, though, they advocated $1,500 per room. In a compromise between House and Senate versions of the legislation, the Byrd limits were raised in the case of cities larger than a half-million people to $5,000 for each unit and $1,250 for each room.[52]

A comparison of these figures with the money spent by the Housing Division provides a sense of the constraints imposed on the new program. Even the highest limits of the United States Housing Act were lower than the $1,421 that the Housing Division averaged per room. Under the PWA, the *average* price per dwelling unit was $4,975, almost exactly the absolute upper limit allowed for the largest cities under the permanent legislation. The PWA figures, moreover, included the South as well as cities under a half-million, and in both situations costs were considerably lower.[53] Thus, the permanent legislation mandated a markedly diminished physical standard for what Americans would come to know as "public housing" as compared with the developments built by the PWA.

Federal Intervention in Housing after the Wagner Act: The Two Tiers of U.S. Housing Policy

The provisions of the Wagner Act were a significant defeat for the Labor Housing Conference program. But in the long run, it was decisions over how to administer the act that may have been the most damaging to prospects for the modern housing approach ever catching on in the United States. The bleak, alienating architecture of housing built under the Wagner Act, often blamed on the influence of modernism, was to a large extent the result of very low budgets. Here the political choices of the program's administrators played an important role, in addition to the formal constraints written into the legislation itself.

The Byrd Amendment forced austerity on the United States Housing Authority (USHA), the agency established to carry out the functions of the new act, but the new agency was even more parsimonious than required. This bare-bones approach was begun under the administration of Nathan Straus, Roosevelt's choice to head the newly formed authority. Heir to the Macy's department store fortune and a long-time political ally of FDR, Straus had a longstanding interest in low-rent housing. In the first phase of Housing Division work, he had sponsored the limited-dividend project in the Bronx called Hillside Houses and was on the board of the New York City Housing Authority. Harold Ickes viewed the appointment of Straus to head the USHA as a serious mistake. He wrote in his private diary that Straus was "a rich man's son, [who] has never had to fight his way through life." Consequently, he had neither the personal qualities nor the organizational experience needed to run a large federal agency successfully. Ickes saw him "as one of that group of starry-eyed people in New York who think they are experts on housing because they write about and talk a lot about it." He included Bauer in this group, referring to her in his diary as "a wild-eyed female."

To some extent, Ickes was reacting with disappointment because he foresaw that Straus's appointment doomed his chances for continuing influence over federal housing operations after the PWA was closed down. But whatever bias prompted Ickes's prediction, he was proved correct. Straus lacked talent as an administrator and did even worse as a political strategist. Reflecting later on his problems with getting congressional appropriations for his agency, he commented that when dealing with congressmen, he was not "a good diplomat" and had not effectively handled their "insistent demand for patronage." From a long-run perspective, Straus's attempt to appease critics of public housing by building very cheaply may have been his most serious error.[54]

Sincerely devoted to the cause of public housing, Straus hoped that by keeping costs to a minimum he could garner political support and at the same time produce the greatest amount of shelter. A 1939 agency memo advised local authorities that "the USHA is confident that much lower costs than the statutory cost limitations . . . can be met." Therefore, the communication explained, plans that were not considerably below the maximums would not be approved.[55] In that year's annual report, Straus wrote that "despite the doubts of many who felt that these statutory limitations [on costs] would seriously retard the rehousing drive, the average room and unit dwelling-facilities costs under the U.S.H.A. program are well below the statutory maxima *and are constantly being driven even further downward.*"[56] As a result of this policy, the new agency spent an average of 30 percent below PWA levels on its construction in the period before World War II.[57]

The cuts had a severe impact. Red Hook and Queensbridge, the first two complexes built in New York City under the new legislation, cost approximately one-half as much per room as the two projects built in the city by the PWA.[58] Lewis Mumford, writing in the *New Yorker,* complained that both developments were "unnecessarily barrackslike and monotonous." He found Red Hook, with its "Leningrad formalism," to be particularly inhumane.[59] The authority carried out its self-proclaimed "policy of eliminating all nonessentials and driving development costs down to a minimum" in a variety of ways.[60] Doors were left off closets, kitchens were not separated from living areas, and interior partitions were cheap and flimsy. At Red Hook, there were no elevator stops at the second, fourth, and sixth floors of buildings.[61]

Probably the most significant economy in terms of guaranteeing that these buildings would forever be poor people's housing was the paring down of room sizes. Thirteen percent below the PWA standard, the rooms at Red Hook were 9 percent smaller than even the average size of pre-Depression apartments built by philanthropic organizations and labor unions in New York City.[62] Room size has a particularly important impact on long-term livability, because the more generous a dwelling's inside space, the more adaptable it is to modification by different users over the years. By contrast, mechanical aspects of a residence, such as plumbing, can be brought up to higher standards later.[63]

The United States Housing Authority's constrained approach to building begun under Straus's administration ultimately proved politically disastrous. Those who hated public housing remained hostile, while the minimal buildings produced by the USHA attracted no new allies and discouraged some of the old ones.[64] The miserly expenditures mandated by the USHA meant that it produced precisely what Mackley Houses architect Oskar Stonorov had hoped to avoid in the field of low-rent shelter: construction that would be immediately identifiable as "those buildings which the government built to house poor people." As it happened, the permanent program of government-built dwellings *did* come to represent what Stonorov had described as "standards of living in a new mode . . . quite different from what individual speculative activity has created." However, the direction in which these standards differed was the exact opposite of what the idealistic architect had envisioned and toward which the best work of the PWA Housing Division had pointed. The result undermined support for the idea of direct federal aid to a non-commercial housing sector.[65]

Meanwhile, the Federal Housing Administration was restructuring the private real estate market so that it was able to serve a larger proportion of the population. This won the agency enthusiastic allies among commercial developers. Labor Housing Conference advocates who opposed the FHA, while correct in their perception about the threat it posed to their own goals, turned out to be mistaken in their prediction that it would merely recreate the property market of the 1920s. Instead, the FHA introduced real changes. The long-term amortized mortgage with its high loan-to-value ratio, which was possible because FHA mortgage insurance reduced risks for commercial lenders, lowered monthly payments. The agency also induced innovations in production patterns such that builders were able to deliver a cheaper product.

Even while making major alterations in the housing sector, the FHA did not provoke antagonism from real estate business groups. In fact, commercial operators were very positive about the agency. A major reason for the amity, as historian Marc Weiss points out, was that the FHA used its authority to promote practices that the larger developers had been championing for some time and it went about its work in a seemingly noncoercive way that fit with "the American image of voluntarism." The agency did not actively try to restrict practices it did not like but, instead, set up structures to reward certain activities. For instance, FHA officials wanted to encourage particular kinds of land-use patterns that they believed would help safeguard residential property values, such as uniform setbacks of houses from the street, cul-de-sac roads, and residential neighborhoods separated from commercial districts. Developers were generally happy to comply, because those whose plans conformed to agency standards were able to get an advance commitment that the FHA would insure mortgages for all the homes they built. Such a commitment made it easier and cheaper for developers to secure financing, since lenders were sure beforehand that sales would be quick and profitable.[66] In this way, the agency was able to influence planning standards throughout the country.

Once able to secure working capital easily, builders increased the size of their operations. Growth brought more profits, and it was also rewarded in another way. Bigger firms were better able to negotiate with federal agencies. Within this environment, small builders tended to expand, while big operators grew larger still.[67] These results were not coincidental. As Weiss points out, the Federal Housing Administration "made a commitment to provide moderate cost housing production through large-scale building operations."[68]

Another way the FHA helped modernize (and subsidize) the industry was by providing builders with research services, something even the largest operators could rarely afford on their own. The government agency developed design standards, projected demand in different areas, and undertook planning studies to make sure that proposed housing was coordinated with utilities, transportation, and schools.[69]

Costs decreased as a result of FHA coordination. The average value of new single-family houses on which loans were accepted for insurance in 1940 was $5,199, approximately 13 percent below the average three years earlier. That same year, 36 percent of the 2,680 subdivisions analyzed by the FHA's Land Planning Department were selling houses for under $4,000, a price well below the average for a new house in the 1920s.[70] Miles Colean, an official with the FHA in this period, concluded that "probably the most important factor in this decline was a shift of FHA financing from houses catering to the high-income classes to medium-priced dwellings."[71]

Thus, through the work of the FHA, aspirations for a modernized construction industry—consisting of big operations benefiting from economies of scale, working on the basis of long-range plans, and using large amounts of low-cost capital—were partly fulfilled. As modern housing supporters, along with earlier generations of reformers, had long predicted, this kind of production was able to achieve a high volume of good quality, moderate-priced shelter. In the early years of the twentieth century, social workers had put forward minimum standards for urban dwellings, calling for such things as adequate ventilation, running water, and a flush toilet for each dwelling unit.[72] Even in the prosperous twenties these standards had seemed impossible at a mass level. After the war, even the most modest of the FHA-insured tracts supplied shelter that met or exceeded these standards, at prices that the majority of Americans could afford. Of course, the construction industry was only capable of such results because of a variety of federal activities, including massive support for road-building throughout the country and reorganization of financial markets.

Conclusion

At the depth of the Depression in the early 1930s, the near collapse of the private real estate market, combined with a liberal upsurge, opened up a small political space for people committed to a new kind of American housing. Those influenced by the innovative ideas and values with regard to housing that were then circulating internationally found limited but real opportunities for experimentation within the temporary housing program of the Public Works Administration. Advocates of the Labor Housing Conference approach hoped that this period might see the birth of a significant noncommercial housing sector in the United States, in the same way that so-called "social" housing had taken root in European countries after the First World War.

Those who espoused ideas associated with the LHC program envisioned a new kind of urban residence that would make it feasible to provide all families with good housing while simultaneously creating neighborhoods with convenient social services and recreational possibilities. They believed that this new kind of housing might prove more appealing to many Americans than conventional suburban living. Through more efficient production, made possible by plentiful, low-interest capital as well as new technologies, they hoped to provide a large supply of such dwellings at moderate cost. And by keeping this housing out of the market, they would prevent speculative increases in its cost. The most democratically oriented advocates of these ideas, such as Bauer and trade unionist Harry Bates, proposed new tenure forms like cooperatives and not-for-profit corporations to give people alternate means of achieving the control of their personal environment that single-family homeownership partially allows. Along with these housing and urban planning goals, the proposals dubbed "modern housing" aimed at giving the government a major macroeconomic lever by which to affect investment and employment levels.

As things worked out, advocates of the modern housing approach were not able to get any major part of it institutionalized in long-term policies. Although opponents were not able to stop the implementation of a permanent program of direct federal provision of housing entirely, they were successful in limiting its scope in ways that made it impossible to achieve the goal of making innovatively designed, moderate-cost, noncommercial housing the focus of federal housing efforts. There were a variety of reasons for this outcome. The basic explanation was that housing activists, with their small grassroots base in the labor movement, had far less political influence with Congress than real estate investors.

With regard to the coalition behind the Labor Housing Conference policy initiative, Bauer's conviction that a highly mobilized constituency behind a program of government-supported not-for-profit housing would have had a chance against real estate interests was never really put to the test. While some might argue that Americans would never embrace alternatives to the ideal of single-family homeownership, Bauer did encounter enthusiasm within parts of the labor movement during LHC organizing drives in 1934 and 1935.

Also, as we have seen in the cases of the Mackley Houses and the Harlem River Houses, many families liked living in the best of the PWA developments. But the Housing Division's program was not able to serve as a springboard to galvanize political support. Fewer than sixty PWA projects were constructed in the entire country and, in the spring of 1937, when the final push for permanent legislation began, only fourteen had been completed. Harlem River Houses opened for occupancy over a month after Roosevelt signed the Wagner Housing Act into law in September 1937. The new ideas about housing design and noncommercial forms of ownership had no chance to take hold at the grassroots before critical battles were joined at the national level.[73]

Moreover, support for nonmarket alternatives that did exist was weaker than it appeared because of widely divergent conceptions of what such a program should do and how it should work. Some liberal reform groups, including the New York City-based Public Housing Conference, envisioned public housing as a means of combating slums and of decently but economically rehousing the very poor, rather than a vehicle to challenge for-profit development practices. Many labor leaders, especially within the powerful construction trades, found Wagner's bills attractive chiefly for the of possibilities they provided expanding employment rather than for the effect they would have on housing per se. Meanwhile, traditional American antipathy to centralized government pervaded the ranks of housing reformers as well as the general public. Few saw a need for a strong federal agency able to plan and coordinate a program at the national level. Not only did liberal reformers raise no coherent opposition to conservative insistence that all initiative reside in local governments, but some even celebrated this outcome as a victory for democracy.[74]

Opposing the small, fragmented, and poorly funded coalition in favor of legislation advancing modern housing ideals were real estate business groups throughout the country, one of the strongest political forces in American political life. While temporarily stunned at the outset of the decade, real estate developers and financial institutions linked to the property market were on the upswing by the mid–1930s, thanks in good part to public aid. Even at the peak of the crisis, property investors in the United States had never been as vulnerable as their European counterparts, given differences in the way societies and governments were organized.

Compared with the situation in the United States, real property interests in Europe were often fairly isolated from other sectors of capital. In Vienna, export-oriented large industrialists, who wanted to keep wages low in order to compete in the world market, positively welcomed the Social Democrats' housing programs that severely disadvantaged the private rental sector. In Britain, the social and economic isolation of landlords gave them no voice in the policies of the Liberal and Conservative Parties before World War I, nor any input into the Labour Party afterwards. Thus, the crisis of the early twentieth-century British property market was resolved at the expense of private landlords through unfavorable taxation policies, rent control, and ultimately the displacement of a large part of the private rental sector by "council" (or public) housing.[75]

In the United States, with its long tradition of land speculation as a central economic activity, property interests were less isolated. Indeed, it was often the case that those who held industrial and landed property could not be clearly differentiated, as exemplified by the extensive property development efforts of the Rockefeller family during the 1920s and 1930s discussed in chapter 6. While leading industrialists did not join in fighting the Wagner Act, neither did they actively support large-scale socialization of residential real estate to solve problems they faced, as was the case in England or Vienna.

The political context was also quite different. The federalized structure of the American government meant that more political decisions were made at the local level, where property investors were often the single most powerful constituency. With regard to decisions at the federal level, real estate entrepreneurs and their allies in the financial sector were a significant force in every congressional district in the country. In addition, they had established national organizations with the capacity to mount effective lobbying campaigns in Washington. Once the Depression-era reforms began restoring optimism and profitability for these groups, they were well situated to strike out in their own defense.

Along with other advantages, commercial real estate operators could draw on the strong sentiment in the United States in favor of owning a home. While often seen as a constant throughout American history, the American homeownership ideal actually was strengthened during the interwar period. Both Hoover and Roosevelt shared the belief that an energetic yet stable housing industry was key to the well-being of the economy as a whole. In addition, both seemed sincerely convinced that owning a house promoted a variety of socially valuable character traits in individuals. Thus, each felt justified in allocating public resources to aid the private real estate market. They explicitly linked such actions to core American values of freedom and democracy. As was the case in other areas, Roosevelt made the greatest progress, but Hoover had already set the federal government on this trajectory during his years as Secretary of Commerce.[76]

Thus, by the end of the 1930s, a long-term pattern for federal housing policy had emerged. It consisted of two tiers. The top one, which implemented most of the proposals that business groups had been making since the end of the First World War, consisted of institutional arrangements employing the federal government to organize and subsidize financial markets, thereby pro-

viding low-cost capital to producers and consumers of market-produced housing. The core programs of the top policy tier were administered by the FHA,
but this agency was only one of several created in this period, including the
Home Loan Bank Board, the temporary Home Owners Loan Corporation, and
the Federal National Mortgage Association (often called Fannie Mae for
short). The Wagner Act, which established public housing as we know it today, defined the lower tier. As it emerged from Congress, Wagner's housing
bill created a form of directly assisted housing that was stingy, physically alienating, and means-tested. In its final form, the legislation did not allow public
aid to go to cooperatives or other private groups interested in developing noncommercial alternatives, nor did it provide possibilities for democracy or self-
determination for residents. These two tiers, created by the federal housing
legislation of the thirties, established the matrix for the development of the
United States housing system—public and private—for the next several decades. The implications of this political choice for American housing and also
for the development of American politics will be explored in the conclusion.

CONCLUSION

The two-tier policy framework for housing that emerged from the New Deal had three goals: improving housing conditions, promoting economic growth in the economy as a whole, and building an enduring Democratic majority coalition. It never accomplished the third goal very well, but it did fulfill large parts of the first two through the 1960s. In the new economic conditions that started emerging in the early 1970s, however, these policies have not functioned as well, either in stimulating the economy or in providing affordable housing to low- and moderate-income families.

For some time, the upper-tier programs contributed to a steady improvement for the American housing market, and this in turn had a salutary impact on the economy. By 1940, new housing starts by private builders broke the half-million mark for the first time since 1929. FHA insurance guarantees facilitated approximately 40 percent of this construction.[1] Although building ground almost to a halt during the war, it took off immediately afterwards. Over one million new units were begun in 1946. By 1950, the number of new starts reached almost 2 million.[2] With the exception of African Americans, most families in the top two-thirds of the income distribution were able to buy comfortable homes in pleasant neighborhoods by the 1950s.

These successes were accompanied by drawbacks. Most new homes were built on the urban periphery, and central cities lost tax revenues as well as population—in particular, middle- and upper-income residents. Also, the low density environment promoted by FHA guidelines destroyed vast expanses of open countryside, was extremely energy intensive, and left some suburbanites isolated.[3] Most seriously, African Americans and poor people of all races benefited little from the advantages that suburban living offered the majority of white families. Although the Supreme Court declared in 1948 that states could not enforce racially exclusive property covenants, the FHA continued to work with developers who refused to sell to blacks. William Levitt, the most famous of the postwar builders, declared that he had "no room in [his] mind or heart for racial prejudice," but still would not sell homes to African-American families for fear of losing white customers. Whether or not all developers were similarly color-blind in their hearts, most pursued similar business policies. Meanwhile, the FHA was wary of insuring apartment construction, steered

have all but withered away. Since the 1970s, American-style public housing has become increasingly discredited, even among liberals. In the 1980s, Housing and Urban Development (HUD) programs targeted at the housing needs of the poor took the biggest cuts of all major social programs. By the mid–1990s, public discussion of "reinventing" HUD has evolved into calls for completely abolishing the agency, leaving no alternative in its place beyond the market. At present, there are no proposals that command support from a major political bloc for sheltering those priced out of the market.

Meanwhile, some upper-tier programs have come under critical public scrutiny. Some policy analysts argue that too much of the nation's capital is being channeled into mortgage debt rather than manufacturing and other industries. Also, the mortgage interest deduction seems to be edging into mainstream political discussion for the first time, as proposals for a so-called flat tax put forward by some conservative Republicans have encouraged serious public debate about the costs and benefits of the present system.[12]

With faith eroded in many of the older policies and no consensus about a new direction, Congress has not funded existing programs at traditional levels. Symptomatic of the political paralysis in this area was the failure of Congress in the 1980s to pass a housing authorization bill for seven consecutive years. In the two years previous to the eventual passage of the bill in early 1988, the FHA had lapsed six times.[13]

In response to these problems, homebuilding and finance groups as well as advocates of the poor have called for a reformulation of national housing policy. As in the 1920s, in the past several years a variety of groups across the political spectrum have expressed dissatisfaction with the American housing system and advocated new or changed roles for government as a way of solving the problems they perceive.

To review the argument thus far: for some time the New Deal programs fulfilled many of the hopes of their originators in terms of stimulating the economy and improving housing conditions for middle-income families. Given the economic changes of the 1970s, however, these programs have operated less successfully. The political implications of New Deal housing reforms have been more ambiguous. Roosevelt supported federal assistance to homeowners because he believed it would promote "political and social stability." In a sense, he was entirely correct.[14] The restructuring of the commercial housing market that occurred as a result of the top tier of federal housing policy created conditions that allowed stably employed, white working families to purchase houses in modest subdivisions in the following decades. As a result, an important segment of the New Deal coalition experienced significantly higher living standards.

What Roosevelt failed to include in his calculations regarding homeownership was that the particular gains it provided undercut allegiance to the coalition he was building in support of an activist federal government. The New Deal reforms significantly modernized the homebuilding industry. Now it was able to routinely deliver good-quality, affordable homes, and moderate-income people could afford to purchase these homes with the low-interest, long-term mortgage loans that had been made possible by federal reorganization of financial institutions. Yet the great impact of public agencies on the housing market, and the public resources upper-tier policies consume, are largely invisible to the average citizen. Thus, the private market rather than the government has received the bulk of the credit for the pleasant living conditions of the suburban neighborhoods in which the majority of American families now live. Poor people aided by bottom-tier programs seem to be getting government assistance in a way that other groups are not, because their housing subsidies are explicit government expenditures and thus highly visible.

The perspective of Tom Nielsen, an autoworker living in western New York, is indicative of how the New Deal housing reforms (as well as other indirect forms of public spending) have affected the political attitudes of many Americans. In the summer of 1994, Nielsen expressed outrage that the state and county had collected a transfer tax on the recent sale of his house of fourteen years as he and his family prepared to move to "a much bigger, more comfortable home." "It's ludicrous," he wrote to the local newspaper. "There were Mario Cuomo [the Governor], Dennis Gorski [Erie County Executive] and their friends cashing in on our equity, our hard work, our investment, and they had done nothing to help earn it." Nielsen believed that he and his family deserved all of the money from the sale since they had "patiently, faithfully" paid their mortgage payments over the years while at the same time maintaining and improving their property. His complaint that the tax was unjustified, because "never once did Mario Cuomo offer to come over and mow the lawn," expressed his perception that he and his family had created all the value embodied in the house on their own. Nielsen showed no awareness of the subsidies and assistance he had received from federal, state, and local governments, such as FHA structuring of the mortgage market (indeed, FHA may have insured his particular mortgage), tax benefits, and infrastructure construction.

Nielsen found the tax particularly galling because he believed that the bulk of it would be spent to help fund the county's transportation authority. This was unfair, he wrote, since "I have never in my life been on a Metro bus, and I can foresee no circumstances in which I will in the future." Despite massive levels of public spending for highways in the United States throughout the twentieth century, the way Nielsen saw it: "Nobody subsidizes my ride to work."[15] Also, since he lived in the suburbs, he probably had few friends or neighbors who relied on public transportation. Nielsen believed that the government did nothing for him, when in fact mass production workers like him have been core beneficiaries of the New Deal policies, in housing and much else. Before the New Deal housing (and labor) legislation, few autoworkers were secure homeowners; fewer still were able to trade up to bigger houses. Nielsen's alienation from government, despite this reality, clearly illustrates how the opaque policy mechanisms developed by New Dealers undermined the possibilities for building a constituency for activist government.

Recent Initiatives to Create Affordable Housing

In response to the escalation of shelter costs and the lack of a clear national program to respond to the situation, there have been widespread local efforts around the country to improve conditions. By the early 1990s, somewhere between 1,500 and 2,000 nonprofit housing providers were operating in the United States. Most had been formed by churches, neighborhood organizations, unions, and tenant groups. During the 1970s, these types of organizations received limited support from the federal government, for instance through HUD's Neighborhood Self-Help Development Program and the Comprehensive Employment and Training Act (CETA). When these programs were cut during the Reagan administration in the 1980s, nonprofits turned to state and local governments, businesses, charities, and foundations to help keep the costs of building and maintaining modest housing units and the rents low-income people pay affordable. One of the few federal subsidies still available is a system of tax credits for building low-rent housing, but these credits can be used only by for-profit firms; nonprofit housing providers draw on them by byzantine arrangements with profit-making enterprises.[16]

In some ways, the work of these local housing providers is reminiscent of the modern housing program. Financially, these are noncommerical operations. Architecturally, the bulk of the housing units are in collective forms of various kinds. While some providers build or renovate standard apartment houses, many have experimented with row or "townhouse" designs. With regard to social amenities, most nonprofit developers attempt to supply residents with usable collective spaces and facilities, at least in the form of a central court with play equipment and benches. As in the interwar era, there are now many talented architects working in the field and many who would like to do so if more funding were available.

Daybreak Grove, a development for single mothers and their children in Escondido, California, exemplifies a number of these trends. Commissioned by the North County Housing Foundation, architects René Davids and Christine Killory designed this thirteen-unit complex based on the traditional California bungalow court. Individual residences are small, two-story townhouses set around a courtyard that contains a children's playground and a separate garden area. Also, there is a common building, with a laundromat, theater, and indoor play area. *Progressive Architecture* magazine recognized the plan for Daybreak Grove with a design award in 1991.[17]

Another way in which contemporary efforts are reminiscent of proposals and experiments of the 1920s and 1930s is the emphasis on lower financing costs as one key to providing inexpensive shelter. Two noncommercial developers have been especially innovative in securing low-cost working capital. In Boston, the Bricklayers and Laborers Non-Profit Housing Company is building townhouses (in brick, of course) using low-interest loans from a bank holding union pension funds. In East Brooklyn, the Nehemiah Project has been financed by no-interest loans from churches. Both of these ventures have also benefited from grants of free land from their city governments and special low-interest state mortgage loan programs.[18]

Just as in the past, recent efforts to increase affordability have included a search for alternatives to the standard American pattern of homeownership. Groups that construct housing on a nonprofit basis tend to favor some form of ownership for residents so they can enjoy the advantages of security and control over their home environment. However, these developers are usually reluctant to sell outright the dwellings they have built or renovated, because, once sold, such units enter the speculative market where the profit added at the point of resale makes them less affordable for future residents. Currently, various experimental forms of ownership, such as limited equity and land trust schemes, which allow people to own their dwellings but not to sell them for a profit, are being tried. The goal is to find mechanisms to ensure that the housing stays outside of the market. Such mechanisms make housing less of a "commodity," so that the focus can be on what Marxists would call its "use value," or how it meets concrete needs, rather than its "exchange value," or how it functions as an investment expected to grow in value over time.[19]

A major difference between housing initiatives in recent years and the proposals and experiments during the New Deal era is that, at present, no politically influential group is articulating an alternative model of shelter and shelter provision for the majority of Americans. New policy proposals focus on specific groups priced out of the market for conventional housing. Yet, there are indications that some middle-income and even affluent Americans are receptive to new patterns for domestic life and might welcome more choices, in terms of tenure patterns, design, and social facilities. The recent proliferation of upscale clustered developments throughout the country testifies to the willingness of some consumers to forego the conventional free-standing house for the right location, amenities, and price.

The Cohousing movement provides another indication that significant numbers of middle-class people feel restless with conventional market alternatives. Cohousing is an attempt to create more cooperative and child-friendly living environments that are planned, designed, and managed by the people who live in them. Residents in cohousing communities typically live in their own apartments or rowhouse units, but often cook and eat together and share childcare. This movement, which originated in Denmark, reached the United States in the early 1990s. Already communities have been established in Davis and Emeryville in California, Bainbridge Island, Washington, and Lafayette, Colorado; approximately 150 more are in the planning stages. Cohousers tend to be well-educated professionals who could easily afford to live in single-family homes but prefer a residential pattern that offers more experience of community and also the practical advantages that come with sharing domestic labor.[20]

Today's housing reformers, while more pragmatic than their predecessors in the 1920s and 1930s in acknowledging the strength of private interests in real estate, may be overlooking the endemic political weakness of programs targeted specifically at the poor rather than the entire population. Historically, government policies designed to serve the majority, such as social security, have fared better than those like welfare that are targeted to a specific group. Relatively "universal" social programs gather political support, while specifically targeted ones tend to fracture and dissipate commitment.

While the inability of recent housing reformers to develop and articulate a broad-ranging alternative to conventional practices seems a weakness, by no means do all of the differences between the two movements reflect negatively on present work. One very important comparative strength of contemporary efforts is that there are now a great many community-based groups, including neighborhood organizations, churches, and labor unions, that are actively working to provide housing. The response to a PWA-type federal agency's appeal for plans from local nonprofit housing organizations would be vastly greater today than it was in the summer of 1933. Then, no national movement of local groups working to increase the supply of affordable urban housing stock existed, and only seven groups in the entire country had the financial resources and planning capacity to make credible proposals. Now there are numerous groups working in all major American cities, many with strong records of successful development and management.[21]

In the last several years, in ways that are reminiscent of the 1920s and 1930s, serious questions have been raised about the standard methods of shelter provision in the United States. Many of the ideas associated with the modern housing program, such as superblock planning, clustered units, large-scale building operations, low-cost capital, and shared facilities are again circulating. Another similarity between the two periods is a growing conviction among those who want to improve access to good housing that no real solution is possible until the federal government becomes involved. Of course, the contemporary situation is far different from that of the 1920s and early 1930s (for one thing, because so much low-density development has taken place in the intervening years). Still, a comparison of housing movements from the two periods suggests much of continuing value in the ideas put forward over a half-century ago.

The Legacy of the Modern Housing Program

In the thirties, the Labor Housing Conference was not able to get its proposals institutionalized in long-term policies or programs. Nevertheless, the modern housing program is historically significant. It represents an attempt to develop mechanisms for public action significantly different from those that emerged from the New Deal: ones that would be more transparent, universalistic, and participatory, and would allow for more public control over the economy.

In contrast to the two-tier policy framework that emerged from the New Deal, which overwhelmingly favors more affluent Americans, the PWA experience suggested and the Labor Housing Conference proposed a unified approach to the housing question. In the United States, advocates of greater economic support for less advantaged groups have most often espoused measures to expand economic growth to improve everyone's situation—in good part because frankly redistributive proposals have tended to be politically unpopular. Supporters of the new housing ideas of the interwar period took a different path. They formulated a radical reconceptualization of the idea of home and neighborhood that would provide benefits not available through the market even to the affluent. Their linking of physical design and social innovation to what was in effect a redistributive program was, to some extent, an attempt to forge a political coalition for egalitarian aims that included the middle class along with the poor.

The perceptiveness of this strategy is borne out by the fulfillment of Bauer's earlier-noted prediction that housing programs focused solely on the poor would be politically unpopular and fail to prosper.[22] She hoped instead to enlist a broad spectrum of Americans behind direct federal support for the kind of housing *they wanted for themselves*. In other words, Bauer believed that only a program that included the majority along with the poor would thrive in the long term.

Bauer's belief that the housing problem could never be satisfactorily solved, "particularly in America, except by the most democratic sort of process" points to another strength of the Labor Housing Conference initiative. As historian James T. Kloppenberg has pointed out, political analysts and would-be reformers often fail to appreciate the positive reasons that "Americans continue stubbornly to cherish the structural and institutional features of this society and polity that obstruct centralized reform." Movements to change American society must confront the enduring power of traditions of self-help and localism, and not simply because they represent an obdurate reality of the United States political context, but also because they embody aspirations for self-determination and democracy that deserve affirmation. While the program of the Labor Housing Conference may seem to have been hopelessly far from the mainstream of American politics, in fact its effort to build in mechanisms for widespread civic participation in federally coordinated programs was much more in line with American political ideology than public housing programs as they came to be institutionalized in the United States. These ideas suggest ways of organizing publicly assisted activity that might find acceptance and possibly even enthusiasm within American political culture, whereas centralized, bureaucratically administered programs probably never will.[23]

The case studies presented in chapters 5 and 6 suggest that there is considerable validity in the ideas championed by Bauer and other modern housing advocates. The Mackley and Harlem River Houses were able to provide an environment that was appealing and very liveable for residents who were far from being the poorest of the poor. At the same time, one key weakness of both developments was their lack of possibilities for self-governance. They did indeed provide amenities (such as on-site social services) that were not available commercially. In terms of physical design, the individual units were on the small side by middle-class standards, but they were of high quality and complemented by fine shared facilities. The PWA program was only in its infancy when the Wagner Act displaced the policy direction it suggested, and in the postwar years government support for suburbanization and single-family homeownership was massive. Given a more level playing field, it seems possible that the kind of living environment described in these two case studies would have appealed to a sizeable number of Americans.

Finally, this policy initiative is important for the way it attempted to fashion instruments by which the federal government would have gained more control over the economy through public investment. While the role of government in the United States has always been suspect, it seems reasonably clear that a healthy economy free of disastrous cyclical downturns can only be maintained with significant government intervention. Furthermore, as the political climate since the 1970s has demonstrated, expensive social programs are difficult to sell to voters in periods of economic stagnation or decline. Thus, governments wishing to advance such policies need to be able to promote economic growth and full employment. Compared to other western nations, the United States government actually has a rather limited repertoire of tools by which to control the economy. Large-scale direct housing programs would have been an important mechanism by which to increase domestic investment and expand employment in times of recession. Such programs could then have been slowed, to avoid overheating the economy, during upturns. They would even have permitted targeting of federal investment to communities and regions in particular need of assistance or development. None of this is possible using the indirect mechanisms to support the commercial market that were fashioned in the New Deal. These mechanisms rely on the decisions of private parties, each acting in isolation from the others. Therefore, housing resources go up or down, and flow to regions of the country or segments of the population, that are determined not by policy decisions but by the aggregate of these atomized decisions.[24]

These advantages of the Labor Housing Conference policy initiative are important to consider in an era when the New Deal political regime seems to have exhausted itself. Especially given the disillusionment that has set in with regard to so many of the economic and social policies that originated in the 1930s, the modern housing program merits renewed attention. This program did not aim simply at supplying everyone with a high minimum standard of the goods and services already being produced by the commercial market, or even at distributing them more equally. Rather, it proposed creating very different kinds of neighborhoods and living environments—ones that its proponents believed would provide a more satisfying life for everyone. Those who tried to move public policy in this direction took the situation of the middle class seriously, as well as that of the poor, in an attempt to build multiclass coalitions in support of a universal program. They developed a program for housing, but much of their basic strategy could be applied to other spheres of public policy. Thus their efforts, whatever the immediate outcome, suggest a political approach that could have the potential to move the United States toward a greater measure of social justice.

NOTES

Introduction

1. Catherine Bauer to C. E. V. Prins, Director, Information Service Division, USHA, 30 July 1940, quoted in Mary Susan Cole, "Catherine Bauer and the Public Housing Movement, 1926–1937," Ph.D. diss., George Washington University, 1975, 673.

2. Catherine Bauer, *Modern Housing* (Boston: Houghton Mifflin, 1934), 247.

3. See, for example, William E. Leuchtenburg, "The Pertinence of Political History: Reflections on the Significance of the State in America," *Journal of American History* 73 (Dec. 1986): 585–600; Alan Brinkley, "The New Deal and the Idea of the State," in *The Rise and Fall of the New Deal Order, 1930–1980*, edited by Gary Gerstle and Steve Fraser (Princeton: Princeton University Press, 1989); Linda Gordon, "The New Feminist Scholarship on the Welfare State," in *Women, the State, and Welfare*, edited by Linda Gordon (Madison: University of Wisconsin Press, 1990); Ellis W. Hawley, "Social Policy and the Liberal State in Twentieth-Century America," in *Federal Social Policy: The Historical Dimension*, edited by Donald T. Critchlow and Ellis W. Hawley (University Park: Pennsylvania State University Press, 1988); Hugh Davis Graham, "The Stunted Career of Policy History: A Critique and an Agenda," *The Public Historian* 15 (Spring 1993): 15–37.

4. For the most prominent example of this approach, see Alan Dawley, *Struggles for Justice: Social Responsibility and the Liberal State* (Cambridge, MA: Harvard University Press, 1991).

5. Linda Gordon provides a clear articulation of this analytical framework in "Social Insurance and Public Assistance: The Influence of Gender in Welfare Thought in the United States, 1890–1935," *American Historical Review* 79 (Feb. 1992): 19–54.

6. "Low-Cost Housing Grows Scarce," *Milwaukee Journal*, 15 Dec. 1991; John Atlas, "Mortgage Interest Deductions, Even for Mansions, Still the Sacred Cow," *Shelterforce*, Jan./Feb. 1993, 16.

7. See for example, Ronald Tobey, Charles Wetherall, and Jay Brigham, "Moving Out and Settling In: Residential Mobility, Home Owning, and the Public Enframing of Citizenship, 1921–1950," *American Historical Review* 95 (Dec. 1990): 1415–20.

Chapter One

1. Senate Select Committee on Reconstruction and Production, *Hearings on S. Res. 350*, 66th Cong., 3d sess., 10 Aug. 1920, vol. 1, p. 89.

2. Michael J. Doucet and John C. Weaver, "Material Culture and the North Ameri-

can House: The Era of the Common Man, 1870–1920," *Journal of American History* 72 (Dec. 1985): 561.

3. Jules Tygiel, "Housing in Late Nineteenth-Century American Cities: Suggestions for Research," *Historical Methods* 12 (Spring 1979): 88–89.

4. U.S. Bureau of the Census, *Historical Statistics, Bicentennial Edition* 2 (Washington, DC: Government Printing Office, 1975), N238–39, p. 646.

5. For wages, see Peter R. Shergold, *Working Class Life: The "American Standard" in International Perspective, 1899–1913* (Pittsburgh: University of Pittsburgh Press, 1982); Doucet and Weaver, "Material Culture," Table 1, 562, quote from 561.

6. Kenneth T. Jackson, *Crabgrass Frontier: The Suburbanization of the United States* (New York: Oxford University Press, 1985), chap. 5; Margaret Marsh, *Suburban Lives* (New Brunswick: Rutgers University Press), 29–31; Gwendolyn Wright, *Building the Dream: A Social History of Housing in America* (1981; Cambridge, MA: MIT Press, 1983), 102, 111–12.

7. Robert G. Barrows, "Beyond the Tenement: Patterns of American Urban Housing, 1870–1930," *Journal of Urban History* 9 (Aug. 1983): 395–420; Sam Bass Warner, Jr., *Urban Wilderness* (New York: Harper and Row, 1972), 201; Eric H. Monkkonen, *America Becomes Urban* (Berkeley: University of California Press, 1988), 192; Martin J. Daunton, "Cities of Homes and Cities of Tenements: British and American Comparisons, 1870–1914," *Journal of Urban History* 14 (May 1988): 283–319.

8. Monkkonen, *America Becomes Urban*, 192; Harold M. Mayer and Richard C. Wade, *Chicago: Growth of a Metropolis* (Chicago: University of Chicago Press, 1969), 254; John Modell and Tamara K. Hareven, "Urbanization and the Malleable Household: An Examination of Boarding and Lodging in American Families," *Journal of Marriage and the Family* 35 (Aug. 1973): 467–79; Warner, *The Urban Wilderness*, 201.

9. Marc Allan Weiss, "Community Builders vs. Curbstoners: The American Real Estate Industry and Urban Land-Use Planning," Ph.D. diss., University of California at Berkeley, 1985, 73, 82–87.

10. Doucet and Weaver, "Material Culture," 565–67; Richard Harris and Chris Hamnett, "The Myth of the Promised Land: The Social Diffusion of Home Ownership in Britain and North America," *Annals of the Association of American Geographers* 77 (1987): 180.

11. Ann Durkin Keating, *Building Chicago: Suburban Developers and the Creation of a Divided Metropolis* (Columbus: Ohio State University Press, 1988), chap. 4; Sam Bass Warner, *Streetcar Suburbs: The Process of Growth in Boston, 1870–1900* (1962; New York: Atheneum, 1973), 184.

12. Perry R. Duis and Glen E. Holt, "Little Boxes, Big Fortunes," *Chicago* 26 (Nov. 1977): 116.

13. Barrows, "Beyond the Tenement," 399.

14. Census, *Historical Statistics*, N238–39, p. 646.

15. Construction cost index in Census, *Historical Statistics*, N139, p. 629. For consumer price index, Census, *Historical Statistics*, E135, p. 211.

16. Doucet and Weaver, "Material Culture," 577; Leo Grebler, David M. Blank,

and Louis Winnick, *Capital Formation in Residential Real Estate: Trends and Prospects* (Princeton: Princeton University Press, 1956), 126–28.

17. Wright, *Building the Dream*, 168; Grebler, Blank, and Winnick, *Capital Formation*, 114–18.

18. Gwendolyn Wright, *Moralism and the Model Home: Domestic Architecture and Cultural Conflict in Chicago, 1873–1913* (Chicago: University of Chicago Press, 1980), 244; Doucet and Weaver, "Material Culture," Table 5, 583.

19. Grebler, Blank, and Winnick, *Capital Formation*, 110, 333. Census, *Historical Statistics*, N156 and N159, p. 640.

20. Jackson, *Crabgrass Frontier*, 175.

21. James J. Flink, *The Car Culture* (Cambridge, MA: MIT Press, 1975), 52–53, 106; James J. Flink, *The Automobile Age* (Cambridge, MA: MIT Press, 1988), 49; Allan Nevins and Frank Ernest Hill, *Ford: Expansion and Challenge, 1915–1933* (New York: Charles Scribner's Sons, 1957), 685, 287.

22. A. C. Shire, "The Industrial Organization of Housing: Its Methods and Costs," *Annals of the American Academy of Political and Social Science* 190 (Mar. 1937): quote on 38. The average volume of work executed by 78.8 percent of construction firms was $8,644. Computed from U.S. Department of Commerce, *Fifteenth Census of the United States: 1930, Construction Industry* (Washington, DC, 1933), Table 1, 1326. The average cost of a nonfarm dwelling unit in 1929 was $5,972. Grebler, Blank, and Winnick, *Capital Formation*, Table J–1, 426. [Miles Colean and Guy Greer], "Facing the Facts on Housing," *Harpers Magazine* 174 (Mar. 1937): 421.

23. Doucet and Weaver, "Material Culture," 565–75, quote on 566.

24. Weiss, "Community Builders vs. Curbstoners," 73–79; Census, *Historical Statistics*, N265 and N263, p. 648.

25. Michael E. Stone, "The Housing Problem in the United States: Origins and Prospects," *Socialist Review*, no. 52 (July–Aug. 1980): 80.

26. Eugene Nelson White, "Before the Glass-Steagall Act: An Analysis of the Investment Banking Activities of National Banks," *Explorations in Economic History* 23 (1986): 34. For the "utopian capitalist" vision of the 1920s, see Alan Dawley, *Struggles for Justice: Social Responsibility and the Liberal State* (Cambridge, MA: Harvard University Press, 1991), 327–33; and Lizabeth Cohen, *Making a New Deal: Industrial Workers in Chicago, 1919–1939* (Cambridge, UK: Cambridge University Press, 1990), 160–83.

27. J. W. Brabner Smith, "The Financing of Large-Scale Rental Housing," *Law and Contemporary Problems* 5 (Autumn 1938): 608; Harold G. Moulton, *Financial Organization and the Economic System* (New York: McGraw-Hill, 1938), 465–66; Louis S. Posner, "The Lesson of Guaranteed Mortgage Certificates," *Harvard Business Review* 26 (Sept. 1948): 561; Alan Rabinowitz, *The Real Estate Gamble: Lessons from 50 Years of Boom and Bust* (New York: AMACOM, 1980), 43; Alexander Halliburton, "The Real Estate Bond House: A Study of Some of Its Financial Practices," Ph.D. diss., Columbia University, 1939, 39.

28. Marc A. Weiss, *The Rise of the Community Builders: The American Real Estate*

Industry and Urban Land Planning (New York: Columbia University Press, 1987), 31–36.

29. The average cost of a house, exclusive of land, in 1922 was $4,705 (measured in 1929 dollars), and in 1929 it was $5,972. Prices for 1920 and 1921 were not used, since in these years building costs were abnormally low, due to instabilities in the economy following the war. Figures are from Grebler, Blank, and Winnick, *Capital Formation*, 426. Other series differ in specifics, but show the same general pattern. See, for example, W. Floyd Maxwell, "The Building Industry Since the War," *The Review of Economic Statistics* 13 (Feb. 1931): 69; and League of Nations, *Urban and Rural Housing* (Geneva, 1939), 143. For wholesale prices of building materials, see Census, *Historical Statistics*, E48, p. 200.

30. For a fuller discussion of changing trends in residential building and transformations in capital markets in the 1920s, see Gail Radford, "New Building and Investment Patterns in 1920s Chicago," *Social Science History* 16 (Spring 1992): 1–21.

31. Eugene White, *The Regulation and Reform of the American Banking System* (Princeton: Princeton University Press, 1983), 169–70; Benjamin J. Klebaner, *American Commercial Banking: A History* (Boston: Twayne, 1990), 118–19, 121–22; Peter Fearon, *War, Prosperity and Depression: The U.S. Economy, 1917–45* (Lawrence: University Press of Kansas, 1987), 75; Victoria J. Pederson, "Urban Mortgage Debts," in *The Internal Debts of the United States*, edited by Evans Clark (New York: Macmillan Co., 1933), 73.

32. John F. Witte, *The Politics and Development of the Federal Income Tax* (Madison: University of Wisconsin, 1985), 78; William C. Baer, "On the Making of Perfect and Beautiful Social Programs," *The Public Interest* 39 (Spring 1975): 92–93.

33. Pearl Janet Davies, *Real Estate in American History* (Washington, DC: Public Affairs Press, 1958), 95; Ray B. Westerfield, *Money, Credit and Banking* (New York: The Ronald Press, 1947), 1017–26.

34. Quote from Senator William Calder, cited in Harry C. Bredemeier, *The Federal Public Housing Movement* (New York: Arno Press, 1980), 40.

35. Census, *Historical Statistics*, D130, p. 137.

36. National Housing Agency, *Housing after World War I: Will History Repeat Itself?* (Washington, DC, 1945), 10.

37. Census, *Historical Statistics*, N156, p. 640.

38. David Montgomery, "New Tendencies in Union Struggles and Strategies in Europe and the United States, 1916–1922," in *Work, Community, and Power*, edited by James E. Cronin and Carmen Sirianni (Philadelphia: Temple University Press, 1983), quote from 91; David Montgomery, "The 'New Unionism' and the Transformation of Workers Consciousness in America, 1909–22," in Montgomery, *Workers' Control in America: Studies in the History of Work, Technology, and Labor Struggles* (Cambridge, UK: Cambridge University Press, 1979), 92–98.

39. Nicholas Adams, "The United States Housing Corporation's Munitions Worker Suburb in Bethlehem, Pennsylvania (1918) and Its Architectural Context," *Pennsylvania Magazine of History and Biography* 108 (Jan. 1984): 62.

40. David Brody, "The American Worker in the Progressive Age: A Comprehen-

sive Analysis," in *Workers in Industrial America: Essays on the Twentieth Century Struggle* (New York: Oxford University Press, 1980), 12.

41. Arthur S. Link and William B. Batton, *American Epoch* vol. 1, 4th ed. (New York: Alfred A. Knopf, 1963), 189; Curtice N. Hitchcock, "The War Housing Program and Its Future," *Journal of Political Economy* 27 (Apr. 1919): 244–49.

42. Public Law 149, 65th Cong., cited in Bredemeier, *The Federal Public Housing Movement*, 48–49.

43. Quotes from Public Law 149, 65th Cong., and Representative Barnhart cited in Bredemeier, *The Federal Public Housing Movement*, 48–49, 42.

44. International Labour Office, *The Housing Situation in the United States* (Geneva, 1925), 12–15; National Housing Agency, *Housing after World War I* (Washington, DC, 1945), 12–13.

45. Quotation from U.S. Shipping Board, *Second Annual Report* (1919), cited in David Barry Cady, "The Influence of the Garden City Ideal on American Housing and Planning Reform, 1900–1940," Ph.D. diss., University of Wisconsin, 1970, 35; Hitchcock, "War Housing Program," 265–7.

46. *Report of the United States Housing Corporation* (1920), cited in William J. O'Toole, "A Prototype of Public Housing Policy: The USHC," *Journal of the American Institute of Planners* 34 (May 1968): 144.

47. Completion figures from Miles Colean, *Housing for Defense* (New York: Twentieth Century Fund, 1940), 155, 157. For projections, see U.S. Department of Labor, *Report of the United States Housing Corporation* 2 (1919), 386. Edith Elmer Wood, *Recent Trends in American Housing* (New York: The Macmillan Co., 1931), 74–82.

48. Marcus Whitman, "The Public Control of House Rents," *Journal of Land and Public Utility Economics* 1 (July 1925): 344; Hubert F. Havlik, "Recent History of the Control of House Rents," *Journal of Land and Public Utility Economics* 6 (Feb. 1930): 95; Wood, *Recent Trends*, 99; International Labor Office, *Housing Situation in the United States*, 51–52.

49. Harris and Hamnett, "Myth of the Promised Land," 176. For a discussion of these factors that focuses specifically on the United States, see Jackson, *Crabgrass Frontier*, 290–96.

50. Census, *Historical Statistics*, E135 and E150, p. 211.

51. National Housing Agency, *Housing after World War I*, 10, 23–33; Fearon, *War, Prosperity and Depression*, 17; Census, *Historical Statistics*, N156, p. 640.

52. Statistics from Bulletins published by U.S. Bureau of Labor Statistics, *Building Permits in the Principal Cities of the United States* (Washington, DC: 1923–1929).

53. Fearon, *War, Prosperity and Depression*, 65–67; George Soule, *Prosperity Decade* (London: Pilot Press, 1947), 317.

54. The Brookings investigation included rural areas where people had relatively low cash incomes, and thus it might be assumed that the situation was considerably better in cities. Yet a Commerce Department survey focused specifically on urban incomes in 1929 found no greater proportion of city families above the $2,000 mark than the Brookings research had found for the country at large (Maurice Leven, Harold G. Moulton, and Clark Warburton, *America's Capacity to Consume* [Washington, DC: The

Brookings Institution, 1934], 56). Data from Financial Survey of Urban Housing indicate that 62.9 percent of families in 33 cities had incomes of less than $1,950 in 1929 (reported in David L. Wickens, *Residential Real Estate: Its Economic Position as Shown by Values, Rents, Family Incomes, Financing, and Construction* [New York: National Bureau of Economic Research, 1941], 146).

For good recent discussions of workers' standard of living in the 1920s, see Frank Stricker, "Affluence for Whom?—Another Look at Prosperity and the Working Classes in the 1920s," *Labor History* 24 (Winter 1983): 5–33; and Cohen, *Making a New Deal*, 102, and chap. 4.

55. Analysts for the Illinois Bell Telephone Company calculated that 25 percent of all heads of families made less than $1,000 a year in 1927. To estimate what this meant in terms of family income, it is necessary to assume that in most cases families augmented low pay from their major wage earner with rent from lodgers and wage labor by spouses and children. Scholars trying to estimate total working-class family income usually add from 12 to 20 percent to the salary of the principal wage earner to take such other income into account. Using a compromise figure of 16 percent makes $1,160 the upper limit of the bottom quartile of Chicago families in the late 1920s, based on the Illinois Bell projections. Telephone company estimates are from Albert P. Allen, "Chicago's Housing Problem," Report to the Chicago Housing Commission, 14 July 1927, Graham Taylor Papers, Newberry Library. The 12-percent estimate for the average supplemental income was used by the Bureau of Labor Statistics 1918 cost-of-living studies; see Albert Farwell Bemis, *The Economics of Shelter*, vol. 2 of *The Evolving House* (Cambridge, MA: The Technology Press, 1934), 123. Lloyd Rodwin uses the 20-percent figure to derive his estimate of $1,560 to $2,683 as the middle of the income scale in Boston in the 1920s, which generates a median of $2,121.50; see Lloyd Rodwin, *Housing and Economic Progress: A Study of the Housing Experiences of Boston's Middle-Income Families* (Cambridge, MA: Harvard University Press and The Technology Press, 1961), 137.

The best-known income study for Chicago in the 1920s was done by Leila Houghteling, who analyzed the budgets of 467 families supported primarily by full-time nonskilled workers in 1924. Houghteling found a median total family income of $1,673. Almost half of the families fell below what professional social workers regarded as a minimal income for their family size. Clearly, many of the families themselves also perceived their incomes to be excessively meager, since 29 percent had applied for some kind of charitable help, such as medical aid or outright relief, during the year of the study. Houghteling made no estimate as to how representative these families were within the city as a whole (Leila Houghteling, *The Income and Standard of Living of Unskilled Laborers in Chicago* [Chicago: University of Chicago, 1927], 127–31, median income interpolated from Table XLIV, 85).

56. William E. Leuchtenburg, *The Perils of Prosperity, 1914–32* (Chicago: University of Chicago Press, 1958), 194. For a similar argument, see Irving Bernstein, *The Lean Years: A History of the American Worker, 1920–1933* (Boston: Houghton Mifflin, 1960), 65. David Montgomery makes the point about falling prices of food in "Think-

ing About American Workers in the 1920s," *International Labor and Working Class History*, no. 32 (Fall 1987): 9.

57. Mike E. Miles et al., *Real Estate Development: Principles and Process* (Washington, DC: Urban Land Institute, 1991), 82; Keating, *Building Chicago*, 76; Wright, *Moralism and the Model House*, 40–45.

58. Daniel J. Prosser, "Chicago and the Bungalow Boom of the 1920s," *Chicago History* (Summer 1981): 86–95.

59. Census, *Historical Statistics*, E135, p. 211.

60. Celia Hilliard, "'Rent Reasonable to Right Parties': Gold Coast Apartment Buildings 1906–1929," *Chicago History* 8 (Summer 1979): 72.

61. Mayer and Wade, *Chicago*, 307. Housing costs calculated by interpolation from Ernest W. Burgess and Charles Newcomb, *Census Data on the City of Chicago, 1930* (Chicago: University of Chicago Press, 1933), xv. Rent equivalents for owned housing are based on the commonly used formula that assumes rent to be equal to one-tenth of the value of the building. See, for example, Leven, Moulton, and Warburton, *America's Capacity to Consume*, 54.

62. Wim de Wit, "Apartment Houses and Bungalows: Building the Flat City," *Chicago History* 12 (Winter 1983–84): 23; Homer Hoyt, *One Hundred Years of Land Values in Chicago* (1933; New York: Arno, 1970), 245.

63. Radford, "New Building and Investment Patterns," 2–9. For a discussion of similar trends in Boston resulting in the striking decline of new "three-deckers," a type of modest residential structure found in many urban areas in New England, see Rodwin, *Housing and Economic Progress*, 31, 36–39, 60. For other discussions of decreasing low-end production in the 1920s, see Robert B. Fairbanks, *Making Better Citizens: Housing Reform and the Community Development Strategy in Cincinnati, 1890–1960* (Urbana: University of Illinois Press, 1988), 68; John F. Bauman, *Public Housing, Race, and Renewal: Urban Planning in Philadelphia, 1920–1974* (Philadelphia: Temple University Press, 1987), 14; and Thomas Lee Philpott, *The Slum and the Ghetto: Middle-Class Reform, Chicago, 1880–1930* (New York: Oxford University Press, 1978), chap. 11.

64. Philpott, *The Slum and the Ghetto*, 259–69; Devereaux Bowley, *The Poorhouse: Subsidized Housing In Chicago 1895–1976* (Carbondale, IL: Southern Illinois University Press, 1978), 5–16; Carl Condit, *Chicago, 1910–29: Building, Planning, and Urban Technology* (Chicago: University of Chicago Press, 1973), 165–67.

65. Carroll Binder, "Housing Demand Found to Lie in Low-Rent Field," *Chicago Daily News*, 10 Aug. 1931, 14.

66. According to Alan W. Evans, the earliest scholarly version of the filtering theory was developed by Ernest W. Burgess in the 1925 article "The Growth of the City" (see Evans, *Urban Economics* [Basil Blackwell, 1985], 15–18). Disillusionment with the filtering model of housing improvement for the poor on the part of Cincinnati housing reformers in the 1920s is discussed in Fairbanks, *Making Better Citizens*, 68–70.

67. Chicago Department of Public Welfare, *Annual Report, 1926* (Chicago, 1926), 46–47, copy at Municipal Research Library, City of Chicago.

68. In 1920, 71.7 percent of Chicago families rented. By 1930, the proportion was

67.9 percent (U.S. Department of Commerce, *Abstract of the Fifteenth Census of the United States* [Washington, DC: Government Printing Office, 1933], 435).

69. Edith Elmer Wood, *The Housing of the Unskilled Wage Earner: America's Next Problem* (New York: Macmillan, 1919), 14.

70. Rosenthal quoted in "Housing Problem Here Called Acute," *Chicago Daily News,* 17 March [1926], Graham Taylor Papers, Newberry Library, Chicago.

71. Burgess and Newcomb, *Census Data,* xv.

72. The following description of conditions relies most heavily on Richard Munger Eddy, "Chicago Housing at Low Rental Levels in 1932," M. A. dissertation, University of Chicago, 1934, 309. Eddy's study, commissioned by the Illinois Housing Commission, analyzed conditions at three rent levels: under $20, $20–29, and $30–42. Translating these three levels to 1930 equivalents (rents had dropped 21 percent between spring 1930 and spring 1932) gives the following ranges: under $25, $25–37, and $38–53. For changes in rents, see "Index Numbers of Rents of Workingmen's Dwellings in Chicago," *Monthly Labor Review* 29 (Aug. 1929): 20; ibid., 36 (Feb. 1933): 433; cited in Hoyt, *Land Values in Chicago,* 476.

73. Edith Abbott, *The Tenements of Chicago, 1908–1935* (Chicago: University of Chicago Press, 1936), 183, 234. Eddy, "Chicago Housing," 110. After 1910, lot widths of thirty feet became standard for residential building because of a new city ordinance requiring windows to be set back three feet from the lot line (Hoyt, *Land Values in Chicago,* 429).

74. Abbott, *Tenements of Chicago,* 286; Eddy, "Chicago Housing," 228, 122.

75. Abbott, *Tenements of Chicago,* 208; Eddy, "Chicago Housing," 71, 74.

76. Abbott, *Tenements of Chicago,* 221; Eddy, "Chicago Housing," 84, 124, 198, 233.

77. A study by the Department of Public Welfare found apartments with furnace heat available at a median rent of $65 to $70 (Elizabeth A. Hughes, *Living Conditions for Small-Wage Earners in Chicago* [Chicago: Department of Public Welfare, 1925], 32).

78. Eddy, "Chicago Housing," 322.

79. Ibid., 309.

80. Mary Faith Adams, "Present Housing Conditions in South Chicago, South Deering and Pullman," M. A. thesis, University of Chicago, 1926, 46.

81. Adams, "Housing Conditions," 20. The Bush was located between 83rd and 87th streets immediately to the west of a group of steel mills on the lakefront.

82. Eddy, "Chicago Housing," 68.

83. Hughes, *Living Conditions,* 23.

84. Ibid., quotes from 24 and 23.

85. Michael E. Stone makes these arguments in "The Housing Problem in the United States," 72.

Chapter Two

1. See, for example, Arthur M. Schlesinger, Jr., *The Coming of the New Deal* (Boston: Houghton Mifflin, 1958), vol. 2 of *The Age of Roosevelt,* 297–98; and William E. Leuchtenburg, *Franklin D. Roosevelt and the New Deal, 1932–40* (New York: Harper and Row, 1963), 133–36.

2. Roy Lubove, *The Progressives and the Slums: Tenement House Reform in New York City, 1890–1917* (1962; Westport, CT: Greenwood Press, 1974), 4–7, quotes from 4 and 7(note).

3. Elizabeth Blackmar, *Manhattan for Rent, 1785–1850* (Ithaca: Cornell University Press, 1989), 240–247, 264–67, quote from 247.

4. Lubove, *Progressives and the Slums*, 33–39, 100–113, 175–76; Eugenie Ladner Birch and Deborah S. Gardner, "The Seven-Percent Solution: A Review of Philanthropic Housing, 1870–1910," *Journal of Urban History* 7 (Aug. 1981): 403–438; Cynthia Zaitzevsky, "Housing Boston's Poor: The First Philanthropic Experiments," *Journal of the Society of Architectural Historians* 42 (May 1983): 157–67; Edith Elmer Wood, *The Housing of the Unskilled Wage Earner* (New York: Macmillan, 1919), 93–114; Alfred T. White, *Thirty-five Years' Experience as an Owner* (New York: National Housing Association, 1912); Lutz Niethammer, "Some Elements of the Housing Reform Debate in Nineteenth-Century Europe," in *Modern Industrial Cities: History, Policy, and Survival*, edited by Bruce Stave (Beverly Hills: Sage Publications, 1981), quote from 156. For a long-term financial analysis of Alfred T. White's Riverside, an early and successful model tenement built in 1890, see "A Tenement Turns Outside In," *Architectural Forum* 71 (Nov. 1939): 406–7.

5. Lubove, *Progressives and the Slums*, 177–79; Edith Elmer Wood, *The Housing of the Unskilled Wage Earner* (New York: Macmillan, 1919), 76–77.

6. Edith Elmer Wood, *Recent Trends in American Housing* (New York: Macmillan, 1931), 11.

7. The influence of English garden city planning on Americans is described in Daniel Schaffer, *Garden Cities for America: The Radburn Experience* (Philadelphia: Temple University Press, 1982), 31–35; David B. Cady, "The Influence of the Garden City Ideal and Federal War Housing on American Housing and Planning Reform," M. A. thesis, University of Wisconsin, Milwaukee, 1966, esp. 42–55; and Francesco Dal Co, "From Parks to the Region: Progressive Ideology and the Reform of the American City," in *The American City: From the Civil War to the New Deal*, edited by Giorgio Ciucci et al. and translated by Barbara Luigia La Penta (Cambridge, MA: MIT Press, 1983), 211. For financial and political dimensions of the garden city, see Joseph L. Arnold, *The New Deal in the Suburbs: A History of the Greenbelt Town Program, 1935–54* (Columbus: Ohio State University Press, 1971), 5–9; and Robert Fishman, *Urban Utopias in the Twentieth Century: Ebenezer Howard, Frank Lloyd Wright, Le Corbusier* (1977; Cambridge, MA: MIT paperback ed., 1982), 24, 46–49.

8. Kenneth T. Jackson, *Crabgrass Frontier: The Suburbanization of the United States* (New York: Oxford University Press, 1985), 79–81, quote from Olmsted, 81.

9. The characterization of goals is from Robert W. DeForest, "The Housing Plan of the Russell Sage Foundation: What It Is, Why It Is, and What It Is Not," 2, Press Release in The Olmsted Associates Collection, Box 255, Library of Congress, n.d., but probably Nov. 1910. The author is indebted to Jon Peterson for this material.

10. Grosvenor Atterbury, "How to Get Low Cost Houses," *Housing Problems in America* 5 (1916): 93; John M. Glenn, Lilian Brandt, and F. Emerson Andrews, *Russell Sage Foundation, 1907–1946*, vol. 1 (New York: Russell Sage Foundation, 1947), 228;

David P. Handlin, *The American Home: Architecture and Society, 1815–1915* (Boston: Little, Brown and Co., 1979), 285–87.

11. Quote from DeForest, "The Housing Plan," 3; Glenn, Brandt, and Andrews, *Russell Sage*, 272; Norman T. Newton, *Design on the Land: The Development of Landscape Architecture* (Cambridge, MA: Harvard University Press, 1971), 478; James Dahir, *Communities for Better Living* (New York: Harper & Brothers, 1950), 184.

12. Benjamin Clarke Marsh, *An Introduction to City Planning: Democracy's Challenge to the American City* (New York: privately published, 1909), 36–37, 50–52, quote from 50.

13. Frederick C. Howe, "The Municipal Real Estate Policies of German Cities," in *Proceedings of the Third National Conference on City Planning* (Philadelphia, 1911), 14–26, quotes from 22 and 23.

14. Carol Aronovici, "Constructive Housing Reform," *National Municipal Review* 2 (Apr. 1913): 210–20; Aronovici, "Housing and the Housing Problem," *The Annals of the American Academy of Political and Social Science* 51 (Jan. 1914): 1, 5; "Carol Aronovici," *National Cyclopaedia of American Biography* 45 (New York: James T. White, 1962), 460.

15. Eugenie Ladner Birch, "Edith Elmer Wood and the Genesis of Liberal Housing Thought, 1910–1942," Ph.D. diss., Columbia University, 1976, 35–41. Quotations from Wood's testimony to Senate Subcommittee on the District of Columbia, *Inhabited Alleyways in the District of Columbia*, 63d Cong., 2d sess., 7 May 1914, 24, 25.

16. Edith Elmer Wood, *The Housing of the Unskilled Wage Earner: America's Next Problem* (New York: Macmillan, 1919), 227–28, 293–300.

17. Wood, *Housing of the Unskilled Wage Earner*, 228; American Federation of Labor, *Report of the Proceedings of the Thirty-fourth Annual Convention of the American Federation of Labor* (Washington, DC, 1914), 355; American Federation of Labor, *Report of the Proceedings of the Thirty-fifth Annual Convention of the American Federation of Labor* (Washington, DC, 1915), 113.

18. Wood, *Housing of the Unskilled Wage Earner*, 225–26; and Edith Elmer Wood, *Recent Trends in American Housing* (New York: Macmillan, 1931), 201.

19. Walter H. Kilham, "Housing by the Commonwealth of Massachusetts," *Journal of the American Institute of Architects* 6 (Mar. 1918): 134. Wood, *Housing of the Unskilled Wage Earner*, 209–22.

20. Roy Lubove, *Community Planning in the 1920's: The Contribution of the Regional Planning Association of America* (Pittsburgh: University of Pittsburgh Press, 1963), 5–9; Richard M. Candee and Greer Hardwicke, "Early Twentieth-Century Reform Housing by Kilham and Hopkins, Architects of Boston," *Winterthur Portfolio* 22 (Spring 1987): 61–62; Dorothy Schaffter, *State Housing Agencies* (New York: Columbia University Press, 1942), 86.

21. For a discussion of more fundamental factors, see articles by David Montgomery cited in chapter 1, note 38.

22. [Charles Harris Whitaker], "The War—The Machine—The Man," *Journal of the American Institute of Architects* 5 (Sept. 1917): 421.

23. Walter H. Kilham, "Housing by the Commonwealth of Massachusetts," *Journal of the American Institute of Architects* 6 (Mar. 1918): 134.

24. For a discussion of the movement to build civic consciousness through working at the local level, see Patricia Mooney Melvin, "'A Cluster of Interlacing Communities': The Cincinnati Social Unit Plan and Neighborhood Organization, 1900–1920," in *Poverty and Public Policy in Modern America*, edited by Donald T. Critchlow and Ellis W. Hawley (Chicago: Dorsey Press, 1989), 82.

25. Facilities were included in twelve of the forty-seven developments (excluding facilities designed for single men only). I have been able to find plans for neighborhood meeting space of some sort for seven of the remaining developments. These calculations are based on information in U.S. Dept. of Labor, Bureau of Industrial Housing and Transportation, *Report of the United States Housing Corporation*, 2 vols. (Washington, DC: Government Printing Office, 1920); Miles L. Colean, *Housing for Defense* (New York: Twentieth Century Fund, 1940), 155–57; Richard M. Candee, *Atlantic Heights: A World War I Shipbuilders' Community* (Portsmouth, NH: Portsmouth Marine Society, 1985); [Charles Piez], *Report of the Director General Charles Piez to the Board of Trustees of the United States Shipping Board Emergency Fleet Corporation* (Washington, DC: Government Printing Office, 1919); General Project Files of the USHC, National Archives, Cartographic and Architectural Branch, Alexandria, Virginia; "An Housing Development at Watertown, N. Y., for the United States Housing Corporation," *Architectural Review* 7 (Dec. 1918): 129–31; "The United States Housing Corporation: Project No. 59 at Bath, Maine," *Architectural Record* 45 (Jan. 1919): 21–25; "A Housing Development That Solves the Lodger Problem: The Naval Ordnance Housing Development, South Charleston, W. Va.," *American Architect* 115 (23 Apr. 1919): 565–69; "The First War Emergency Government Towns: IV. Groton, Connecticut," *Journal of the American Institute of Architects* 6 (Nov. 1918): 510–17; "Buckman Village: U.S. Shipping Board Housing at Chester, PA.," *Architectural Forum* 32 (May 1920): 183–88; "The First War Emergency Government Towns: II. Hilton, Virginia," *Journal of the American Institute of Architects* 6 (July 1918): 333–45.

26. William E. Groben, "Union Park Gardens: A Model Garden Suburb for Shipworkers at Wilmington, Delaware," *Architectural Record* 45 (Jan. 1919): 60.

27. Christian Topalov, "Housing Reform for the Poor and the Working Class: New York, Paris, 1900–1940," paper presented at the conference on the History of Low-Income Housing in New York City, Columbia University, October 1984, in possession of author; Topalov, "Scientific Planning and the Ordering of Daily Life: The First 'War Housing' Experiment in the United States, 1917–1919," *Journal of Urban History* 17 (November 1990): quote from 33.

28. Phrase from Gwendolyn Wright, *Moralism and the Model Home: Domestic Architecture and Cultural Conflict in Chicago, 1873–1913* (Chicago: University of Chicago Press, 1980), 2. For the design component of utopian reform, see Dolores Hayden, *Seven American Utopias: The Architecture of Communitarian Socialism, 1790–1975* (1976; Cambridge, MA: MIT Press Paperback, 1979).

29. Quotes from Groben, "Union Park Gardens," 60; and Electus D. Litchfield, "Yorkship Village," *The American Review of Reviews* 60 (Dec. 1919): 599.

30. Quoted in Dolores Hayden, *The Grand Domestic Revolution: A History of Feminist Designs for American Homes, Neighborhoods, and Cities* (Cambridge, MA: MIT Press, 1981), 250.

31. Virginia Yeaman, "The House That Moorestown Built," *The American City* 39 (Aug. 1928): 95–96. This building still stands and functions as a neighborhood center.

32. "Reconstruction Program, A. F. of L.," in *American Federation of Labor: History, Encyclopedia Reference Book* 2 (Washington, DC, 1924), 258. Richard Plunz notes that the platform of the New York Labor Party in 1920 called for government to take over all housing production (see Plunz, *A History of Housing in New York City: Dwelling Type and Social Change in the American Metropolis* [New York: Columbia University Press, 1990], 126–27). For a bibliography of articles from this period supportive of the war housing agencies' work, see Francesco Dal Co, "From Parks to the Region: Progressive Ideology and the Reform of the American City," in *The American City: From the Civil War to the New Deal*, edited by Giorgio Ciucci et al. and translated by Barbara Luigia La Penta (1973; Cambridge, MA: MIT Paperback, 1983), notes on pages 178–87, and 282–84.

33. Frederick L. Ackerman, "Government Housing—Federal, State, Municipal— Is It Desirable?" in National Housing Association, *Housing Problems in America, Proceedings of the Seventh National Conference of the National Housing Association* 7 (1918): 70–81, quotations from 75 and 75–76.

34. For discussions of George's ideas, see Blackmar, *Manhattan for Rent*, 265–67; and John D. Fairfield, *The Mysteries of the Great City: The Politics of Urban Design, 1877– 1937* (Columbus: Ohio State University Press, 1993), chapter 1, esp. 38–41.

35. Charles Harris Whitaker, *The Joke About Housing* (Boston: Marshall Jones Company, 1920), quotes from 135 and 83.

36. Richard S. Childs, "What Is a House? V," in Charles Harris Whitaker et al., *The Housing Problem in War and Peace* (Washington, DC: Journal of the American Institute of Architects, 1918), 59; George Gove, "Housing the Workers—An Unfinished Job," *American City* 20 (Jan. 1919): 23–25; "Government Housing Chaos," *Nation* 108 (18 Jan. 1919): 84–85. Efforts to transform World War I federal housing developments into nonprofit cooperatives are discussed in Kristin Szylvian Bailey, "The Federal Government and the Cooperative Housing Movement, 1917–1955," Ph.D. diss., Carnegie Mellon University, 1988, 14–19.

37. Frederick Law Olmsted, "Lessons from Housing Developments of the United States Housing Corporation," *Monthly Labor Review* 8 (May 1919): 1259–60, quotes from 1259.

38. Samuel P. Hayes, *Conservation and the Gospel of Efficiency* (1959; New York: Atheneum, 1979), 266.

39. J. Horace McFarland, "War-Time Housing and the Government," *American Review of Reviews* 60 (Dec. 1919): quote from 597–98; George Holden Tinkham, "Urgent Need for a Department of Housing and Living Conditions in the Department of Labor, *American City* 22 (Mar. 1920): 222; Roy Lubove, "Homes and 'A Few Well

Placed Fruit Trees': An Object Lesson in Federal Housing," *Social Research* 27 (Winter 1960): 485–86.

40. Joseph A. Spencer, "New York City Tenant Organizations and the Post-World War I Housing Crisis," in *The Tenant Movement in New York City, 1904–1984*, edited by Ronald Lawson (New Brunswick: Rutgers University Press, 1986), 51–52, 59–63.

41. Quoted in Lubove, *Community Planning*, 20.

42. Wood, *Recent Trends*, 240–41; Lubove, *Community Planning*, 23.

43. Alfred E. Smith, "A Housing Policy for New York," *The Survey* 45 (2 Oct. 1920): 3–4; Wood, *Recent Trends*, 202, 106–109; Harry C. Bredemeier, *The Federal Public Housing Movement* (New York: Arno Press, 1980), 68. For the Land Bank of New York, see Miles L. Colean, *The Impact of Government on Real Estate Finance in the United States* (New York: National Bureau of Economic Research, 1950), 91.

In 1926, Smith again tried for a program by which the state could channel low-cost capital into particular kinds of residential building through a state housing bank. That year his proposals were cut back to a State Housing Board authorized to study conditions and oversee limited-dividend (that is, low-profit) companies established to provide housing at moderate rents. These companies were granted tax exemptions on their buildings, but without easy access to cheap capital, they were difficult to organize. Only eleven limited-dividend housing companies were set up, and they built approximately 7,000 apartments; see Roy Lubove, *Community Planning*, 73–82; James Ford, *Slums and Housing* (Cambridge, MA: Harvard University Press, 1936), 234–36; Miles L. Colean, *American Housing* (New York: Twentieth Century Fund, 1944), 273–74.

44. Lubove, *Community Planning*, 17–29, quote from 22; Wood, *Recent Trends*, 252–58.

45. Marcus Whitman, "The Public Control of House Rents," *Journal of Land and Public Utility Economics* 1 (July 1925): 345; Herbert F. Havlik, "Recent History of the Control of House Rents," *Journal of Land and Public Utility Economics* 6 (Feb. 1930): 95–98; Allan David Heskin, *Tenants and the American Dream: Ideology and the Tenant Movement* (New York: Praeger, 1983), 28–29; quote from Wood, *Recent Trends*, 95.

46. Spencer, "New York City Tenant Organizations," 84–85, quote from 85.

47. Wood, *Recent Trends*, 101. Havlik, "Recent History," 95.

48. John L. Weaver, President of the National Association of Real Estate Boards, testimony before House Committee on Ways and Means, *Hearing on Real Estate Mortgage Taxes (H.R. 8080 and H. R. 14062)*, 66th Cong., 2d sess., 26 May 1920, 20.

49. Marc A. Weiss, *The Rise of the Community Builders: The American Real Estate Industry and Urban Land Planning* (New York: Columbia University Press, 1987), chaps. 4 and 5.

50. House, Ways and Means, *Real Estate Mortgage Taxes*, 6, 9.

51. Ibid., 9.

52. Senate Committee on Banking and Currency, *Hearing on Federal Building Loans (S. 2492)*, 66th Cong., 1st sess., 8 Oct. 1919; House Committee on Banking and Currency, *Hearing on Federal Building Loan Act (H.R. 7597)*, 66th Cong., 1st sess., 31 Oct. 1919. For federal land banks, see Ray B. Westerfield, *Money, Credit and Banking* (New York: The Ronald Press, 1947), 1017–26. See also M. J. Daunton, "Home Loans versus

Council Houses: The Formation of American and British Housing Policy, 1900–1920," *Housing Studies* 3 (Oct. 1988); Miles L. Colean, *The Impact of Government on Real Estate Finance in the United States* (New York: National Bureau of Economic Research, 1950); and H. Morton Bodfish, *History of Building and Loan in the United States* (Chicago: United States Building and Loan League, 1931), 207–14.

53. House Committee on Ways and Means, *Hearings on Real Estate Mortgage Taxes (H.R. 8080 and H. R. 14062 [also H. R. 14473])*, 66th Cong., 3d sess., 11 Dec. 1920, quotes from 66.

54. House, Ways and Means, *Real Estate Mortgage Taxes*, quotes from Oldfield, 69–70, and Smith, 70.

55. "Cities Build Homes for Workers," *Illustrated World* 34 (Sept. 1920): 121, quote from 122; Wood, *Housing of the Unskilled Worker*, 130–31.

56. Joan M. Meister, "Civic Park: General Motors' Solution for the Housing Shortage," in Michigan History Division, Department of State, *A Wind Gone Down: Smoke into Steel* (Michigan Department of State, 1978), 5–14; Carolyn S. Loeb, "Entrepreneurial Vernacular: Developers' Subdivisions in the 1920s," Ph.D. diss., City University of New York, 1990, 27–49.

57. Wood, *Recent Trends*, 207.

58. Loeb, "Entrepreneurial Vernacular," 34. Allan Nevins and Frank Ernest Hill, *Ford: Expansion and Challenge, 1915–1933* (New York: Charles Scribner's Sons, 1957), 510.

59. "Effect of Housing Shortage on Industry," *Monthly Labor Review* 19 (July 1924): 184–85, quote from 185.

60. David Barry Cady, "The Influence of the Garden City Ideal on American Housing and Planning Reform, 1900–1940," Ph.D. diss., University of Wisconsin, 1970, 81–86, 96–98, quotes from 86.

61. Cady, "Garden City Ideal," 98–104, commission quotes from 84; Schuchardt quoted in Wayne Attoe and Mark Latus, "The First Public Housing: Sewer Socialism's Garden City for Milwaukee," *Journal of Popular Culture* 10 (Summer 1976): 145; Wisconsin Writers Program, *Wisconsin: A Guide to the Badger State* (1941; St. Clair Shores, MI: Somerset, 1974), 263.

62. Cady, "Garden City Ideal," 87, 108; "The Municipal and Cooperative Housing Law in Wisconsin," *American City* 22 (Feb. 1920): 156–57; Attoe and Latus, "First Public Housing," 143; Emil Seidel, "Garden Homes Steps Out," *Historical Messenger of the Milwaukee County Historical Society* 28 (Summer 1972): 73–78, quote from 76.

63. Wood, *Recent Trends*, 176.

64. Cady, "Garden City Ideal," 95, 102–108, tenant quoted on 122, note 111.

65. Fred A. Bjornstad, "'A Revolution in Ideas and Methods': The Construction Industry and Socioeconomic Planning in the United States, 1915–1933," Ph.D. diss., University of Iowa, 1991, 19–28; Hoover quoted in "Statement by Secretary Hoover for *Christian Science Monitor*," 25 Mar. 1925, 5, in Commerce Department Files, Herbert Hoover Presidential Library (hereafter HHPL). The author thanks Mark Rose for material from the Hoover Library. For Hoover's work with the Housing Division, see also Craig Lloyd, *Aggressive Introvert: A Study of Herbert Hoover and Public Relations*

Management, 1912–1932 (Columbus: Ohio State University Press, 1972), 130–33; Herbert Hoover, *The Memoirs of Herbert Hoover: The Cabinet and the Presidency, 1920–1933* (New York: Macmillan, 1952), 92–96; and Ellis W. Hawley, "Herbert Hoover, the Commerce Secretariat, and the Vision of an 'Associative State,' 1921–1928," *Journal of American History* 61 (June 1974): 125, 133.

66. Herbert Hoover to James R. Angell, Carnegie Corporation, 28 Sept. 1921, Commerce Department File, HHPL.

67. Press release, "The Value of Standardization," 25 Oct. 1921, in Commerce Department Files, HHPL.

68. Hoover quote from "Statement to *Christian Science Monitor*," 4. See also, Janet Hutchison, "The Cure for Domestic Neglect: Better Homes in America, 1922–1935," in *Perspectives in Vernacular Architecture, II*, edited by Camille Wells (Columbia: University of Missouri Press, 1986): 168–78.

69. William R. Tanner, "Secretary of Commerce Hoover's War on Waste, 1921–1928," in *Herbert Hoover and the Republican Era: A Reconsideration*, edited by Carl E. Krog and William R. Tanner (Lanham: University Press of America, 1984), 13–14.

70. Tanner, "Hoover's War on Waste," 22.

71. Wood, *Recent Trends*, 62.

72. William Linous Cody Wheaton, "The Evolution of Federal Housing Programs," Ph.D. diss., University of Chicago, 1953, 7, 21–37.

73. Quoted in John M. Gries and James Ford, Introduction to *Housing Objectives and Programs*, vol. 11 of *President's Conference on Home Building and Home Ownership*, edited by John M. Gries and James Ford (Washington, DC, 1932), xv.

74. Elizabeth A. Hughes, *Living Conditions for Small Wage Earners in Chicago* (Chicago: Department of Public Welfare, 1925), 17. Rosenthal quote from "Housing Problem Here Called Acute," *Chicago Daily News*, 17 Mar. [1926], Graham Taylor Papers, Newberry Library, Chicago.

75. Karl de Schweinitz, "Are the Poor Really Poor?" *Survey* 59 (15 Jan. 1928), quotes from 517, 519; Clark A. Chambers, *Seedtime of Reform: American Social Service and Social Action, 1918–1933* (Minneapolis: University of Minnesota Press, 1963), 133–38, 178–79. See also Allen F. Davis, *Spearheads for Reform: The Social Settlements and the Progressive Movement 1890–1914* (New York: Oxford University Press, 1967), chap. 4.

76. Robert Hunter, *Tenement Conditions in Chicago* (Chicago: City Homes Association, 1901).

77. *The National Cyclopaedia of American Biography* C (New York: James T. White, 1930), 517; Ellen Fitzpatrick, *Endless Crusade: Women Social Scientists and Progressive Reform* (New York: Oxford University Press, 1990), 87.

78. Edith Abbott, *The Tenements of Chicago, 1908–1935* (Chicago: University of Chicago Press, 1936), 64–65, 73.

79. Edith Elmer Wood, *Slums and Blighted Areas in the United States*, Housing Division Bulletin, No. 1 (Washington, DC: Federal Emergency Administration of Public Works, 1936), 40.

80. Mary Faith Adams, "Present Housing Conditions in South Chicago, South Deering and Pullman," M. A. thesis, University of Chicago, 1926, 18, quote 21.

81. Abbott, *Tenements of Chicago*, 486.

82. Hughes, *Living Conditions*, quotes from 9 and 32.

83. Ibid., 39.

84. Quote from Elizabeth Hughes, "Chicago Takes Another Step," 6, article reprinted from *Welfare Magazine*, March 1927, in Chicago Municipal Research Library; Abbott, *Tenements of Chicago*, 483.

85. Clark Chambers notes that the National Federation of Settlements published a policy statement in 1922 calling for "the housing problem to be recognized as a community problem" because private capital could not earn a profit on housing for low-income families (Chambers, *Seedtime of Reform*, 135). The AFL, after going on record in 1919 for continuing the Labor Department's Housing Corporation, stopped making public statements on the housing question. However, during the decade, a number of individual unions, most notably the Amalgamated Clothing Workers, experimented with mechanisms outside of normal commercial channels by which to produce housing. These efforts will be discussed in chapter 5.

86. The term "professional houser" is from John F. Bauman, *Public Housing, Race, and Renewal: Urban Planning in Philadelphia, 1920–1974* (Philadelphia: Temple University Press, 1987), 5–6. Marquette is quoted in Robert B. Fairbanks, *Making Better Citizens: Housing Reform and the Community Development Strategy in Cincinnati, 1890–1960* (Urbana: University of Illinois Press, 1988), 69. Veiller's philosophy is described in Lubove, *The Progressives and the Slums*, 175–82. For a specific proposal along these lines, which Veiller made in 1929 to housing reformers in Cincinnati, see Fairbanks, *Making Better Citizens*, 73. For the changing position of Bernard Newman, executive director of the Philadelphia Housing Association, see Bauman, *Public Housing, Race, and Renewal*, 5–6; and Bauman, "Black Slums/Black Projects: The New Deal and Negro Housing in Philadelphia," *Pennsylvania History* 49 (July 1974): note 2, 313.

87. Wood, *Recent Trends*, 1, punctuation as in original.

88. Michael E. Stone, *Shelter Poverty: New Ideas on Housing Affordability* (Philadelphia: Temple University Press, 1993), 87; Bernard Newman, "Housing Research in Philadelphia," *Architectural Record* 74 (Sept. 1933).

Chapter Three

1. Catherine Bauer, *Modern Housing* (Boston: Houghton Mifflin, 1934). Bibliographies of Bauer's articles from the 1930s can be found in Mary Susan Cole, "Catherine Bauer and the Public Housing Movement, 1926–1937," Ph.D. diss., George Washington University, 1975, 682–84; and Bernard J. Frieden and William W. Nash, Jr., *Shaping an Urban Future: Essays in Memory of Catherine Bauer Wurster* (Cambridge, MA: MIT Press, 1969), 205–6.

2. For discussions of the political situation at this time, see Élie Halévy, "The World Crisis of 1914–1918: An Interpretation," in Halévy, *The Era of Tyrannies*, translated by R. K. Webb (Garden City: Anchor Press, 1965): 209–48; and Charles S. Maier, *Recasting Bourgeois Europe* (Princeton: Princeton University Press, 1975), part 1. See also

Glen Yago, *The Decline of Transit: Urban Transportation in German and U.S. Cities, 1900–1970* (Cambridge, UK: Cambridge University Press, 1984), 95; and Mark Swenarton, *Homes Fit for Heroes: The Politics and Architecture of Early State Housing in Britain* (London: Heinemann Educational Books, 1981), 189–94.

3. Ada Louise Huxtable, "Inventing American Reality," *New York Review of Books*, 3 Dec. 1992, 28.

4. Elizabeth Denby, *Europe Re-housed* (New York: W. W. Norton, 1938), 154; Helmut Gruber, "Socialist Party Culture and the Realities of Working-Class Life in Red Vienna," in *The Austrian Socialist Experiment: Social Democracy and Austromarxism, 1918–1934*, edited by Anson Rabinbach (Boulder: Westview Press, 1985), 230–31; Peter Marcuse, "A Useful Installment of Socialist Work: Housing in Red Vienna in the 1920s," in *Critical Perspectives on Housing*, edited by Rachel G. Bratt, Chester Hartman, and Ann Meyerson (Philadelphia: Temple University Press, 1986).

5. Barbara Miller Lane, *Architecture and Politics in Germany, 1918–1945* (Cambridge, MA: Harvard University Press, 1968), 89; Richard Pommer and Christian F. Otto, *Weissenhof 1927 and the Modern Movement in Architecture* (Chicago: University of Chicago Press, 1991), 1–4; Sima Ingberman, "Normative and Evolutionary Housing Prototypes in Germany and Austria: The Viennese Superblocks, 1919–1934," *Oppositions* 13 (Summer 1978): 77. In Vienna, the emphasis on maintaining high levels of employment discouraged experimentation with new building methods. See Gruber, "Socialist Party Culture," 232–33.

6. Vittorio Magnago Lampugnani, *Architecture and City Planning in the Twentieth Century* (1980; New York: Van Nostrand Reinhold, 1985), 99–100; Ronald Wiedenhoeft, *Berlin's Housing Revolution: German Reform in the 1920s* (Ann Arbor: UMI Research Press, 1985), 33–51, 119–20. Henry Wright, *Rehousing Urban America* (New York: Columbia University Press, 1935), 86–96. John Robert Mullin, "City Planning in Frankfurt, Germany, 1925–32," *Journal of Urban History* 4 (November 1977): 18–19.

7. Wiedenhoeft, *Berlin's Housing Revolution*, 20.

8. Richard Pommer and Christian F. Otto, *Weissenhof 1927 and the Modern Movement in Architecture* (Chicago: University of Chicago Press, 1991), 2.

9. Wolfgang Pehnt, *Expressionist Architecture*, translated by J. A. Underwood and Edith Kustner (London: Thames and Hudson, 1973; paperback ed., 1979), 196–97.

10. Helen Searing, "*Eigen Haard*: Workers' Housing and the Amsterdam School," *Architectura* (1971): 148–74. Helen Searing, "With Red Flags Flying: Housing in Amsterdam, 1915–1923," in *Art and Architecture in the Service of Politics*, edited by Henry Á. Millon and Linda Nochlin (Cambridge, MA: MIT Press, 1978), 230–69. Pehnt, *Expressionist Architecture*, 181–93.

11. Matthew Josephson to Cole, 9 Nov. 1974, in Cole, "Catherine Bauer," 99. The sketch of the person Josephson calls "Miss D." in his memoir is based on Bauer; see Josephson, *Life Among the Surrealists* (New York: Holt, Rinehart and Winston, 1962), 368–69.

12. Cole, "Catherine Bauer," 87–93; Catherine Bauer, "We Present Catherine Bauer in Her Own Words," *Journal of Housing* 1 (Nov. 1944): quote from 27.

13. Cole, "Catherine Bauer," 87–93.

14. Catherine Bauer, "Machine-Age Mansions for Ultra-Moderns," *New York Times Magazine*, 15 Apr. 1928, 10.

15. Bauer, "Machine-Age Mansions," 10.

16. Bauer, "Machine-Age Mansions," 22. For a fascinating discussion of Le Corbusier's experimental low-cost housing development near Bordeaux, built in the mid–1920s, see Philippe Boudon, *Lived-in Architecture: Le Corbusier's Pessac Revisited*, translated by Gerald Onn (1969; paperback edition: Cambridge, MA: MIT Press, 1979).

17. Bauer, "Own Words," 27; Lewis Mumford, *The Golden Day: A Study in American Experience and Culture* (New York: Boni and Liveright, 1926); Lewis Mumford, *My Works and Days: A Personal Chronicle* (New York: Harcourt Brace Jovanovich, 1979), 302; Donald L. Miller, *Lewis Mumford: A Life* (New York: Weidenfeld and Nicolson, 1989), 288–89, 305–307; Cole, "Catherine Bauer," 101–2.

18. Roy Lubove, *Community Planning in the 1920s: The Contribution of the Regional Planning Association of America* (Pittsburgh: University of Pittsburgh Press, 1963), 39–40, 96–97; Lewis Mumford, "Introduction" to Clarence S. Stein, *New Towns for America* (1957; Cambridge, MA: MIT Press Paperback, 1969); Cole, "Catherine Bauer," 87; Miller, *Lewis Mumford*, 332.

19. Buder, *Visionaries and Planners*, 166, 170–73. The RPAA's theories are discussed in various articles in *Survey* 54 (1 May 1925); quote from title of Clarence S. Stein's article in this issue, 134. See also, Lewis Mumford, "Regionalism and Irregionalism," *Sociological Review* 19 (Oct. 1927): 277–88; Mumford, "The Theory and Practice of Regionalism," ibid. 20 (Jan. 1928): 18–33; Mumford, "The Theory and Practice of Regionalism (Continued)," ibid. 20 (Apr. 1928): 131–41.

20. Lubove, "Homes and 'A Few Well Placed Fruit Trees': An Object Lesson in Federal Housing," *Social Research* 27 (Winter 1960): 470–71; Edith Elmer Wood, *Recent Trends in American Housing* (New York: Macmillan, 1931), 66.

21. Frederick L. Ackerman, "What Is a House? IV," *Journal of the American Institute of Architects* 5 (Dec. 1917): 591–621; reprinted in *The Housing Problem in War and Peace*, edited by Charles H. Whitaker (Washington, DC: Journal of the American Institute of Architects, 1918).

22. Robert D. Kohn, "The Housing Division of the Emergency Fleet Corporation during the War," *Journal of the American Institute of Architects* 7 (Jan. 1919): 41; Mumford, "Introduction," 12.

23. Cole, "Catherine Bauer," 40–41.

24. Henry Wright, "The Road to Good Houses," *The Survey* 54 (1 May 1925): 166.

25. Lewis Mumford, "Houses—Sunnyside Up," *The Nation* 120 (4 Feb. 1925): 116.

26. Kenneth T. Jackson, *Crabgrass Frontier: The Suburbanization of the United States* (New York: Oxford University Press, 1985), 174–77.

27. Wright, "Road to Good Houses," 166. A number of scholars have described and examined the ideas of the Regional Planning Association of America. See Roy Lubove, *Community Planning in the 1920's*; Daniel Schaffer, *Garden Cities for America: The Radburn Experience* (Philadelphia: Temple University Press, 1982); and David Berry Cady,

"The Influence of the Garden City Ideal on American Housing and Planning Reform, 1900–1940," Ph.D. diss., University of Wisconsin, 1970, chaps. 5–8.

28. For a fascinating account of efforts to achieve cost breakthroughs at the level of the individual house, see H. Ward Jandl, *Yesterday's Houses of Tomorrow: Innovative American Homes, 1850–1950* (Washington, DC: Preservation Press, 1991).

29. Lewis Mumford, "Mass Production and the Modern House," *Architectural Record* 67 (Jan. 1930): 17–20, quote from 18.

30. Lewis Mumford, "Mass Production and the Modern House—Part Two," *Architectural Record* 67 (Feb. 1930): quote from 113.

31. Schaffer, *Garden Cities for America*, 121–26; Lubove, *Community Planning*, 58–61; cost figure from Schaffer.

32. Lubove, *Community Planning*, 62; Schaffer, *Garden Cities for America*, 175, 192–93, 164.

33. Cole, "Catherine Bauer," 103. Quotes from Catherine Bauer Wurster, "The Social Front of Modern Architecture in the 1930s," *Journal of the Society of Architectural Historians* 24 (Mar. 1965): 48.

34. Nicholas Bullock, "Housing in Frankfurt and the New *Wohnkultur*, 1925–1931," *Architectural Review* 63 (June 1978): 335.

35. Cole, "Catherine Bauer," 102; Catherine K. Bauer, "Prize Essay: Art in Industry," *Fortune* 3 (May 1931): 95.

36. Bauer, "Prize Essay," 94.

37. Susan R. Henderson, "The Work of Ernst May, 1919–1930," Ph.D. diss., Columbia University, 1990, esp. chap. 5; Bullock, "Housing in Frankfurt," 350–51.

38. Cole, "Catherine Bauer," 105. See also introduction to Bauer, "Prize Essay," 94; William H. Jordy, *American Buildings and Their Architects: The Impact of European Modernism in the Mid-Twentieth Century* (Garden City: Doubleday and Co., 1972), 289.

39. Bauer, "Prize Essay," 94.

40. Henderson, "The Work of Ernst May," 9–10; Bullock, "Housing in Frankfurt," 350, 336; Leonardo Benevolo, *The History of Modern Architecture: The Modern Movement* (1960; Cambridge, MA: MIT Press, 1971), 509–11; John Robert Mullin, "City Planning in Frankfurt, Germany, 1925–1932: A Study in Practical Utopianism," *Journal of Urban History* 4 (Nov. 1977): 3–28; Glen Yago, *The Decline of Transit: Urban Transportation in German and U.S. Cities, 1900–1970* (Cambridge, England: Cambridge University Press, 1984), 97–99.

41. Frederic J. Osborn quoted in Cole, "Catherine Bauer," 103.

42. Bauer, "Prize Essay," 94; Henderson, "The Work of Ernst May," 325–34.

43. Bauer, "Prize Essay," 101–102, May quoted on 101. Henderson, "The Work of Ernst May," 334–38. For discussions of the meaning of the Frankfurt Kitchen within the context of gender relations and economic change in Germany at this time, see Mary Nolan "'Housework Made Easy': The Taylorized Housewife in Weimar Germany's Rationalized Economy," *Feminist Studies* 16 (Fall 1990): 549–77; and Susan R. Henderson, "A Revolution in Woman's Sphere: Grete Lihotzky and the Frankfurt Kitchen," in *Architecture and Feminism*, edited by Debra Coleman, et al. (Princeton, NJ: Princeton Architectural Press, 1996).

44. Bauer, "Prize Essay," 110.

45. Bauer, "Own Words," 27.

46. Cole, "Catherine Bauer," 106.

47. Miller, *Lewis Mumford*, 323. Cole, "Catherine Bauer," 118, Mumford quote from letter to Cole, 8 Aug. 1972, 125.

48. Miller, *Lewis Mumford*, 323–24; quote from letter from Bauer to Frederick Gutheim, 19 Nov. 1932, in Cole, "Catherine Bauer," 127, see also 120–23. Editors of *Fortune, Housing America* (New York: Harcourt, Brace and Company, 1932), quotes from 21. Lewis Mumford, "Taxes Into Houses," *Fortune* 7 (May 1933): quotes from 89.

49. Quotes from letters from Bauer to Frederick Gutheim, n.d. and 19 Nov. 1932, cited in Cole, "Catherine Bauer," 127.

50. Letter from Mumford to Bauer, 7 June 1933, quoted in Miller, *Lewis Mumford*, 333, see also 330–40.

51. Letter from Bauer to Mumford, 1933, quoted in Miller, *Lewis Mumford*, 332.

52. Cole, "Catherine Bauer," 130.

53. William E. Leuchtenburg, *Franklin D. Roosevelt and the New Deal, 1932–1940* (1963; New York: Harper Torchbooks, 1965), 53.

54. This was Edith Elmer Wood's *Housing Progress in Western Europe* (New York: E. P. Dutton, 1923).

55. Resume in Papers of Executive Secretary of the Labor Housing Conference, State Historical Society of Wisconsin, Madison, Wisconsin, file: National Resources Board; Cole, "Catherine Bauer," 131; Quotes from letter from Bauer to Frederick Gutheim, 21 Mar. 1933, and from Ferris Greenslet to Bauer, 15 Mar. 1933, both cited in Cole, "Catherine Bauer," 131–32.

56. Bauer to Lovell Thompson, 24 Apr. 1934, cited in Cole, "Catherine Bauer," 261, note 3.

57. Bauer, *Modern Housing*, xv, 199–204.

58. Ibid., quotes from 147 and 124–25.

59. Ibid., 124, 126–27.

60. Ibid., 125, 132–34.

61. Ibid., 130–31.

62. Ibid., 176–87, 200, 207–10.

63. Ibid., 149–50, quote from 150.

64. Ibid., 150–52, quote from 152.

65. Ibid., 136.

66. Ibid., 242.

67. Ibid., 78–91, 253. Recent scholarly investigation supports Bauer's conclusion. Historians credit improvements in housing quality in late nineteenth-century Britain solely to increasing real wages starting in 1850. Philanthropic reforms are seen as having had negligible effect. Contemporary scholarship is reviewed in Richard Rodger, *Housing in Urban Britain, 1780–1914* (London: Macmillan, 1989), 9–12, 47.

68. Bauer, *Modern Housing*, 87–91, 93–94. For a discussion of the role of housing societies in Germany, see Lane, *Architecture and Politics in Germany*, 88–89, 104. Helen Searing describes working-class housing associations in the Netherlands and especially

the role of these organizations in supporting the development of the Amsterdam School of Architecture in "With Red Flags Flying: Housing in Amsterdam, 1915–1923," in *Art and Architecture in the Service of Politics*, edited by Henry A. Millon and Linda Nochlin (Cambridge, MA: MIT Press, 1978), 230–69.

69. Friedrich Engels, "How Proudhon Solves the Housing Question," originally published 1872, reprinted in Engels, *The Housing Question* (1954; Moscow: Progress Publishers, 1975), 18.

70. Bauer, *Modern Housing*, 96. Leonardo Benevolo discusses this issue in *The Origins of Modern Town Planning*, translated by Judith Landry (1963; Cambridge, MA: MIT Press Paperback, 1971), 105–47.

71. Bauer, *Modern Housing*, 87, 133, quote from 254.

72. Ibid., 122.

73. Ibid., 122.

74. Ibid., 252–3.

75. Ibid., 255.

76. Ibid., 255, 254.

77. Quotes from Newman in *Annals of the American Academy of Political and Social Science* 181 (Sept. 1935): 203; and Haskell, "Housing and America," *The Nation* 140 (20 Feb. 1935): 228.

78. Haskell, "Housing and America," 228; and Langdon W. Post, "The Exploitation of Land and People," *Saturday Review of Literature* 11 (26 Jan. 1935): 442.

79. For discussions of how such structural factors facilitated the creation of non-commercial housing sectors in Britain, see Steve Schifferes, "The Dilemmas of British Housing Policy," in *Critical Perspectives on Housing*, edited by Rachel G. Bratt, Chester Hartman, and Ann Meyerson (Philadelphia: Temple University Press, 1986), 533; and Martin J. Daunton, "Introduction" to Daunton, ed., *Councillors and Tenants: Local Authority Housing in English Cities, 1919–1939* (Leicester, England: Leicester University Press, 1984), 1–33. For Vienna, see Peter Marcuse, "A Useful Installment," 581–83; and Marcuse, "The Housing Policy of Social Democracy: Determinants and Consequences," in Rabinbach, *The Austrian Socialist Experiment*, 201–21.

80. Bauer, *Modern Housing*, 254.

81. Bauer to Dale Warren, 9 May 1934, cited in Cole, "Catherine Bauer," 264.

Chapter Four

1. For Sunnyside and Radburn, see chapter 3. The apartments of the Amalgamated Clothing Workers are discussed in chapter 5.

2. Cities could not accomplish a great deal on their own, given their limited resources and their lack of authority over land-use decisions throughout the metropolitan region in which they were located.

3. U.S. Bureau of the Census, *Historical Statistics, Bicentennial Edition*, vol. 1 (Washington, DC: Government Printing Office, 1975), N156, 640. Hereafter: Census, *Historical Statistics*.

4. Census, *Historical Statistics*, Series F79 and F89, 231.

5. John H. Fahey, "The Resumption of Home Building," *Real Estate Record and Builders' Guide* 134 (29 Sept. 1934): 5.

6. Gertrude S. Fish, "Housing Policy During the Great Depression," in *The Story of Housing*, edited by Gertrude Sipperly Fish (New York: Macmillan, 1979), 183.

7. Census, *Historical Statistics*, N156, 640.

8. Herbert Hoover, "Address," in *Housing Objectives and Programs*, vol. 11 of *President's Conference on Home Building and Home Ownership*, edited by John M. Gries and James Ford (Washington, DC: President's Conference on Home Building and Home Ownership, 1932), 1.

9. Hoover, "Address," 2–5.

10. 47 Stat. 725 (1932). Gries and Ford, "Introduction" to *Housing Objectives and Programs*, edited by Gries and Ford, 21. William Linous Cody Wheaton, "The Evolution of Federal Housing Programs," Ph.D. diss., University of Chicago, 1953, 21–37.

11. Robert P. Lamont, Foreword to *Home Ownership, Income and Types of Dwellings*, vol. 4 of *President's Conference*, edited by Gries and Ford, viii.

12. Robert P. Lamont, "Foreword" to *Negro Housing*, vol. 6 of *President's Conference*, edited by Gries and Ford, vii—viii.

13. Richard T. Ely, "Economic Factors Underlying Housing, and Experience of Limited Dividend Companies," in *Slums, Large-Scale Housing and Decentralization*, vol. 3 of *President's Conference*, edited by Gries and Ford, 155.

14. Ray Lyman Wilber, "Foreword" to *Slums, Large-Scale Housing, and Decentralization*, vol. 3 of *President's Conference*, edited by Gries and Ford, xii.

15. *Emergency Relief and Construction Act*, 47 Stat. 709 (1932). Gilbert A. Cam, "United States Government Activities in Low-Cost Housing, 1932–38," *Journal of Political Economy* 47 (June 1939): 358.

16. Kenneth T. Jackson, *Crabgrass Frontier: The Suburbanization of the United States* (New York: Oxford University Press, 1985), 193; Census, *Historical Statistics*, N156, 640; William Leuchtenburg, *Franklin Roosevelt and the New Deal* (New York: Harper and Row, 1963), 53.

17. Timothy L. McDonnell, *The Wagner Housing Act: A Case Study of the Legislative Process* (Chicago: Loyola University Press, 1957), 54–55, 29. Citations from *The National Industrial Recovery Act*, Public Law 67, 48 Stat. 195 (1933).

18. John H. Mollenkopf, *The Contested City* (Princeton: Princeton University Press, 1983), 58. Charles W. Eagles, *Democracy Delayed: Congressional Reapportionment and Urban-Rural Conflict in the 1920s* (Athens, GA: University of Georgia Press, 1990), 31, 11–124, Rankin quoted on 82.

19. Mollenkopf, *Contested City*, 54–72. Mollenkopf calculates that non-Southern Democrats also had working majorities in the House after the congressional elections of 1934, 1936, 1964, 1974, 1976, and 1978. See also Kristi Anderson, *The Creation of a Democratic Majority, 1928–1936* (Chicago: University of Chicago Press, 1979), esp. 19–42; Zane L. Miller and Patricia M. Melvin, *The Urbanization of Modern America*, 2d ed. (San Diego: Harcourt Brace Jovanovich, 1987), 158–62. The analysis in this section assumes a strong relationship between voting and policy formation but also acknowledges the importance of institutional structures in the emphasis on reapportion-

ment. For discussions of the connections between electoral behavior and pubic policy, see Barbara Deckard Sinclair, "Party Realignment and the Transformation of the Political Agenda: The House of Representatives, 1925–1938," *American Political Science Review* 71 (Sept. 1977): 940–53; and Benjamin Ginsberg, "Elections and Public Policy," *American Political Science Review* 70 (Mar. 1976): 41–49. For arguments as to why institutional structures are significant in shaping public policy, see Theda Skocpol, "Bringing the State Back In: Strategies of Analysis in Current Research," in *Bringing the State Back In*, edited by Peter B. Evans, Dietrich Rueschemeyer, and Theda Skocpol. (New York: Cambridge University Press, 1985), 3–37; and Skocpol and Kenneth Finegold, "State Capacity and Economic Intervention in the Early New Deal," *Political Science Quarterly* 97 (Summer 1962): 255–78.

20. Leuchtenburg, *Franklin Roosevelt and the New Deal*, 44–62; Arthur M. Schlesinger, Jr., *The Coming of the New Deal* (Boston: Houghton Mifflin, 1958), vol. 2 of *The Age of Roosevelt*, 98–102.

21. Senator Albert Fall, quoted in Harry C. Bredemeier, *The Federal Public Housing Movement: A Case Study of Social Change*, (New York: Arno Press, 1980), 44.

22. Leonard Freedman, *Public Housing: The Politics of Poverty* (New York: Holt, Rinehart and Winston, 1969), 160.

23. Federal Emergency Administration of Public Works [hereafter FEAPW], *Urban Housing: The Story of the PWA Housing Division, Bulletin No. 2*, (Washington, DC: Government Printing Office, 1936), 37; Miles L. Colean, *American Housing: Problems and Prospects* (New York: Twentieth Century Fund, 1944), 276–77; Harold L. Ickes, "Activities of Housing Division of the Federal Emergency Administration of Public Works," report submitted to Senate Committee on Education and Labor, 75th Cong., 1st Sess. (1937), *Hearings on S. 1685* (Washington, DC: Government Printing Office, 1937), 20. Different authors calculate the total number of projects in different ways. Statistics given here conform to the data published in Ickes's 1937 congressional testimony.

24. Michael W. Straus and Talbot Wegg, *Housing Comes of Age* (New York: Oxford University Press, 1938), 31–31; "Housing Upheaval," *Architectural Forum* 61 (July 1934): 67; Roy Lubove, "Homes and 'A Few Well Placed Fruit Trees': An Object Lesson in Federal Housing," *Social Research* 27 (Winter 1960): 478.

25. James Stuart Olson, *Herbert Hoover and the Reconstruction Finance Corporation, 1931–1933* (Ames: Iowa State University Press, 1977), 88–89; Cam, "United States Government Activities in Low-Cost Housing," 357–59; Jack F. Isakoff, "The Public Works Administration," *University of Illinois Bulletin* 36 (18 Nov. 1938): 127–28; Ernest M. Fisher, "Housing Legislation and Housing Policy in the United States," *Michigan Law Review* 31 (Jan. 1933): 320–21, quote on 320.

26. Jack Levin, Legislative Reference Service, Library of Congress, "Your Congress and American Housing: Actions of Congress on Housing from 1852 to 1951," *House Documents*, vol. 18, Miscellaneous, 82d Cong., 2d Session, H. Doc. 532 (U.S. Gov't Printing Office, 1952), 6; Cam, "United States Government Activity," 358; Richard Plunz, *A History of Housing in New York City: Dwelling Type and Social Change in the American Metropolis* (New York: Columbia University Press, 1990), 210.

27. Straus and Wegg, *Housing Comes of Age*, 31–43; "The New Deal's Housing Activities," *Congressional Digest* 15 (Apr. 1936): 110; Cam, "Government Activity in Low-Cost Housing," 357–60; Horatio B. Hackett, "Problems and Policies of the Housing Division of the P.W.A.," in *Housing Officials' Year Book, 1935*, edited by Coleman Woodbury (Chicago: National Association of Housing Officials, 1935), 1; FEAPW, *Urban Housing*, 28–30; Harold L. Ickes, *Back to Work: The Story of PWA* (New York: Macmillan, 1935), quote from 183.

28. Ickes, *Back to Work*, 183; Barry Dean Karl, *Executive Reorganization and Reform in the New Deal: The Genesis of Administrative Management, 1900–1939* (Cambridge: Harvard University Press, 1963), 200–202.

29. "State Housing: American Style," *Fortune* 9 (Feb. 1934): 114.

30. Public Works Administration, *America Builds: The Record of the PWA* (Washington, DC: U.S. Government Printing Office, 1939), 209.

31. FEAPW, *Urban Housing*, 30.

32. Straus and Wegg, *Housing Comes of Age*, 35.

33. Ibid., 56.

34. Ibid., 36.

35. Ibid., 55–79, quote on 57.

36. Eugene H. Klaber, "Limited Dividend Corporations Under the National Housing Act," *Architectural Record* 77 (Feb. 1935): 78; Charles Abrams, *The Future of Housing* (New York: Harper and Brothers, 1946), 234.

37. Straus and Wegg, *Housing Comes of Age*, 42. The bulk of the data on financial aspects of limited-dividend housing that did exist at this time came from projects supervised by the New York State Board of Housing in New York City. These data were not generally applicable, however, since costs in New York were much higher than for other urban areas.

38. Ickes, "Activities of Housing Division," 21.

39. Barry D. Karl, *The Uneasy State: The United States from 1915–1945* (Chicago: University of Chicago Press, 1983), 123–24, 164–65.

40. Harold L. Ickes, "The Federal Housing Program," *New Republic* 81 (19 Dec. 1934): 155.

41. Ickes, "Activities of Housing Division," 21.

42. "Kohn Explains Housing Views," *Real Estate Record and Builders' Guide* 132 (7 Oct. 1933): 3.

43. "Housing Corporation to Hasten Slum Clearance," *Architectural Record* 74 (Dec. 1933): 1.

44. Isakoff, "Public Works Administration," 129.

45. Straus and Wegg, *Housing Comes of Age*, 44–50; Cam, "United States Government Activity in Low Cost Housing," 360.

46. John Thurston, "Government Proprietary Corporations," *Virginia Law Review* 21 (Feb. 1935): 354–56.

47. Otis L. Graham, Jr., *Toward a Planned Society: From Roosevelt to Nixon* (New York: Oxford University Press, 1976), 49–64.

48. Straus and Wegg, *Housing Comes of Age*, 47–50. Isakoff, "Public Works Admin-

istration," 60–61; Cam, "United States Government Activity in Low-Cost Housing," 360; McDonnell, *The Wagner Housing Act*, 36–38. Quote from Harvey Pinney, "The Legal Status of Federal Government Corporations," *California Law Review* 27 (Sept. 1939): 736.

49. Straus and Wegg, *Housing Comes of Age*, 124–25; *George-Healey Act*, 49 Stat. 2025 (1936).

50. Lewis Mumford, "New Homes for a New Deal, III: The Shortage of Dwellings and Direction," *New Republic* 78 (28 Feb. 1934): 69–72, quote on 71; Catherine Bauer, "'Slum' Clearance or 'Housing,'" *Nation* 137 (27 Dec. 1933): 730–31, quotes from 731. See also, Catherine Bauer, "Slums Aren't Necessary," *American Mercury* 31 (Mar. 1934): 296–305; Albert Mayer, "New Homes for a New Deal, I: Slum Clearance—But How?" *New Republic* 78 (14 Feb. 1934): 7–9; Henry Wright, "New Homes for a New Deal, II: Abolishing Slums Forever," *New Republic* 78 (21 Feb. 1934): 41–43; Albert Mayer, Henry Wright, and Lewis Mumford, "New Homes for a New Deal, IV: A Concrete Program," *New Republic* 78 (7 Mar. 1934): 91–94.

51. Harold L. Ickes, "The Federal Housing Program," *New Republic* 81 (19 Dec. 1934): 155.

52. "Housing Upheaval," 61.

53. FEAPW, *Urban Housing*, 32; "Housing Upheaval," 67.

54. Isakoff, "Public Works Administration," 130–31; Ickes, "Activities of Housing Division," quote on 32; Straus and Wegg, *Housing Comes of Age*, 81.

55. Ickes's quotes from "PWA Pledges Action on Low-Cost Housing and Slum Clearance," *American City* 49 (Sept. 1934): 99; and Ickes, *Back to Work*, 185.

56. Straus and Wegg, *Housing Comes of Age*, 86–88, court opinion cited on 88; Isakoff, "Public Works Administration," 130–31.

57. Ickes, "Activities of Housing Division," 26–28, 32.

58. Nathaniel S. Keith, *Politics and the Housing Crisis Since 1930* (New York: Universe Books, 1973), 28; FEAPW, *Urban Housing*, quote from 32; Rosalie Genevro, "Site Selection and the New York City Housing Authority, 1934–1939," *Journal of Urban History* 12 (Aug. 1986): 336–38; Hackett, "Problems and Policies," 5.

59. Richard Sterner, *The Negro's Share: A Study of Income, Consumption, Housing and Public Assistance* (New York: Harper and Brothers, 1943), 316–17; Robert C. Weaver, "An Experiment in Negro Labor," *Opportunity* 14 (1936): 297, quote from 298; Raymond Wolters, "The New Deal and the Negro," in *Women and Minorities during the Great Depression*, edited by Melvyn Dubofsky and Stephen Burwood (New York: Garland, 1990), 31–32.

60. Christopher G. Wye, "The New Deal and the Negro Community: Toward a Broader Conceptualization," *Journal of American History* 59 (Dec. 1972): 625–26. See also, John B. Kirby, "The Roosevelt Administration and Blacks: An Ambivalent Legacy," in *Twentieth-Century America: Recent Interpretations*, edited by Barton Bernstein and Allen J. Matusow (New York: Harcourt Brace Jovanovich, 1972), 276.

61. Abrams, *The Future of Housing*, 249–58, quotes from 255 and 251.

62. Ibid., 257.

63. Howard A. Gray, "The Housing Division's Third Year," *Housing Officials' Year*

Book, edited by Coleman Woodbury (Chicago: National Association of Housing Officials, 1937), 3.

64. Straus and Wegg, *Housing Comes of Age*, quotes from 122. Straus and Wegg dedicated their book to Ickes, "whose social vision led public housing from theory to fact in the United States. . . ."

65. William E. Leuchtenburg, *Franklin D. Roosevelt and the New Deal, 1932–40* (1963; New York: Harper Torchbooks, 1965), 70–71.

66. Abrams, *The Future of Housing*, 257.

67. The analysis of the Housing Division presented here relies heavily on Karl, *The Uneasy State*; and Skocpol, "Bringing the State Back In: Strategies of Analysis in Current Research," 3–37.

68. The importance of an "interventionist role definition" for effective public administration is discussed in Skocpol and Finegold, "State Capacity and Economic Intervention in the Early New Deal," 275–76.

69. Paul F. Wendt, *Housing Policy—The Search for Solutions* (Berkeley: University of California Press, 1963), 111–13.

70. Ickes, "Activities of Housing Division," 21–24. For Roosevelt's ambivalence toward public works spending, see Leuchtenburg, *Franklin D. Roosevelt*, 71; Frank Freidel, *Franklin D. Roosevelt: Launching the New Deal* (Boston: Little, Brown, 1973) 430–32.

71. See for example, Skocpol and Finegold, "State Capacity and the Early New Deal," 260–61.

72. For a discussion of Johnson in this regard, see Skocpol and Finegold, "State Capacity," 264–65; for Jones, see Graham, *Toward a Planned Society*, 47–49; for FDR, see Karl, *Uneasy State*, 154.

73. Richard Plunz, "Institutionalization of Housing Form in New York City, 1920–1950," in *Housing Form and Public Policy in the United States*, edited by Richard Plunz (New York: Praeger, 1980), 178. Richard Pommer, "The Architecture of Urban Housing in the United States during the Early 1930s," *Journal of the Society of Architectural Historians* 37 (Dec. 1978): 262–63. For another positive assessment of PWA housing, see Carl W. Condit, *Chicago, 1930–70: Building Planning and Urban Technology* (Chicago: University of Chicago Press, 1974), 39–43.

74. *Congressional Record*, 3 Apr. 1936, 4890, cited in McDonnell, *Wagner Housing Act*, 166.

75. R. Allen Hays, *The Federal Government and Urban Housing: Ideology and Change in Public Policy* (Albany: State University of New York Press, 1985), 92–93.

76. *George-Healey Act*, 49 Stat. 2025 (1936).

77. Stonorov to unspecified federal official, 15 Nov. 1935, in papers of the Labor Housing Conference at the Wisconsin Historical Society, Box 2, File: Stonorov.

Chapter Five

1. Catherine Bauer, "Housing Project Number One!" *Hosiery Worker*, 18 Jan. 1935.

2. John W. Edelman, *Labor Lobbyist: The Autobiography of John W. Edelman*, edited

by Joseph Carter (Indianapolis: Bobbs-Merrill Co., 1974), 98; Peter Marcuse, "A Useful Installment of Socialist Work: Housing in Red Vienna in the 1920s," in *Critical Perspectives on Housing*, edited by Rachel G. Bratt, Chester Hartman, and Ann Meyerson (Philadelphia: Temple University Press, 1986), 573; Joachim Schlandt and O. M. Ungers, "The Vienna Superblocks," translated by Sima Ingberman, *Oppositions* 13 (Summer 1978): 88.

3. Edelman, *Labor Lobbyist*, 12–16, 37, 3, 39–41; Donald D. Egbert and Paul E. Sprague, "In Search of John Edelman, Architect and Anarchist," *AIA Journal* 45 (Feb. 1966): 35–41. The union was affiliated to the AFL through the United Textile Workers of America. In 1933, the union assumed jurisdiction over the seamless hosiery industry and changed its name to the American Federation of Hosiery Workers (Lawrence Rogin, *Making History in Hosiery: The Story of the American Federation of Hosiery Workers* [Philadelphia: American Federation of Hosiery Workers, 1938], 5–7, 25).

4. "Biographical Sketch of Emil Rieve," Sept. 1934, Textile Workers Union of America Archives, Box 16, State Historical Society of Wisconsin, Madison, Wisconsin (hereafter TWUAA); "American Federation of Full-Fashioned Hosiery Workers," *Fortune* 5 (Jan. 1932): 50; Interview with Larry Rogin, who followed John Edelman as research and education director for the union, 8 June 1984, George Meany Center for Labor Studies, Silver Spring, Maryland; quotes from Rogin in letter to author, 9 May 1985.

5. David J. Pivar, "The Hosiery Workers and the Philadelphia Third Party Impulse, 1929–1935," *Labor History* 5 (Winter 1964): 23; Edelman quote from "The Reminiscences of John W. Edelman" (1960), Oral History Collection of Columbia University, 94, cited in Mary Susan Cole, "Catherine Bauer and the Public Housing Movement, 1926–1937," Ph.D. diss., George Washington University, 1975, 221. For Philadelphia politics, see articles by Arthur P. Dudden and Margaret B. Tinkcom in *Philadelphia: A 300-Year History*, edited by Russell F. Weigley (New York: W. W. Norton, 1982), esp. 581–87, 619–28.

6. George W. Taylor, *The Full-Fashioned Hosiery Worker: His Changing Economic Status* (Philadelphia: University of Pennsylvania Press, 1931), 6, 13; "American Federation of Full-Fashioned Hosiery Workers," 50; U.S. Bureau of the Census, *Historical Statistics, Bicentennial Edition*, vol. 1 (Washington, DC: Government Printing Office, 1975), Series D804, p. 170.

7. "American Federation of Full-Fashioned Hosiery Workers," 50–53; Rogin, *Making History in Hosiery*, 19.

8. "American Federation of Full-Fashioned Hosiery Workers," 53, 104, 107; "Intelligent Unionism," *New Republic* 62 (26 Mar. 1930): 141; Rogin, *Making History in Hosiery*, 20.

9. Paul Blanshard, "Class Struggle in a Ball-Room," *New Republic* 26 (4 May 1921): 283.

10. For the basic features of the ACW approach, see Steve Fraser, "Dress Rehearsal for the New Deal: Shop-Floor Insurgents, Political Elites, and Industrial Democracy in the Amalgamated Clothing Workers," in *Working-Class America: Essays on Labor, Community, and American Society*, edited by Michael H. Frisch and Daniel J. Walkowitz

(Urbana: University of Illinois Press, 1983), 212–55; and Steve Fraser, "The 'New Unionism' and the 'New Economic Policy',", in *Work, Community, and Power: The Experience of Labor in Europe and America: 1900–1925*, edited by James E. Cronin and Carmen Sirianni (Philadelphia: Temple University Press, 1983), 173–96.

11. Rogin, *Making History in Hosiery*, 20–21; Pledge quoted from "Intelligent Unionism," 141; "American Federation of Full-Fashioned Hosiery Workers," 52.

12. Membership in the Hosiery workers was 15,000 in 1929, compared with 100,000 in the Amalgamated. Membership figures from: "American Federation of Full-Fashioned Hosiery Workers," 50; and Steven Fraser, *Labor Will Rule: Sidney Hillman and the Rise of American Labor* (New York, Free Press, 1991), 207.

13. Matthew Josephson, *Sidney Hillman: Statesman of American Labor* (Garden City, NY: Doubleday, 1952), 245; David Montgomery, "New Tendencies in Union Struggles and Strategies in Europe and the United States, 1916–1922," in *Work, Community, and Power*, edited by Cronin and Sirianni, 98; "Housing Activities of Labor Groups," *Monthly Labor Review* 27 (Aug. 1928): 222–26. For a discussion of the appeal of cooperative endeavors in this period, see Dana Frank, *Purchasing Power: Consumer Organizing, Gender, and the Seattle Labor Movement, 1919–1929* (Cambridge: Cambridge University Press, 1994), chaps. 2 and 3.

14. "Cooperative Homes for Garment Workers," *New York Times*, 26 Apr. 1925, Section 11, 2; "Rockefeller Opens Cooperative Flats," *New York Times*, 10 Feb. 1927, 48; Richard Plunz, "Reading Bronx Housing, 1890–1940," in *Building a Borough: Architecture and Planning in the Bronx, 1890–1940* (New York: Bronx Museum of the Arts, 1986), 49–51; Robert A. M. Stern, Gregory Gilmartin, and Thomas Mellins, *New York, 1930: Architecture and Urbanism between the Two World Wars* (New York: Rizzoli, 1987), 485; "Thomas Garden Apartments," *Architecture and Building* 59 (Apr. 1927): 111–12; Edith Elmer Wood, *Recent Trends in American Housing* (New York: The Macmillan Co., 1931), 222–24.

15. For a nuanced discussion of the appeal of cooperation to the Jewish working class in this period, see Fraser, "'The New Unionism,'" 177.

16. Wood, *Recent Trends*, 177–78; "Housing Activities of Labor Groups," 217–22; Plunz, "Bronx Housing," 51–52, 70–76; Calvin Trillin, "U.S. Journal: The Bronx—The Coops," *New Yorker*, 1 Aug. 1977, 49–54; Deborah Dash Moore, *At Home in America: Second Generation New York Jews* (New York: Columbia University Press, 1981), 55.

17. From text of resolution at 1918 ACW convention, quoted in Earl Strong, *The Amalgamated Clothing Workers of America* (Grinnell, IA: Herald-Register Publishing Co., 1940), 217.

18. Montgomery, "New Tendencies," 98; Fraser, "The 'New Unionism,'" 173.

19. Abraham Kazan, *30 Years of Amalgamated Cooperative Housing, 1927–57* (New York: James Peter Warbasse Memorial Library, n.d. [1958]), n. p. [3]; "Housing Activities of Labor Groups," 210–12; Wood, *Recent Trends*, 260–69, 180–81; Strong, *Amalgamated Clothing Workers*, 222; Eugene Rachlis and John E. Marqusee, *The Land Lords* (New York: Random House, 1963), 131–34, 144–53.

20. Wood, *Recent Trends*, 171–72; "Housing Activities of Labor Groups," 214.

21. Abraham E. Kazan, "Cooperative Housing in the United States," *The Annals of the American Academy of Political and Social Science* 191 (May 1937): 141.

22. Wood, *Recent Trends*, 182–83; "Housing Activities of Labor Groups," 214; Asher Achinstein, *Report of the State Board of Housing on the Standard of Living of 400 Families in a Model Housing Project: The Amalgamated Housing Corporation* (Albany: State of New York, 1931), 65–72.

23. Rachlis and Marqusee, *The Land Lords*, 155–60; "The Cooperative Plan—One Answer to the Low Cost Housing Problem," *Architectural Forum* (Feb. 1931): 241–43.

24. "Low Cost Housing—What the Rest of the Country Can Learn from Philadelphia," *The American City* 40 (April 1929): 102; U.S. Bureau of the Census, "Table 10: Homes by Tenure and Value or Monthly Rental for Philadelphia Census Tracts 1930," Temple University Urban Archives (hereafter TUUA).

Philadelphia had a population of 1,950,961 in 1930. The other twelve cities with a population of over a half-million in 1930 and their homeownership rates were: Baltimore (pop. 804,874) 50 percent, Boston (pop. 781,188) 26 percent, Buffalo (pop. 573,076) 43 percent, Chicago (pop. 3,376,438) 31 percent, Cleveland (pop. 900,429) 37 percent, Detroit (pop. 1,568,662) 41 percent, Los Angeles (pop. 1,238,048) 37 percent, Milwaukee (pop. 578,249) 42 percent, New York (pop. 6,930,446) 20 percent, Pittsburgh (pop. 669,817) 40 percent, St. Louis (pop. 821,960) 31 percent, San Francisco (634,394) 32 percent (U.S. Bureau of the Census, *Abstract of the Fifteenth Census of the United States* [Washington, DC: U.S. Government Printing Office, 1933], Table 13, p. 21, and Table 44, pp. 435–36).

25. Horace Russell, *Savings and Loan Associations*, 2d ed. (Albany, NY: Matthew Bender and Co., 1960), 23; Daniel J. Prosser, "Chicago and the Bungalow Boom of the 1920s," *Chicago History* (Summer 1981): 86–95; "Low Cost Housing—What the Rest of the Country Can Learn from Philadelphia," 102–4.

26. Morton Keller, *Regulating a New Economy: Public Policy and Economic Change in America, 1900–1933* (Cambridge, MA: Harvard University Press, 1990), 176; I. M. Rubinow, "Housing in the City of Homes," *The Survey* 55 (15 Dec. 1925): 355–58.

27. Bureau of the Census, *Abstract of the Fifteenth Census* (Washington, DC: U.S. Government Printing Office, 1933), Table 44, 436; Bernard Newman, "Housing Research in Philadelphia," *Architectural Record* 74 (Sept. 1933): 170–74, quote from 173. National statistics, starting in 1926, gathered by the Federal Home Loan Bank Board show foreclosures increasing 80 percent between 1926 and 1928; see Stuart Chase, "The Case Against Home Ownership," *Survey Graphic* 27 (May 1938): 263.

28. Bernard Newman, "Sheriff Sales," *Housing in Philadelphia, 1935* (Philadelphia: Philadelphia Housing Association, 1936), 21–22; Bernard Newman, "Can We Afford Not to Build?" *Housing in Philadelphia, 1933* (Philadelphia: Philadelphia Housing Association, 1934), 6.

29. Bernard Newman, "Dwelling Construction," *Housing in Philadelphia, 1931* (Philadelphia: Philadelphia Housing Association, 1932), 27; "Housing Problems in Philadelphia," *Monthly Labor Review* 37 (Sept. 1933): 630.

30. W. W. Jeanes, *Housing of Families of the American Federation of Full-Fashioned Hosiery Workers, Local Nos. 1 and 39, Philadelphia* (Philadelphia: n. p., 1933), 9, 48.

31. Edelman, *Labor Lobbyist*, 97–98.

32. The Palace of the Soviets was originally conceived as the Soviet alternative to the League of Nations. The project, which was to have been a combined government center and cultural complex, was never erected. After a total of three international competitions and a cost of 25 million ruples, plans for building were abandoned. The enormous foundations that were dug were later used for an underground water heating and filtration plant for an all-year open-air swimming pool in Moscow. In part, the project fell victim to the shift occurring at the time away from avant-garde abstract architecture toward Socialist Realism in the Soviet Union. Stonorov and Kastner's submission was an unabashedly functionalist design, while the winning entry in the final round of competition in 1932 was a stripped neoclassical design topped by a massive 300–foot high statue of Lenin. See Ursula Cliff, "Oskar Stonorov: Public Housing Pioneer," *Design and Environment* 2 (Fall 1971): 52, 57; Frederick Gutheim, "The Social Architecture of Oskar Stonorov," *L'architecttura* 28 (June 1972): 78–79; Peter Lizon, "The Palace of the Soviets—Change in the Direction of Soviet Architecture," Ph.D. diss., University of Pennsylvania, 1971, 6–7, 84, 175; S. Frederick Starr, *Melnikov: Solo Architect in a Mass Society* (Princeton: Princeton University Press, 1978), 156; Edelman, *Labor Lobbyist*, 99; "Oskar Stonorov, Architect, Killed," *New York Times*, 11 May 1970.

33. Interview with William Jeanes, 21 Nov. 1983, Earlville, Maryland.

34. [Oskar Stonorov], "Architect's Discussion," in Jeanes, *Housing of Families*, 57; A. K. Kendrick, "Experimental Plan Considered in Attempt to Aid Employment and Improve Living Conditions," *Hosiery Worker* 10 (1 Apr. 1932): 3.

35. Kendrick, "Experimental Plan," 3; "Stonorov Outlines Permanent Program," *Hosiery Worker*, 11 Jan. 1935, p. 10.

36. "Plan Model Homes for Philadelphia," *New York Times*, 3 Apr. 1932, clipping file of the *Evening Bulletin* (Philadelphia), folder: Hosiery Workers—Housing Project, TUUA. All newspaper stories, except for those in the *Hosiery Worker*, are from this source.

37. John Edelman, "Housing Crisis Near as 2,000 Properties Go Under Hammer," *Hosiery Worker*, 20 May 1932, 3.

38. Jeanes, *Housing of Families*, 24 and 30–34.

39. [Stonorov], "Architect's Discussion," 61.

40. Draft of a letter from Stonorov to the PWA Housing Division, 15 Nov. 1935, Labor Housing Conference Papers, University of Wisconsin Historical Society, Box 2, Stonorov File.

41. For May's political vision, see Susan R. Henderson, "The Work of Ernst May, 1919–1930," Ph.D. diss., Columbia University, 1990, esp. chap. 7.

42. Jeanes, *Housing of Families*, 61.

43. Alfred Kastner, "The Architect's Place in Current Housing," in *Housing Yearbook*, edited by Coleman Woodbury (Chicago: National Association of Housing Officials, 1938), quotes from 230, 227, 229.

44. Edelman, *Labor Lobbyist*, 102. Jeanes calculated monthly carrying costs at $55.30 on a $6,000 house and assumed that shelter expenses should come to no more

than one-fourth of income. While it is true that some new houses were available in Philadelphia for as little as $4,000, the price Jeanes used to estimate standard costs was much more typical. According to studies made by Bernard Newman, director of the Philadelphia Housing Association, over 80 percent of houses built in the city during the 1920s sold for at least $6,000. The survey of Hosiery Workers found the average cost of mortgaged homes for this group to be $5,720 (Jeanes, *Housing of Families*, 40, 31, 18). For Newman's research, see Robert Stuart Glover, Jr., "Survey of the Housing Situation in Philadelphia," Masters thesis, Wharton School of the University of Pennsylvania, 1933, 67.

45. Richard Pommer, "The Architecture of Urban Housing in the United States during the Early 1930s," *Journal of the Society of Architectural Historians* 37 (Dec. 1978): 239.

46. Edelman, *Labor Lobbyist*, 102; survey reprinted in Jeanes, *Housing of Families*, 69.

47. Jeanes, *Housing of Families*, 1.

48. "Housing Idea Here Wins Hosiery Unit," *Public Ledger* (Philadelphia), 20 Aug. 1933.

49. "Community Development for the American Federation of Full Fashioned Hosiery Workers," Stonorov Papers, Juniata Park Misc., Box 19, University of Wyoming Archives (the author is indebted to Eric J. Sandeen for sending her this document); "Plan Model Homes for Philadelphia," *New York Times*, 3 Apr. 1932.

50. Jeanes, *Housing of Families*, 50.

51. Pommer, "Architecture of Urban Housing," 240.

52. "Governor Pinchot to Confer on Hosiery Housing Plan," *Hosiery Worker*, 23 Sept. 1932, 3; Edelman, *Labor Lobbyist*, 105–6; Timothy L. McDonnell, *The Wagner Housing Act* (Chicago: Loyola University Press, 1957), 32. See chapter 4 for specifics on the Emergency Relief and Construction Act of 1932 and the NIRA.

53. Harold L. Ickes, *History of the Housing Division and Its Activities* (1 Apr. 1937), report submitted to the Committee on Education and Labor for Hearings on S. 1685, 75th Cong., 1st sess., 28.

54. Joseph Oberman and Stephen Kozakowski, *History of Development in the Delaware Valley Region* (Philadelphia: Delaware Valley Regional Planning Commission, 1976), 70.

55. *Evening Bulletin* (Philadelphia), 9 Nov. 1933, 4 Dec. 1933, 7 Dec. 1933; *Philadelphia Record*, 10 Nov. 1933.

56. *Evening Bulletin* (Philadelphia), 9 Nov. 1933; "Council Committee Ignores Silly Protests, Passes Bills," *Hosiery Worker*, 8 Dec. 1933, 3; "Names of Foes," *Hosiery Worker*, 8 Dec. 1933, 3; Edelman quoted in "Answers Realty Board," *Evening Bulletin* (Philadelphia), 4 Dec. 1933; Stonorov quoted in "Housing Idea Here Wins Hosiery Unit," *Public Ledger* (Philadelphia), 20 Aug. 1933.

57. "Veto by Mayor Halts $3,000,000 Housing Project," *Evening Bulletin* (Philadelphia), 20 Nov. 1933.

58. *Kensington Critic* (Philadelphia), 9 Feb. 1934; *Evening Bulletin* (Philadelphia), 3 Feb. 1934.

59. Pommer, "Architecture of Urban Housing," 240, 242.

60. *Hosiery Worker*, 20 Oct. 1933.

61. *Hosiery Worker*, 13 Oct. 1933.

62. Jeanes interview, 21 Nov. 1983. Irene Cohen estimated that approximately twelve teachers lived at Mackley; telephone interview with Irene Cohan, 15 Oct. 1994.

63. Alfred Kastner, "The Architect's Place in Current Housing," *Housing Yearbook*, edited by Coleman Woodbury (Chicago: National Association of Housing Officials, 1938), 235. Kastner's residential history is taken from rental records, courtesy of Betty Robinson, Mackley administrative office, 7 April 1986.

64. Jeanes, *Housing of Families*, 42–43; Simon Breines, "The Philadelphia Experiment in Low-Cost Housing," *Real Estate Record*, 135 (20 Apr. 1935): 20. In comparison with all Philadelphia renters, this average put them at the 34th percentile (Bureau of the Census Worksheet: Table 10, 1930, TUUA).

65. Letter from William W. Jeanes to Bernard J. Newman, 4 Oct. 1935, Files of the Housing Association of Delaware Valley, Box 44, TUUA.

66. "Statement of John W. Edelman," *Hearing before the Committee on Education and Labor, U.S. Senate*, 74th Cong., 1st sess., S. 2392, 4–7 June 1935, 128–29; Flo Pryor, "Housing and the Hosiery Workers," *American Federationist* 42 (July 1935): 736.

67. Much of this section is based on interviews with people who lived or still live in the Carl Mackley Houses or who were involved in managing the development. The author talked at length with seventeen such people. Since there was no way to contact a scientific sample of initial residents or of those who were tenants while the complex was being run as a social experiment, this interview evidence cannot be generalized with confidence to the entire population of residents. However, a number of networks were used to contact a range of people in an effort to get as unbiased a picture as possible of the kind and quality of social life that existed.

68. Interview with Adolph and Nan Taffler, 28 Feb. 1985, Huntingdon Valley, Pennsylvania.

69. Jeanes interview.

70. Rogin interview.

71. Jeanes quoted in Jean Coman, "Report of Recreation and Welfare Activities of the Carl Mackley Houses," Jul. 31–Aug. 6, 1936, 13–14, pamphlet #245–11, TUUA.

72. Rogin interview.

73. Jean Coman, *Report of Recreation and Welfare Activities of the Hillside Homes* (Washington, DC: Federal Emergency Administration of Public Works, Housing Division, 1936), 14, 13, 19.

74. Jean Coman, *Report of Recreation and Welfare Activities of the Boulevard Gardens Apartments* (Washington, DC: Federal Emergency Administration of Public Works, Housing Division, 1936), 11.

75. *Mackley Messenger*, Dec. 1935, 2, copy in possession of author.

76. Interview with Irene and Bernard Cohan, 29 Jan. 1986, Philadelphia.

77. Interview with Irving and Eleanor Fleet, 7 Oct. 1985, Philadelphia.

78. *Mackley Messenger*, March 1936, 2; Dec. 1935, 3–4; Apr. 1936, 3, copies in possession of author.

79. Interview with Margaret Burge, 21 Mar. 1986, Cresskill, New Jersey; Fleet interview; Coman, "Activities of Mackley Houses," 15, 44, 53.

80. Quote from interview with William Rafsky, 12 Mar. 1986, Philadelphia.

81. Interview with Ruth Haight, 15 Nov. 1983, Philadelphia; interview with Joan Striplin, 23 Apr. 1985, Philadelphia; interview with William Jeanes.

82. Quote from Edelman and other information from interview with Rebecca Smaltz, 24 Feb. 1986, Philadelphia; Coman, "Activities of Mackley Houses," 24.

83. Coman, "Activities of Mackley Houses," 22, 26; Elizabeth Fones-Wolf, "Industrial Unionism and Labor Movement Culture in Depression-Era Philadelphia," *The Pennsylvania Magazine of History and Biography* 109 (Jan. 1985): 19; Rogin interview; Smaltz interview.

84. Coman, "Activities of Mackley Houses," 22, 24, 26; Interview with Elizabeth Stonorov, 20 Feb. 1986, Phoenixville, Pennsylvania.

85. "Carl Mackley Nursery School" (n.p., [1946]), [2], Pamphlet #238–2, TUUA; Cohan interview.

86. "Carl Mackley Nursery School," [1].

87. Smaltz interview. Statistics from records of the school in possession of Rebecca Smaltz, with copies in possession of author.

88. Telephone interview with Selma Rafsky, Mar. 1986, Philadelphia.

89. Haight interview; Striplin interview; Cohan interview.

90. Jeanes interview.

91. Rafsky interview.

92. Alan Brinkley, *The End of Reform: New Deal Liberalism in Recession and War* (New York: Knopf, 1995), 250–58; Paul K. Conkin, *Tomorrow a New World: The New Deal Community Program* (1959; New York: Da Capo Press, 1976), 224–33, 322–25; Joseph Arnold, *The New Deal in the Suburbs: A History of the Greenbelt Town Program, 1935–54* (Columbus: Ohio State University Press, 1971), chap. 13; Jeanes interview.

93. The Teachers Union in Philadelphia was a left-wing organization of public school teachers. In the early 1940s it lost its status as a local of the American Federation of Teachers, on charges of Communist influence. See Marjorie Murphy, *Blackboard Unions: The AFT and the NEA, 1900–1980* (Ithaca: Cornell University Press, 1990), 170–74. Telephone interview with Isadore Reivich, 15 Oct. 1994; telephone interview with Irene Cohan, 15 Oct. 1994; Murphy, *Blackboard Unions*, 193; Teachers Union of Philadelphia, *The Case Against the School Board* (n.p., 1955), in pamphlet collection TUUA.

94. "Emil Rieve," in *Biographical Dictionary of American Labor*, edited by Gary M. Fink (Westport, CT: Greenwood Press, 1984), 485–86; "McKeown, 67 and Ill, Retiring as Head of Once-Great Union He Helped Build," *Sunday Bulletin* (Philadelphia), 5 May 1957, XB–18; Jeanes interview; letter from Jerome Markovitz to Patricia Eames, 15 Nov. 1963, Box 644, Folder: Juniata Apts. (1963–65), TWUAA; *Evening Bulletin* (Philadelphia), 20 Feb. 1965.

95. "Report to Executive Council on Juniata Park Housing Corporation," 16 Feb. 1968, Box 644, Folder: Juniata Park Housing Corp., TWUAA.

96. Interview with Margaret Traynor, 16 Apr. 1985, Philadelphia.

97. Piero Santostefano, *Le Mackley Houses di Kastner e Stonorove a Philadelphia 1931–1935* (Rome: Officina Edizioni, 1982), 11, author's translation.

98. Fleet interview.

99. Rafsky interview.

Chapter Six

1. *New York Times*, 5 Jan. 1934, 3.

2. Harlem in the 1930s, according to *The WPA Guide to New York City*, was that part of Manhattan which was "blocked in by the high ridges of Morningside Heights and St. Nicholas Terrace, by the East and Harlem rivers, and by Central Park. Along the East River is the Italian section; north and east of Central Park, the Spanish; and further north, the Negro district, its boundaries extending into the Italian and Spanish neighborhoods and creeping northward into Washington Heights" (Federal Writer's Project, *The WPA Guide to New York* [1939; New York: Pantheon, 1982], 253).

3. Quoted in Nathan Irvin Huggins, *Harlem Renaissance* (New York: Oxford University Press, 1971), 4.

4. Claude McKay, *Harlem: Negro Metropolis* (1940; New York: Harcourt Brace Jovanovich, Harvest Books, 1968), 16.

5. Gilbert Osofsky, *Harlem: The Making of a Ghetto: Negro New York, 1890–1930*, 2d ed. (New York: Harper Torchbooks, 1971), 74–80, 87–91, quote from 75–76; Norval White, *New York: A Physical History* (New York: Atheneum, 1987), 61; Joseph Cunningham and Leonard O. DeHart, *The Manhattan Els and the I.R.T.*, vol. 1 of *A History of the New York City Subway System* (New York: n.p., 1976), 7, 9, 18; the author thanks Clifton Hood for this reference.

6. Osofsky, *Harlem*, 90, 78; income figure from U.S. Bureau of the Census, *Historical Statistics, Bicentennial Edition*, vol. 1 (Washington, DC: Government Printing Office, 1975), G566, p. 322.

7. *WPA Guide*, 256.

8. Osofsky, *Harlem*, 90; Stanley Lebergott, *The Americans: An Economic Record* (New York: W. W. Norton, 1984), 396.

9. Norval White and Elliot Willensky, *AIA Guide to New York City*, rev. ed. (New York: Collier Books, 1978), 127, 270; Carl W. Condit, *The Port of New York*, vol. 1 of *A History of the Rail and Terminal System from the Beginnings to Pennsylvania Station* (Chicago: University of Chicago Press, 1980), 239, 266, 284.

10. Osofsky, *Harlem*, 3, 13.

11. Osofsky, *Harlem*, 93–104, 113–17; E. Franklin Frazier, "Negro Harlem: An Ecological Study," *American Journal of Sociology* 43 (July 1937): 75.

12. According to Larry A. Greene, the number of single adults in Harlem during the 1930s was nearly double the average for the city as a whole (16 percent compared with the citywide ratio of 8.3 percent). In Harlem, 47.9 percent of living groups con-

sisted of one or two people. See Greene, "Harlem in the Great Depression: 1928–1936," Ph.D. diss., Columbia University, 1979, 278–79.

13. Osofsky, *Harlem*, 135–36; Davies quoted in Cheryl Lynn Greenberg, *"Or Does It Explode?" Black Harlem in the Great Depression* (New York: Oxford University Press, 1991), 29; Urban League statistics from Greene, "Harlem in the Great Depression," 6.

14. Edith Elmer Wood, *Slums and Blighted Areas, Housing Division Bulletin, No. 1* (Washington, DC: Government Printing Office, 1936), 28; James Ford, *Slums and Housing*, vol. 1 (Cambridge, MA: Harvard University Press, 1936), 317; Anthony Jackson, *A Place Called Home: A History of Low-Cost Housing in Manhattan* (Cambridge, MA: MIT Press, 1976), 189; Greene, "Harlem in the Great Depression," 14.

15. "Hungry Harlem Hides Behind Gay Exterior," *New York Herald-Tribune*, 8 Oct. 1933, reprinted by the New York Urban League, New York City Housing Authority Records, 15A6: 22, Fiorello H. LaGuardia Archives, LaGuardia Community College, City University of New York, New York City (hereafter called NYCHAR); Greenberg, *Or Does It Explode?*, 185; Robert C. Weaver, *The Negro Ghetto* (New York: Harcourt, Brace, 1948), 35; Franklin O. Nichols, *Harlem Housing* (New York: Citizens' Housing Council of New York, 1939), 10, 16 (copy at University of Pennsylvania School of Social Work Library).

16. Mark Naison, *Communists in Harlem during the Depression* (Urbana: University of Illinois Press, 1983), 16, 19–22.

17. Mark Naison, "From Eviction Resistance to Rent Control: Tenant Activism in the Great Depression," in *The Tenant Movement in New York City, 1904–1984*, edited by Ronald Lawson (New Brunswick, NJ: Rutgers University Press, 1986), 99, 115–116, quote from 116.

18. Joel Schwartz, "The Consolidated Tenants League of Harlem: Black Self-Help vs. White, Liberal Intervention in Ghetto Housing, 1934–1944," *Afro-Americans in New York Life and History* 10 (Jan. 1986): 42, Watson quoted, 43. Information about James Watson from Kenneth Cobb, New York City Municipal Archives.

19. Naison, "From Eviction Resistance," 102–112, 114; Greenberg, *Or Does It Explode?*, chaps. 4–5.

20. White and Willensky, *AIA Guide to New York City*, 284; Naison, "From Eviction Resistance," 114–16; Schwartz, "Consolidated Tenants League," 31–32; Greene, "Harlem in the Great Depression," 251–52.

21. Naison, "From Eviction Resistance," 115; Schwartz, "Consolidated Tenants League," 33.

22. Anthony Platt, "Introduction" to chapter 4 in *The Politics of Riot Commissions 1917–1970*, edited by Anthony Platt (New York: Macmillan, 1971), 161; Greenberg, *Or Does It Explode?*, 3–5; Schwartz, "Consolidated Tenants League," 33.

23. *Complete Report of Mayor LaGuardia's Commission on the Harlem Riot of March 19, 1935* (New York: Arno Press and the New York Times, 1969), 74. This publication is a transcript of the report published in the *Amsterdam News* (New York City), 18 July 1936.

24. Platt, "Introduction," 162; Alain Locke, "Dark Weather Vane," *Survey Graphic* 25 (Aug. 1936), reprinted in *Politics of Riot Commissions*, edited by Anthony Platt, 190.

25. Lester Taylor to Langdon Post, 18 Dec. 1933, NYCHAR, 15A7: 14.

26. Rivers to Shreve, 8 Dec. 1933, NYCHAR 49B2: 7; Edwin R. Lewinson, *Black Politics in New York City* (New York: Twayne Publishers, 1974), 66–67; Wilhelmena S. Robinson, *Historical Negro Biographies* (New York: Publishers Co., 1967), 242; "There Is No Housing of Consequence Yet," *Architectural Forum* 60 (Feb. 1934): 161; Wood, *Slums and Blighted Areas*, 28–30; memo by Shreve, 13 Dec. 1933; and Rivers to Shreve, 13 Dec. 1933, both in NYCHAR, 49B2: 7; Robert P. Ingalls, *Herbert H. Lehman and New York's Little New Deal* (New York: New York University Press, 1975), 189.

27. James Hubert, executive director of the New York Urban League, to Shreve, 15 Dec. 1933, NYCHAR 49B2: 7; James Egert Allan, president, New York Branch NAACP, to Langdon Post, 3 Jan. 1934, NYCHAR, 15A6: 10; Myles A. Paige, secretary, North Harlem Community Council, to LaGuardia, 9 Apr. 1934, NYCHAR 15A6: 23.

28. New York State passed legislation to allow cities to establish housing authorities on 31 Jan. 1934. The New York City Housing Authority was established as a public corporation by the Municipal Assembly on 6 Feb. 1934. The board, which consisted of five unpaid members, was picked by Mayor La Guardia. Langdon Post, already serving as Tenement House Commissioner, was appointed chairman. Other members were: Mary K. Simkhovitch, head of Greenwich House and president of the National Public Housing Conference; B. Charney Vladeck, a former member of the Board of Aldermen and general manager of the *Jewish Daily Forward*; Rev. E. Roberts Moore, director of the Division of Social Action for the Catholic Charities of the Archdiocese of New York; and Louis H. Pink, a former member of the State Housing Board ("New York City Housing Authority: A Legislative and Fiscal History," NYCHAR 39C1: 11). New York City Housing Authority [hereafter NYC Housing Authority], *Toward the End to Be Achieved: The New York City Housing Authority, Its History in Outline* (New York: New York City Housing Authority, 1937), 5–6; pamphlet in NYCHAR collection. For an account of the state-level legislative history of the housing authority, see Ingalls, *Herbert H. Lehman*, 188–91.

29. "Harlem's Claim for Housing Reform and Slum Clearance," *Real Estate Record and Builders Guide* 134 (11 Aug. 1934): 5.

30. Rosalie Genevro, "Site Selection and the New York City Housing Authority, 1934–1939," *Journal of Urban History* 12 (Aug. 1986): 334–41.

31. Langdon Post, *The Challenge of Housing* (New York: Farrar and Rinehart, 1938), 224.

32. Harold L. Ickes, *Back to Work: The Story of the PWA* (New York: Macmillan, 1935), 183–86. The "Columbia University Housing Orientation Study," written by Carol Aronovici, reported property prices at $10 to $15 a square foot in Manhattan in the mid–1930s; see *New York Times*, 22 Mar. 1934, 18. Even on the dilapidated Lower East Side, the Housing Authority found assessments for land and buildings averaged between $10.27 and $13.33 per square foot. See James Ford, *Slums and Housing*, vol. 2, 728; Michael W. Straus and Talbot Wegg, *Housing Comes of Age* (New York: Oxford University Press, 1938), 96.

33. Linda J. Lear, *Harold Ickes: The Aggressive Progressive, 1879–1933* (New York:

Garland Publishing, 1981), 109, 119, 394; Harold L. Ickes, *The Inside Struggle, 1936–1939*, vol. 2 of *The Secret Diary of Harold L. Ickes* (New York: Simon and Schuster, 1954), 215; Post, *Challenge of Housing*, 176.

34. Post headed the Tenement House Commission as well as the Housing Authority. As Tenement House Commissioner, he was in charge of building demolitions, and he used his authority in this role to allocate the income from the sale of used bricks to the housing authority. See Ford, *Slums and Housing*, vol. 2, 728; Post, *Challenge of Housing*, 180–90, quote from 230; Peter Marcuse, "The Beginnings of Public Housing in New York," *Journal of Urban History* 12 (Aug. 1986): 356–65; Alfred Medioli, "Housing Form and Rehabilitation in New York City," in *Housing Form and Public Policy in the United States*, edited by Richard Plunz (New York: Praeger, 1980), 142–43 and *passim*.

35. Straus and Wegg, *Housing Comes of Age*, 86–91; citations from Müller decision in Ingalls, *Herbert H. Lehman*, 192.

36. Although cheap for New York City, the property was still more expensive than any other acquired by the Housing Division for its national program. See Straus and Wegg, *Housing Comes of Age*, 96; New York City Housing Authority, "Report of the Secretary for the Period February 20–November 30, 1934," 1 Dec. 1934, 22–23, quote from 22, NYCHAR, 15A4: 7; "Report of Secretary," 23; *New York Times*, 16 May 1934, 21.

37. Federal Administration of Public Works, "Williamsburg Houses," proof copy of pamphlet, n.d., 11, NYCHAR, MS1; List and map of Slum Clearance Committee, NYCHAR, 49B2: 1.

38. Housing Authority Board Minutes, 29 Jan. and 13 Feb. 1935, cited in Joel Schwartz, "Site Planning at the New York City Housing Authority in the 1930s," paper presented at the History of Public Housing Session, Annual Meeting of the Association of Collegiate Schools of Planning, 2 Nov. 1985, 7–8; *New York Age*, 6 July 1935, 1.

39. Raymond B. Fosdick, *John D. Rockefeller, Jr.: A Portrait* (New York: Harper and Brothers, 1956); Osofsky, *Harlem*, 155, 157; Ford, *Slums and Housing*, vol. 2, 743–48.

40. Advertising brochure quoted and commented on in Edith Elmer Wood, *Recent Trends in American Housing* (New York: Macmillan, 1931), 227–28.

41. Ford, *Slums and Housing*, vol. 2, 747; Osofsky, *Harlem*, 157–58, quote from 158.

42. Ford, *Slums and Housing*, vol. 2, 743; Alvin Moscow, *The Rockefeller Inheritance* (Garden City, NY: Doubleday and Co., 1977), 101; Osofsky, *Harlem*, 155; Michael Wallace, "Visiting the Past: History Museums in the United States," *Radical History Review*, no. 25 (Oct. 1981): 77.

43. "A Phenomenon of Exploitation," *Architectural Forum* 61 (Oct. 1934): 298; Post to LaGuardia, "Memorandum on the Question of Purchasing the Paul Lawrence Dunbar Apartments," 27 June 1935, NYCHAR, 15B1: 18.

44. New York City Housing Authority, "Report of the Secretary," 22–37.

45. Post to LaGuardia, "Memorandum on the Question of Purchasing Paul Lawrence Dunbar Apartments," 3.

46. Slum Clearance Committee of New York, "Maps and Charts Prepared by the Slum Clearance Committee of New York, 1933–34," acknowledgment page, copy of volume presented to New York City Housing Authority, 3 Apr. 1934, Avery Library,

Columbia University; Post to Stacy May at Rockefeller Foundation, 19 Nov. 1934, NYCHAR, 15A7: 7.

47. *Amsterdam News* (New York City), 18 May 1935, 1; Schwartz, "Consolidated Tenants League," 35, 37.

48. *New York Times*, 23 May 1935, 27.

49. *Amsterdam News* (New York City), 6 July 1935, 1.

50. Handbills in Fiorello H. LaGuardia Papers (hereafter FHLP), New York City Archives, cited in Schwartz, "Consolidated Tenants League," 38.

51. Margaret Reynolds, "Report of CTL Mass Meeting," 27 July 1935, FHLP, quoted in Schwartz, "Consolidated Tenants League," 38.

52. Interview with Dr. Cyril H. Dolly, n.d., FHLP, cited in Schwartz, "Consolidated Tenants League," 33; biographical sketch of Post in "There Is No Housing," 161; Post, *Challenge of Housing*, quotation 158.

53. Reynolds, "Report of CTL Mass Meeting."

54. *Amsterdam News* (New York City), 27 July 1935; Memo from W. C. Charles, Acting Corporation Counsel, to Post, 6 Aug. 1935, NYCHAR, Box 17A7: 7; *New York Times*, 1 Nov. 1935, 23.

55. New York Chapter American Institute of Architects, Committee on Housing, *The Significance of the Work of the New York City Housing Authority* (New York: American Institute of Architects, 1949), 21.

56. Interview with John L. Wilson by Clifton Hood, 16 Sept. 1987, tape at Fiorello H. LaGuardia Archives, LaGuardia Community College/CUNY, New York City (hereafter called FLA).

57. Hood interview with Wilson; Robert A. M. Stern, Gregory Gilmartin, and Thomas Mellins, *New York 1930: Architecture and Urbanism Between the Two World Wars* (New York: Rizzoli, 1987), 449; Roy Strickland and James Sanders, "Harlem River Houses," *Harvard Architectural Review* 2 (Spring 1981): 281; "A. M. Brown Dies, Architect Was 75," *New York Times*, 30 Nov. 1956, 23.

58. Richard Pommer, "The Architecture of Urban Housing in the United States during the Early 1930s," *Journal of the Society of Architectural Historians* 37 (Dec. 1978): note 45, 255–56, quote from 255; "Public Housing," *Architectural Forum* 68 (May 1938): 364; Post to A. R. Clas, PWA Housing Division, 29 July 1935, NYCHAR, 16D3: 1.

59. "A. M. Brown Dies," 23; Wilson "Biography," New York Housing Authority Photography Department Files, folder: Ceremonies/Harlem River Houses; Hood interview with Wilson.

60. Henry Wright, *Rehousing Urban America* (New York: Columbia University Press, 1935), 29. For a discussion of the garden apartment form and its "undisputed master strategist," Andrew J. Thomas, see Stern, Gilmartin, and Mellins, *New York 1930*, 419–21, 479–86.

61. The rich were not as drawn to the form, tending to favor luxury high-rises in more costly central-city locations. As Plunz explains, the "obvious site amenities" of a building enclosing a garden court were less necessary to wealthy families who lived in the country part of the year (Richard Plunz, "Institutionalization of Housing Form in

New York City, 1920–1950," in *Housing Form and Public Policy*, edited by Richard Plunz, 172).

62. Straus and Wegg, *Housing Comes of Age*, 217.

63. Talbot Faulkner Hamlin, "New York Housing: Harlem River Houses and Williamsburg Houses," *Pencil Points* 19 (May 1938): 282.

64. Katharine Hamill, "2,196 Families Are Living in the Williamsburg and Harlem River Housing Projects," *Harper's Bazaar*, Aug. 1939, quotes from 101–2 and 132.

65. Strickland and Sanders, "Harlem River Houses," 56.

66. Federal Emergency Administration of Public Works, *Harlem River Houses* (publicity brochure, n.d. but probably 1937); New York Chapter of AIA, *The Significance of the Work*, 21–29.

67. Federal Emergency Administration of Public Works, "Harlem River Houses"; Strickland and Sanders, "Harlem River Houses," 53; Langdon W. Post, "Harlem River Houses," *Opportunity: Journal of Negro Life* 15 (Aug. 1937): 233.

68. Author's interview with John Lewis Wilson, 8 June 1988, New York City.

69. New York Chapter AIA, *Significance of Work of New York City Housing Authority*, 98.

70. Hood interview with Wilson.

71. Williamsburg, the PWA development in Brooklyn, contained 1,622 units, for which the authority received 20,000 applications. See NYC Housing Authority, *Toward the End to Be Achieved*, 11–12; NYC Housing Authority, *Must We Have Slums?* (New York: New York City Housing Authority, 1937), 12.

72. NYC Housing Authority, *Toward the End to Be Achieved*, 12; Post, *Challenge of Housing*, 187, 186, 187.

73. In addition to information from archival sources about the Harlem River Houses, the author conducted seven interviews with residents and four interviews with persons associated with the development and used two interviews available at the Fiorello LaGuardia Archives. As with the Mackley, the information required to construct a random sample was not available.

74. NYC Housing Authority, *Toward the End to Be Achieved*, 13; Interview with Lorinda Johnson (pseudonym for person who wishes to remain anonymous) by Elliot Sparkman, 3 Sept. 1987, tape and transcript at FLA.

75. Harold L. Ickes, "Activities of Housing Division of the Federal Emergency Administration of Public Works," report submitted to Senate Committee on Education and Labor, 75th Cong., 1st sess. (1937), Hearings on S. 1685 (Washington, DC: Government Printing Office, 1937), 37; NYC Housing Authority Management Division, "Income Study of 4,832 Applicants for Apartments," 8 Mar. 1937, 2–3, NYCHAR, 15D1: 14; NYC Housing Authority, *Toward the End to Be Achieved*, 12; Post, *Challenge of Housing*, 194.

76. "New York City Housing Authority Memorandum," 18 Nov. 1937, NYCHAR, 15D1: 14; statistics on incomes, occupations, and unemployment rates from U.S. Bureau of Labor Statistics, "Urban Study of Consumer Purchases," cited in Nichols, *Harlem Housing*, 26; Interview with Miriam Burns, 21 June 1987, New York City; Greenberg, *Or Does It Explode?*, 66.

77. Ruth E. Lewis, "Report on Project Activities: Harlem River Houses," 27 May 1939, NYCHAR, 16B7: 11.

78. Catherine F. Lansing, "Children's Centers Linked to Great Housing Projects," text of article from *New York Times*, 12 Feb. 1939, reprinted in *U.S. Housing Authority Publications, 1938–39* (n.p.) at Avery Library, Columbia University.

79. Interview with Nixcola Ramsay, 3 Dec. 1986, New York City.

80. Joel Schwartz, "Tenant Unions In New York City's Low-Rent Housing, 1933–1949," *Journal of Urban History* 12 (Aug. 1986): 426–27.

81. Hamill, "2,196 Families," 132, 103.

82. Federal Writers Project, "Harlem River Houses," FHLP, Box 3646, cited in Schwartz, "Tenant Unions," 427.

83. Roger Flood, "New Environment Builds Social Program," *Shelter,* April 1938, 19–20, quote from 20; Ramsay interview; quote from R. Vincent Hammond, interviewed 7 June 1988, New York City.

84. Burns interview.

85. Hamill, "2,196 Families," 132.

86. Schwartz, "Tenant Unions," 422.

87. Interview with Priscilla Reed, 13 July 1987, New York City.

88. Interview with David W. Scott, 14 July 1987, New York City; Interview with Edward B. McClendon, 22 June 1988, New York City.

89. Telephone interview with Edward B. McClendon, 29 Dec. 1994.

90. Hammond interview.

91. Alex Jetter, "Mississippi Learning," *New York Times Magazine,* 21 Feb. 1993, 32.

92. Hammond interview.

93. Ramsay interview.

94. Burns, Scott, Hammond, and McClendon interviews.

95. Reed interview; interview with William Booker, 18 June 1987.

96. Interview with Val Coleman, 22 June 1988, New York City.

97. The author attended both celebrations.

98. Priscilla Reed, "Closing Remarks," given at Harlem River Houses Fiftieth Anniversary Celebration, 12 Sept. 1987, copy in possession of author.

99. New York City Landmarks Preservation Commission, "Harlem River Houses," 23 Sept. 1975; interview with Horace Carter of the Emanuel Pieterson Historical Society, Dec. 1986, New York City; Hammond interview; news release by NYC Housing Authority, "40th Anniversary of Historic Harlem River Houses to Be Celebrated Saturday," 9 Sept. 1977, copy in author's possession.

100. Reed, "Closing Remarks."

101. As we will see in chapter 7, various factors, including legal restrictions on construction expenditures for public housing, reduced the quality of later federally assisted housing.

Chapter Seven

1. "Housing," *Real Estate Record and Builders' Guide* 132 (25 Nov. 1933): 3.

2. Peter Arnold, "Public Housing in Atlanta: A National First," *Atlanta Historical*

Bulletin 13 (Sept. 1968): 10–13; Mark B. Lapping, "The Emergence of Federal Public Housing: Atlanta's Techwood Project," *The American Journal of Economics and Sociology* 32 (Oct. 1973): 380–81.

3. Gertrude S. Fish, "Housing Policy During the Great Depression," in *The Story of Housing*, edited by Gertrude Sipperly Fish (New York: Macmillan, 1979), 185–86.

4. Kenneth T. Jackson, "Race, Ethnicity and Real Estate Appraisal: The Home Owners Loan Corporation and the Federal Housing Administration," *Journal of Urban History* 6 (Aug. 1980): 421; Arthur M. Schlesinger, Jr., *The Coming of the New Deal* (Boston: Houghton Mifflin, 1958), vol. 2 of *The Age of Roosevelt*, 298; FDR quoted in Peter Marcuse, "The Ideologies of Ownership and Property Rights," in *Housing Form and Public Policy in the United States*, edited by Richard Plunz (New York: Praeger, 1980), 46.

5. Marriner S. Eccles, *Beckoning Frontiers* (New York: Alfred A. Knopf, 1951), 144–52, quote from 144.

6. Eccles, *Beckoning Frontiers*, quotes from 149, 151; Kenneth T. Jackson, *Crabgrass Frontier: The Suburbanization of the United States* (New York: Oxford University Press, 1985), 204–5; U.S. Housing and Home Finance Agency, *Tenth Annual Report, 1956* (Washington, DC: Government Printing Office, 1957), Table A–1, 266.

7. Paul F. Wendt, *Housing Policy—The Search for Solutions: A Comparison of the United Kingdom, Sweden, West Germany and the United States Since World War II* (Berkeley: University of California Press, 1963), 152.

8. Catherine Bauer, "Housing for, of, and by Workers," *Hosiery Worker*, 11 May 1934, 2; "Philadelphia Labor Housing Chiefs Confer with Foreign Experts," *Hosiery Worker*, 28 Sept. 1934, 6; Mary Susan Cole, "Catherine Bauer and the Public Housing Movement, 1926–1937," Ph.D. diss., George Washington University, 1975, 261–62; Labor Housing Conference, "First Annual Report," March 1936, 1, in Files of the Executive Secretary of the Labor Housing Conference (hereafter FESLHC), State Historical Society of Wisconsin, Box 1, File: Labor Housing Conference.

9. Resolution by John A. Phillips, president of the Pennsylvania Federation of Labor, *Report of the Proceedings of the Fifty-Fourth Annual Convention of The American Federation of Labor* (Washington, DC: Judd and Detweiler, 1934), 580.

10. *American Federationist* 39 (Nov. 1932): 1247; and ibid. (Dec. 1932): 1389, cited in Timothy L. McDonnell, *The Wagner Housing Act: A Case Study in the Legislative Process* (Chicago: Loyola University Press, 1957), 68–69.

11. Catherine Bauer, "Housing: Paper Plans, or a Workers' Movement," in *America Can't Have Housing*, edited by Carol Aronovici (New York: Museum of Modern Art, 1934), 20.

12. Catherine Bauer, "The Social Front of Modern Architecture in the 1930s," *Journal of the Society of Architectural Historians* 24 (Mar. 1965): 52.

13. Lewis Mumford, "The Social Imperatives in Housing," in *America Can't Have Housing*, edited by Aronovici, 19. For discussions of collectivist evolutionary thinking in the United States in this period, see Richard Pells, *Radical Visions and American Dreams: Culture and Social Thought in the Depression Years* (New York: Harper and Row, 1973), 19–21; Ellis W. Hawley, *The New Deal and the Problem of Monopoly: A Study in*

Economic Ambivalence (Princeton, NJ: Princeton University Press, 1966), 170–77; and James Gilbert, *Designing the Industrial State: The Intellectual Pursuit of Collectivism in America* (Chicago: Quadrangle Books, 1972), 6–7, and passim.

14. Bauer, "Housing: Paper Plans," 22.

15. Catherine Bauer, *Modern Housing* (Boston: Houghton Mifflin, 1934), 253; Bauer, "Housing: Paper Plans," 20.

16. Bauer, "Housing: Paper Plans," quotes from 22, 23, 22.

17. Bauer to Mrs. Jacob L. Bauer, 1 May 1934, cited in Cole, "Catherine Bauer," 262.

18. Catherine Bauer, "Housing for, of, and by Workers," *Hosiery Worker*, 6 July 1934, 2.

19. Cole, "Catherine Bauer," 297–300.

20. Bauer, "Housing for, of, and by Workers," 2.

21. Cole, "Catherine Bauer," 307.

22. *Report of the Fifty-fourth Convention of AFL*, 580–81, quote from 581; McDonnell, *Wagner Housing Act*, 70–72; Cole, "Catherine Bauer," 307–8.

23. "Housing Bodies Planned for Twenty Cities," *Hosiery Worker*, 4 Jan. 1935, 1; "Bauer Finds Labor Housing Growing," *Hosiery Worker*, 1 Mar. 1935, 2; Cole, "Catherine Bauer," 372–93.

24. Bauer to Mrs. Jacob L. Bauer, n.d., cited in Cole, "Catherine Bauer," 386.

25. Bauer to Mrs. Margaret Smith, 6 Mar. 1935, cited in Cole, "Catherine Bauer," 403.

26. John Edelman to Douglass Haskell, 25 Jan. 1967, cited in Cole, "Catherine Bauer," 385.

27. Bauer to Anna Bogue, n.d., cited in Cole, "Catherine Bauer," 392–93.

28. S. 2392, 74th Cong., 1st sess., (1935).

29. McDonnell, *Wagner Housing Act*, 88–92. Wagner's 1935 bill is reprinted in McDonnell, *Wagner Housing Act*, 405–25. J. Joseph Huthmacher, *Senator Robert F. Wagner and the Rise of Urban Liberalism* (New York: Atheneum, 1968), 207.

30. McDonnell, *Wagner Housing Act*, 97–99; Carter, ed., *Labor Lobbyist*, 109.

31. Ellenbogen's bill, H. R. 7399, 74th Cong., 1st sess. (1935), reprinted in McDonnell, *Wagner Housing Act*, 404–24, quote from Sec. 1.

32. Differences in outlook between the two groups are described in Eugenie Ladner Birch, "Edith Elmer Wood and the Genesis of Liberal Housing Thought, 1910–1942," Ph.D. diss., Columbia University, 1976, 195.

33. Resolution by Charles F. Hollopeter, New Jersey State Federation of Labor, in *Report of the Proceedings of the Fifty-fifth Annual Convention of the American Federation of Labor*, (Washington, DC: Judd and Detweiler), 614.

34. McDonnell, *Wagner Housing Act*, 120–21.

35. U.S. Congress, Senate, Committee on Education and Labor, *Hearings on S. 4424*, 74th Cong., 2d sess., 1936, 41.

36. U.S. Congress, Senate, Committee on Education and Labor, *Hearings on S. 2392: Slum and Low-Rent Public Housing*, 74th Cong., 1st sess., 1935, 87.

37. *Hearings on S. 2392*, quotes from 91, 86, 87.

38. *Hearings on S. 4424*, 45.

39. *Hearings on S. 2392*, 84.

40. *Hearings on S. 4424*, 175, quotes from 179.

41. *Hearings on S. 4424*, 44.

42. AFL statement on the Federal Housing Administration is reprinted in *Hearings on S. 4424*, 49–50.

43. Quotes from Albert Mayer, "Let Us Demand a Housing Program," *The Nation* 139 (10 Oct. 1934): 403; and Carter, *Labor Lobbyist*, 115.

44. Nathaniel S. Keith, *Politics and the Housing Crisis Since 1930* (New York: Universe Books, 1973), 29–30; McDonnell, *Wagner Housing Act*, 60–62.

45. Michael Jacobs, "The Origins of Federal Housing Policy and the Needs of the State," in *Housing Form*, edited by Plunz, 79; McDonnell, *Wagner Housing Act*, 140–42.

46. Michael J. Doucet and John C. Weaver, "Material Culture and the North American House: The Era of the Common Man, 1870–1920," *Journal of American History* 72 (Dec. 1985): 570.

47. McDonnell, *Wagner Housing Act*, 61, 316.

48. Walter S. Schmidt, "Report Concerning Certain Federal and Private Activities in the Field of Real Estate and Housing," 1935, NAREB Files, Chicago, quoted in McDonnell, *Wagner Housing Act*, 138–39.

49. Quoted in John H. Mollenkopf, *The Contested City*, (Princeton: Princeton University Press, 1983), 70. Nelson, though he fought public housing on the grounds it was communistic, was hardly a crusader for democracy. In 1949, he explained to what must have been a startled House Committee: "I do not believe in democracy. I think it stinks. I don't think women should be allowed to vote at all. Ever since they started, our public affairs have been in a worse mess than ever before." Quoted in Barry Checkoway, "Large Builders, Federal Housing Programs, and Postwar Suburbanization," in *Critical Perspectives on Housing*, edited by Rachel G. Bratt, Chester Hartman, and Ann Meyerson (Philadelphia: Temple University Press, 1986), 136.

50. James T. Patterson, *Congressional Conservatism and the New Deal: The Growth of the Conservative Coalition in Congress, 1933–1939* (Lexington: University of Kentucky Press, 1967), 155.

51. McDonnell, *Wagner Housing Act*, 301–2, 323–59, and 389–402; Lawrence M. Friedman, *Government and Slum Housing: A Century of Frustration* (Chicago: Rand McNally, 1968), 111–12; R. Allen Hays, *The Federal Government and Urban Housing: Ideology and Change in Public Policy* (Albany: State University of New York Press, 1985), 90–91, quote from 90; Bruce Headey, *Housing Policy in the Developed Economy: The United Kingdom, Sweden and the United States* (New York: St. Martin's Press, 1978), 204–5; Charles Abrams, "Housing Policy–1937 to 1967," in *Shaping an Urban Future: Essays in Memory of Catherine Bauer Wurster*, edited by Bernard J. Frieden and William W. Nash, Jr. (Cambridge, MA: MIT Press, 1969), quote from 35–36.

52. McDonnell, *Wagner Housing Act*, 326–32, 394–95; Friedman, *Government and Slum Housing*, 112–13.

53. Miles L. Colean, *American Housing: Problems and Prospects* (New York: Twen-

tieth Century Fund, 1944), 277. In the South, per-room costs under the PWA averaged $1,177 according to a study by the Bureau of Labor Statistics. See Herman B. Byer and Clarence A. Trump, "Labor and Unit Costs in PWA Low-Rent Housing," *Monthly Labor Review* 49 (Sept. 1939): 579.

54. Harold Ickes, *The Inside Struggle* (New York: Simon and Schuster, 1954), vol. 2 of *The Secret Diary of Harold L. Ickes*, 218; Straus quote from Roger Biles, "Nathan Straus and the Failure of U.S. Public Housing, 1937–1942," *The Historian* 53 (Autumn 1990): 41.

55. Federal Works Agency, United States Housing Authority, "Summary of General Requirements and Minimum Standards for USHA-Aided Projects" (13 July 1939), 2, copy at Avery library, Columbia University.

56. United States Housing Authority, *Annual Report for Fiscal Year 1939* (Washington, DC: Government Printing Office, 1940), 5, emphasis added.

57. Computed from Colean, *American Housing,* Table 60, 439.

58. Richard Pommer, "The Architecture of Urban Housing in the United States during the Early 1930s," *Journal of the Society of Architectural Historians* 37 (Dec. 1978): 256.

59. Mumford, "Versailles for the Millions," *The New Yorker* 16 (17 Feb. 1940): 44 and 42.

60. "26 Million to Be Saved in Development Costs," *Public Housing Weekly News,* 25 June 1940, 4.

61. Described in Plunz, "Institutionalization of Housing Form," 180–81. See also "A Lesson in Cost Reduction," *Architectural Forum* 69 (Nov. 1938): 405–8.

62. Calculated from "A Lesson in Cost Reduction," 406; and U.S. Federal Emergency Administration of Public Works, Housing Division, *Unit Plans* (Washington, DC: Government Printing Office, 1935). The worker housing standard is from Elizabeth Coit, "Notes on Design and Construction of the Dwelling Unit for the Lower-Income Family—Part I," *The Octagon* 13 (Oct. 1941): 25.

63. For discussions of the relationship of space to long-term usability and acceptability of residential form, see Philip Boudon, *Lived-in Architecture: Le Corbusier's Pessac Revisited,* translated by Gerald Onn (1969; Cambridge, MA: MIT Press, 1979), 30, 65–66, 161–65; and Alfred Medioli, "Housing Form and Rehabilitation in New York City," in *Housing Form,* edited by Plunz, 129–56; Coit, "Notes on Design," 23–25.

64. Mark I. Gelfand, *A Nation of Cities* (New York: Oxford University Press, 1975), 64.

65. Draft of a letter by Stonorov to the PWA housing Division, 25 Mar. 1935, Box 2, Stonorov File, FESLHC.

66. Marc Weiss, *The Rise of the Community Builders: The American Real Estate Industry and Urban Land Planning* (New York: Columbia University Press, 1987), 147, quote from 152; Jackson, *Crabgrass Frontier,* 203–8.

67. Checkoway, "Large Builders," 129.

68. Weiss, *Community Builders,* 146.

69. Ibid., 148–49.

70. Ibid., 155.

71. Colean, *American Housing*, 50.

72. Minimum requirements for a good dwelling formulated by the National Conference of Charities and Correction, cited in Edith Elmer Wood, *Recent Trends in American Housing* (New York: Macmillan Co., 1931), 39–40.

73. Harold L. Ickes, "Activities of Housing Division of the Federal Emergency Administration of Public Works," report submitted to Senate Committee on Education and Labor, 75th Cong., 1st sess. (1937), *Hearings on S. 1685* (Washington, DC: Government Printing Office, 1937), 29, 34.

74. See, for example, Charles Abrams, *The Future of Housing* (New York: Harper and Brothers, 1946), 258.

75. These interpretations are based on work by Peter Marcuse and M. J. Daunton. See Marcuse, "A Useful Installment of Socialist Work: Housing in Red Vienna in the 1920s," in *Critical Perspectives*, edited by Rachel G. Bratt, Chester Hartman, and Ann Meyerson (Philadelphia: Temple University Press, 1986), esp. 581–83; Marcuse, "The Housing Policy of Social Democracy: Determinants and Consequences," in *The Austrian Socialist Experiment: Social Democracy and Austromarxism, 1918–1934*, edited by Anson Rabinbach, 201–21; Daunton, "Introduction" to Daunton, ed., *Councillors and Tenants: Local Authority Housing in English Cities, 1919–1939* (Leicester: Leicester University Press, 1984), 1–33; and Daunton, *House and Home in the Victorian City: Working Class Housing 1850–1914* (London: E. Arnold, 1983).

76. Ronald Tobey, Charles Wetherall, and Jay Brigham, "Moving Out and Settling In: Residential Mobility, Home Owning, and the Public Enframing of Citizenship, 1921–1950," *American Historical Review* 95 (Dec. 1990): 1415–20.

Conclusion

1. Nathaniel Keith, *Politics and the Housing Crisis* (New York: Universe Books, 1973), 39; Kenneth T. Jackson, *Crabgrass Frontier: The Suburbanization of the United States* (New York: Oxford University Press, 1985), 205.

2. U.S. Bureau of the Census, *Historical Statistics, Bicentennial Edition*, 2 (Washington, DC: Government Printing Office, 1975) N156, p. 639.

3. For good discussions of these issues, see Dolores Hayden, *Redesigning the American Dream: The Future of Housing, Work, and Family Life* (New York: W. W. Norton, 1984), esp. chap. 3; and David Harvey, "The Political Economy of Urbanization in Advanced Capitalist Societies: The Case of the United States," in *The Social Economy of Cities*, edited by Gary Grappert and Harold Rose, vol. 9 of *Urban Affairs Annual Review* (Beverly Hills: Sage, 1975), 139.

4. Levitt quoted in Hayden, *Redesigning the American Dream*, 6; Jackson, *Crabgrass Frontier*, 230.

5. R. Allen Hays, *The Federal Government and Urban Housing: Ideology and Change in Public Policy* (Albany: State University of New York Press, 1985), 96.

6. Census, *Historical Statistics*, Series N176, p. 641.

7. World Bank, *World Development Report 1986*, cited in Graham Hallett, ed., *Land and Housing Policies in Europe and the USA: A Comparative Analysis* (London: Routledge, 1988), 5.

8. For discussions of the link between McCarthyism and resistance to public hous-
ing, see Donald Craig Parson, "Urban Politics during the Cold War: Public Housing,
Urban Renewal and Suburbanization in Los Angeles (California)," Ph.D. diss., Uni-
versity of California at Los Angeles, 1985; and Thomas Hines, "Housing, Baseball and
Creeping Socialism: The Battle of Chavez Ravine, Los Angeles, 1949–59," *Journal of
Urban History* 8 (Feb. 1982): 123–43.

9. Elizabeth A. Roistacher, "Housing Finance and Housing Policy in the United
States: Legacies of the Reagan Era," in *Government and Housing: Developments in Seven
Countries*, edited by Willem van Vliet and Jan van Weesep (Newbury Park, CA: Sage
Publications, 1990), 166; Ann Meyerson, "The Changing Structure of Housing
Finance in the United States," in *International Journal of Urban and Regional Research*
4 (Dec. 1986): 465–95; H. I. MacDonald, "Special Interest Politics and the Crisis of
Financial Institutions in the USA," *Environment and Planning C* 10 (1992), 123.

10. Kenneth Harney, "FHA Might Stand for 'Flexible' Housing Administration
in '95," *Buffalo News*, 11 Feb. 1995, Homefinder section, 13. Other homeowner tax
expenditures include the "rollover" deferral of capital gains on home sales, which was
estimated by the Treasury Department for 1994 at $30 billion, and the zeroing out of
all federal taxation on the first $125,000 of capital gains for home sellers 55 years of
age or older, estimated at $5 billion. Estimates as to the proportion of tax subsidies
going to taxpayers at various income levels from Peter Drier and John Atlas, *U.S.
Housing Policy at the Crossroads: A Progressive Agenda to Rebuild the Housing Constituency*
(Los Angeles: International and Public Affairs Center of Occidental College, 1996),
8. Dan Stets, "U.S. Help for Home Buyers Is Urged: Ownership is Down, Head of
Realtors' Group Says," *Philadelphia Inquirer*, 10 May 1987, K–1; Timothy B. Clark,
"Challenges for Housing," *National Journal*, 24 Jan. 1987, 192, 191; John Cunniff,
"Buying 1st Home Tough for Young," *Philadelphia Inquirer*, 9 Aug. 1987, H–1; National
Association of Home Builders, National Association of Realtors, Mortgage Bankers
Association of America, "Toward a National Housing Policy," (n.p., 1987); Low-
Income Housing Information Service, "Special Memorandum: The 1989 Low-Income
Housing Budget," Apr. 1988, 9; "New Housing Law: U.S. Housing Policy Gets an
11th-hour Boost From Congress," *Chicago Tribune*, 17 Jan. 1988, Real Estate–1.

11. Chester Hartman, "The Housing Part of the Homelessness Problem," in *The
Mental Health Needs of Homeless Persons*, edited by E. L. Bassuk (San Francisco: Jossey-
Bass, 1986), 72; Clark "Challenges for Housing," 191; Kim Hoper and Jill Hamberg,
"The Making of America's Homeless: From Skid Row to New Poor, 1945–1984," in
Critical Perspectives on Housing, edited by Rachel G. Bratt, Chester Hartman, and Ann
Meyerson (Philadelphia: Temple University Press, 1986), 20; Peter Rossi, *Down and
Out in America: The Origins of Homelessness* (Chicago: University of Chicago Press,
1989); Drier and Atlas, *U.S. Housing Policy*, 6.

12. See Anthony Downs, "Too Much Capital for Housing," *Brookings Review* (Summer 1980); David Cay Johnson, "The Pitfall in the Flat Tax: The Republicans Tiptoe
around the Mortgage Deduction," *New York Times*, 12 Jan. 1996, D1.

13. "New Housing Law: U.S. Housing Policy Gets an 11th-hour Boost from Congress," *Chicago Tribune*, 17 Jan. 1988, Real Estate–1.

14. Quoted in Peter Marcuse, "The Ideologies of Ownership and Property Rights," in *Housing Form and Public Policy in the United States*, edited by Richard Plunz (New York: Praeger, 1980), 46.

15. Tom Nielsen, "Look Who's Cashing in on the Sale of Our Home," *Buffalo News*, 28 July 1994, B–3.

16. Peter Drier and J. David Hulchanski, "Social Housing: U.S. Prospect, Canadian Reality," in *The Affordable City: Toward a Third Sector Housing Policy*, edited by John Emmeus Davis, 51–53; Edward G. Goetz, *Shelter Burden: Local Politics and Progressive Housing Policy* (Philadelphia: Temple University Press, 1993), chap. 5.

17. Sam Davis, *The Architecture of Affordable Housing* (Berkeley: University of California Press, 1995), 184–88.

18. Ian Alper et al., *Building Our Communities: Unions and Affordable Housing* (Beverly, MA: Trade Union Housing Corporation of the North Shore, n.d.), 16–17; David Bensman, "BAC's Comeback: The Bricklayers' Renewal Program," *Labor Research Review* 7 (Fall 1988): 67–68; Karen Sue Smith, "Churches Enter Building Industry to Fill Housing Gap," *National Catholic Reporter*, 23 May 1986, 5; I. D. Robbins, "Affordable Single-Family Housing Grows in Brooklyn," *Real Estate Finance Journal*, Winter 1987: 49–55; Jim Gittings, "Churches in Communities: A Place to Stand: East Brooklyn Churches and the Nehemiah Project," *Christianity and Crisis* 47 (2 Feb. 1987): 5–11.

19. John Emmeus Davis gives an excellent overview of alternative models of tenure in "Beyond the Market and the State: The Diverse Domain of Social Housing," in *The Affordable City*.

20. Kathryn M. McCamant and Charles R. Durrett, "Cohousing in Denmark," in *New Households, New Housing*, edited by Karen A. Franck and Sherry Ahrentzen (New York: Van Nostrand Reinhold, 1989). Recent efforts in the United States are described in Nick Ravo, "Where Condos Meet Communes: Housing with Togetherness Built In," *New York Times*, 25 Feb. 1993, B4. Dorit Fromm describes contemporary forms of housing with shared facilities in the United States, including Cohousing, in *Collaborative Communities: Cohousing, Central Living, and Other New Forms of Housing with Shared Facilities* (New York: Van Nostrand Reinhold, 1991).

21. For overviews, see Davis, *The Affordable City*; Michael Ball, Michael Harloe, and Maartje Martins, *Housing and Social Change in Europe and the USA* (London: Routledge, 1988); Rachel G. Bratt, *Rebuilding a Low-Income Housing Policy* (Philadelphia: Temple University Press, 1989); Peter Dreier, "Community-based Housing: A New Direction in Federal Housing Policy," *Shelterforce*, Sept.–Oct. 1987: 12–14; Churches' Conference on Shelter and Housing, *Making Room at the Inn: Congregational Investment in Affordable Housing* (Washington, DC: n.p., n.d.); Edward G. Goetz, *Shelter Burden: Local Politics and Progressive Housing Policy* (Philadelphia: Temple University Press, 1993).

22. Bauer to C. E. V. Prins, Director of Information, USHA, 30 July 1940, quoted in Cole, "Catherine Bauer," 673.

23. Bauer to Monroe E. Deutsch, 17 April 1940, cited in Cole, "Catherine Bauer," 672; James T. Kloppenberg, "Who's Afraid of the Welfare State?" *Reviews in American History* 18 (Sept. 1990): 404.

24. For the importance of public intervention in the economy, see Alan Brinkley "Liberals and Public Investment: Recovering a Lost Legacy," *American Prospect* (Spring 1993): 81–86. Gosta Esping-Anderson discusses the link between economic growth and political support for generous social programs in *Politics Against Markets: The Social Democratic Road to Power* (Princeton: Princeton University Press, 1985), 34–36.

INDEX

Illustrations and tables are indicated by **boldface** page numbers.